INSTITUTIONS AND IMAGINARIES

The School of the Art Institute of Chicago
Department of Exhibitions and Exhibition Studies
Sullivan Galleries
33 S. State Street, 7th floor
Chicago, Illinois 60603
www.saic.edu/exhibitions

Series Editors
Mary Jane Jacob and Kate Zeller

Editorial Assistants
Raven Munsell
Elisabeth Smith

Design
Jess Mott Wickstrom

Design Concept
Corey Margulis

Copyeditor
Rosemary Adams

Print
The University of Chicago Press

Distribution
The University of Chicago Press
1427 E. 60th Street
Chicago, Illinois 60637

ISBN-13: 978-0-982-87986-3

The *Chicago Social Practice History Series* was
developed by the School of the Art Institute of
Chicago's Department of Exhibitions and Exhibition
Studies as part of the series of exhibitions, programs,
and symposium launched in 2014 as "A Lived Practice."

Chicago Social Practice History Series

INSTITUTIONS AND IMAGINARIES

Edited by Stephanie Smith
Series Editors Mary Jane Jacob and Kate Zeller

The School of the Art Institute of Chicago
Distributed by the University of Chicago Press

CONTENTS

Preface

Mary Jane Jacob

Institutions and imaginaries may not be a familiar coupling or regular rubric, but in Chicago they have come to define and shape each other. To create a city out of whole cloth, in the American way where no ancient tracks remain in sight, is an act of invention. Part of that task is to signify in stone what you are—or aspire to be—and then fill the halls with those records and mementos that monumentalize and memorialize. Most importantly, they become the foundation for the future. And in the grand city-building agenda, institutions put forward the concept of a place, while the dreams of that place fuel their reason for coming into being.

History is at stake in both institutions and imaginaries. Cultural institutions are not only repositories of history; they speak to the very existence of history. And imaginaries, well, those are the histories that are continually being reinvented—a concept that connotes the transitoriness and conflicted nature of any single history, while acknowledging the imagistic way we engage in living the experience of a place. Inextricably linked, history and imagination each imbue the other with power and purpose.

In Chicago, city making was cultural institution making. Much unfolded from its signature event on the world stage, the 1893 World's Columbian Exposition; the classical architecture of those defining museums was intentional, even if the style was not imaginative at a time when progressive modernism was also being born. But the imaginary it supported, one of deep and lasting roots, sought to transform a place in the prairie into a Paris of the Middle West. This desire to be part of the ongoing story is with us still.

Successive decades bring new institutions (whether they themselves cozy up to that moniker or not). They arise, most often it seems, as challenges by newcomers, upstarts, and detractors, or those who at the very least make the claim that they are filling a void in the cultural landscape and addressing omissions: culturally specific constituencies, artists living and working here, practioners in other aligned or emerging fields, a creative need for experimentation at a moment.

Reflection is necessary to the health of any organism. This means reassessing vis-à-vis existing institutions and needs, and at the same time, realigning according to the evolving imaginaries. Thus, imaginaries (desires to be) motivate change, and imaginaries (who we are) provide a groundedness and enable us to describe ourselves to others. If this is perceived over time to be too rigid, then a competing imaginary, with possible alternative institution building, begins anew.

This continual dynamic of organizational identities and missions, built structures and programs, money and other resources, demands change over time. And while individual institutions may be slow, unable, or unwilling to change, and power struggles between institutions can come into play, rooted as they are in the perceptions of enduring imaginaries, in the grand scheme of things there is continual fluidity: a wide range of institutions are all components of the civic ecology.

It is important to clarify the directions of this volume in the *Chicago Social Practice History* series in relation to *Support Networks*, guest edited by Abigail Satinsky. That book looked to mechanisms of artists to realize their work with others in short- and longer-lived ways, and with a drive toward diversity, equity, and social justice. In turn, Stephanie Smith takes us to the edges of large institutions where they meet artists' interventions, sometimes covert, and to other established institutions at key moments of relooking at themselves through a daring program.

Stephanie's own exhibitions during her tenure as curator and later deputy director at the David and Alfred Smart Museum of Art at the University of Chicago demonstrated how an established mid-size museum could be a testing ground for ideas—able to flex and show work that feeds a larger community that is the institutional and artistic ecology of this place. Her approach was to work within an institutional team during a period of change that, in Smith's words, was "knee-deep into the question of how to be a truly hospitable and dynamic civic museum." For example, her 2009 show *Heartland*, co-curated with Charles Esche, probed the imaginary of the Midwest through contemporary projects by artists within the region. Meanwhile, her dedication to Chicago-area artists through her national and international shows, namely *Beyond Green* in 2006 and *Feast: Radical Hospitality in Contemporary Art* in 2012, further recommended her for this assignment. We thank Stephanie for taking on this considerable task and bringing it to completion during the period in which she transitioned to taking on the role of chief curator at the Art Gallery of Ontario. We are glad this project afforded her a chance to reflect on what, as she commented, she learned during her years in Chicago and how that period might shape her work in a new city and country.

Stephanie would like to thank, along with the other volume editors and series editors, a group of friends who helped her to think more clearly about art, citizens, and Chicago: Marshall Brown, Tania Bruguera, Viviana Checchia, Charles Esche, Ika Knezevic, Matthew Jesse Jackson, Conor O'Neil, Geof Oppenheimer, Dan Peterman, Michael Rakowitz, Gina Reichert, Monika Szewcyzk, Jacqueline Terrassa, Dan Wang, and Lori Waxman. She found ways to bring all of their voices into this book, directly or indirectly. She also wishes to thank her family for their support.

In closing, we thank our continuing publication team that has been so dedicated to this series: my co-editor Kate Zeller, editorial assistants Raven Munsell and Elisabeth Smith, and designer Jess Mott Wickstrom. With this volume we are pleased to be joined by Rosemary Adams who served as volume editor and Terry Ann R. Neff, editorial consultant. At the University of Chicago we thank Carol Kasper, marketing director, and Robby Desmond and Kewon Bell, print production. Finally, we are grateful for the support of the SAIC's Earl and Brenda Shapiro Center for Research and Collaboration, the Graham Foundation for Advanced Studies in the Fine Arts, Elizabeth Firestone Graham Foundation, and the Illinois Arts Council, a state agency.

Introduction

Stephanie Smith

Institutions

This volume explores the roles of institutions, as well as the power of imaginaries, in shaping the history of socially engaged practice in Chicago. Apart from a few highly visible moments that might fall under the category of "institutional critique," the roles played by major cultural institutions have not yet been fully woven into this history. This volume aims to make clear that institutions have played an important part both within the story of social practice in Chicago and within a broader consideration of the changing roles of twenty-first century cultural institutions. Nonetheless, we must concede that over the past century much of Chicago's most important socially engaged practice has unfolded outside of the city's impressive core.

This disjuncture has to do both with the methods and the ethos of socially engaged practice. In terms of method, socially engaged art practice prioritizes relationships, process, and action. It often occupies space fluidly and temporarily rather than settling into fixed objects or static places. It thrives out in the world and in non-art-related and non-institutional spaces that foster a messier sort of intersection between art and life, places less marked by normative power. And in terms of ethos, over the past two centuries in Europe and North America, much progressive art and thinking—including some now associated with socially engaged practice—has been anti-institutional or at least extremely skeptical in relation to institutional power. This feels almost definitional as institutions are by their nature bound up with existing power structures. In other words, the ethics embodied by major cultural and educational institutions have rarely felt like home to socially engaged practitioners.

It would be easy to frame the situation in Chicago as one of mutual lack of interest or antagonism between socially engaged practitioners and institutions but the story is and has always been more nuanced. This volume includes texts that consider Chicago's institutions as frames, supports, and foils for socially engaged practice and its precursors. The texts address the intersection of major cultural and educational institutions (libraries, museums, universities, and public schools) with independent projects and artist-run initiatives. These interactions include explicit, anti-institutional modes of working, that we might call direct critique. There is also institutional infiltration, such as Temporary Services' secret placement of books in the Harold Washington Library Center, or guerrilla actions, such as the performance orchestrated by Tania Bruguera discussed in the final chapter. Another spectrum ranges from mutual support, in which allegiances formed around shared goals amplify the work of all parties, as characterized by Michael Rakowitz's *Enemy Kitchen (Food Truck)* project, part of a 2012 exhibition that I organized for the University of Chicago's Smart Museum of Art, to what I would call wary collaboration, in which both parties temporarily work together despite generally different agendas, as exemplified by the Museum of Contemporary Art and the Conservative Vice Lords' collaboration on the project space Art & Soul more than forty years earlier.

Sometimes it is necessary to create new institutional or quasi-institutional organizations that actively or implicitly challenge the status quo of larger institutions. This was the case with Randolph Street Gallery, as discussed by Peter Taub and Iñigo Manglano-Ovalle. At other times, in institutions small enough for a fundamental shift to happen, change can occur from within. Such was the case with Sculpture Chicago, whose *Culture in Action* program is revisited by Lisa Corrin, or the Jane Addams Hull-House Museum's sex-positive programming undertaken by Lisa Junkin Lopez. Meanwhile, Gregory Sholette's approach to teaching arts administration at the School of the Art Institute of Chicago and David Senior's consideration of the archiving of radical histories at the Newberry Library and the Museum of Modern Art demonstrate that even large institutions can move through specific programs.

Varied forms of interrelation among socially engaged practitioners and cultural institutions will continue to evolve, perhaps quite quickly. Socially engaged practice is having an institutional moment right now. Current interest in social practice is building on other long strands of thinking, including decades of work by museums seeking to reach and welcome wider and more diverse audiences, and a rich discourse around collaborative and community-based art—as this book and the series of which it is a part shows. The twinned tasks of assessing and learning from the histories and current modes of interaction between socially engaged practitioners and institutions thus feel urgent now, both here in Chicago and within wider art worlds. Some of the questions considered in the texts that follow include: What's at stake when artists committed to socially engaged work move into relation with institutions like museums, public schools, universities, and libraries—whether as active affiliates or invited guests or through guerrilla interventions? When and how can institutions be productive partners that offer needed resources and serve as repositories of inspiration? What's gained or lost on both sides—and is "sides" still (or was it ever) a constructive metaphor, especially given the rapid rise of institutional interest in socially engaged art? And when an institution does open itself either to invited collaborators or surprise visitors, what kinds of responsibilities fall on both host and guest?

Imaginaries

In the waning days of the nineteenth century, a reformer named Henry Demarest Lloyd wrote a speculative fable in which Chicagoans come together to create a new community they call No Mean City. While certainly informed by prior utopian models, Lloyd's strongest inspiration came from an exhibition—the 1893 world's fair, known popularly as the White City and officially as the World's Columbian Exposition. In his fable, Lloyd saw the fair as an aspirational version of the city itself. He described the demolition of the White City at the close of the fair as a loss that galvanizes Chicagoans to take action, to reach again for something beyond the inequities and flat comforts of everyday life. People from all walks of life—including, notably, artists—begin to work together, eventually creating this fictional new community adjacent to Chicago. Over time, it grows into a kind of paradisical zone in which a newly equalized class of citizens lives in harmony, a place that hums and sparkles as a kind of research-and-development site for progressive urbanism and civil coexistence. (It does this so well, in fact, that it eventually eclipses Chicago.) So, rather than seeing the world's fair as merely a boosterish, expensive civic spectacle—a reasonable critique—Lloyd spun a tale in which the fair inspires a different sort of grand endeavor.

Lloyd's utopian fable describes a collective project based in ideals of social justice and equality. An exhibition provides direct inspiration for the collective work of social change. Artists are named among the citizens working together toward this change. And No Mean City grows into something that we might think of as an institution that incubates and tests new ways of living and working.[1]

The limits of Lloyd's text leap out at modern readers, particularly its purple prose and over-earnest optimism in relation to a particular kind of progress. But we can draw something still from the text's too-much-ness, its dark spots, its weirdnesses. Especially within the context of a conversation about social practice and civic good, it feels useful to be reminded that we sometimes need to embrace the irrational. We need to continue to seek out both resonant true histories and tall tales from the city's past as well as from its complex present. Over time, through mutual consideration and debate, these unearthed stories about institutions and imaginaries might inspire new ways of envisioning the intricate and ever-evolving interplay among art, citizens, and city.

Chicago's civic imaginary is in part built; it is the cityscape itself. As I write, landmarks of Chicago culture surround me. I'm in a sun-filled coffee shop on the ground floor of the Fisher Building, a gracious early skyscraper located just inside the Loop's southern edge. Across the way, I can see the Harold Washington Library and the hulking postmodern gargoyles that perch along its roofline. Around the corner, Alexander Calder's classic mid-century sculpture arcs up from a public plaza, all red curves against the crisp dark backdrop of Mies van der Rohe's modernist buildings. A short walk over to the lakefront would immerse me in the crowds exploring the city's big museums and swarming around Anish Kapoor's *Cloud Gate,* watching as their distorted reflections stretch across the sculpture's gleaming surface to merge with city and sky.

Ironically, this setting feels appropriate to the task of introducing a book that deals with the history of socially engaged practice in Chicago—a political, ethical, and/or activist approach that is not necessarily linked to any particular aesthetic form or method. The iconic surroundings—classic buildings, gleaming sculpture, great institutions—might be thought of as key components of an internationally visible "brand" that projects an image of contemporary Chicago as a sleekly powerful Midwestern city embellished with properly glossy and venerable cultural accouterments. Yet this contemporary vision pushes against other fabled imagery of the city and its rough-and-tumble past: the Great Fire of 1871 and the mythic story of its subsequent up-by-bootstraps civic rebirth; gangsters and corrupt machine politics; the radical work of labor activists, muckraking journalists, and civic reformers. The polished sleekness also sits in uneasy relation to infamous aspects of the city's present, including the massive gaps between rich and poor and between whites and people of color. The imbalance expresses itself concretely in the high murder rates, closed schools, and necessary day-to-day resilience that mark life for the many Chicagoans who live in deteriorating neighborhoods beyond the city's core. This contradictory brew of Chicago-ness is both absorbed daily by its citizens and exported—a civic imaginary—inflected by factors such as age, race, class, neighborhood, and tribe that cause us to find different imaginaries at play. It has engendered a sense of artistic energy particular to this city that has played out in the past and shows no signs of abating.

The texts in the first section of the book—Imagining Chicago—lay groundwork for a broad consideration of both Chicago's civic imaginary view of society and ways in which activism is practiced. Studs Terkel's classic essay "Bound for Glory" reflects the verve and swagger of the city's quest for a stature all its own. His indelible voice delivers an unsentimental but deeply humane sensibility that provides ballast and inspiration for many current social practitioners. Sociologists Terry Nichols Clark, Daniel A. Silver, and Stephen W. Sawyer offer another approach to understanding the city. In a text rich with informative facts, they consider how data, analysis, and imagery generated by the University of Chicago's sociologists over the past century profoundly shaped not only that field of inquiry but also perceptions of the city. Their viewpoint influenced those living here and those around the world for whom The Chicago School defined twentieth-century urban research. The final two texts in the section move into consideration of recent social practice. Hamza Walker in conversation with Ronne Hartfield, Edward Maldonado, and Robert Peters sheds light on Chicago milestones during the 1980s that were extensions of the dramatic changes associated with the 1960s. They speak about Urban Gateways' mission of artists in schools as giving the decade's slogan of multiculturalism real meaning through all aspects of its operations; repurposing the city's former main library into the Cultural Center, which has come to be a place for all citizens to see their city and be represented; and Randolph Street Gallery as a site for purposefully bringing together art and politics. Each had transformative effects on the art scene in this city. This inside view is complemented by that of Dieter Roelstraete, sharing his outside-in view as a European curator new to Chicago as he encounters the city through artists' eyes and questions whether some forms of socially engaged art practice can be expected to result in actual social change. Three sections follow the introductory chapter. Each section considers the intersection of socially engaged practice with Chicago's institutions and imaginaries through a different, loosely structured theme: Reworking Education, Collecting Stories, and Public Propositions. Brief introductions follow that summarize the contents of each section.

---

1 Lloyd developed his ideas around the same time that many of the city's key cultural institutions were founded—not only the University of Chicago (1896) and the Art Institute of Chicago (1890) but also smaller, more experimental projects that gave concrete form to ideas about progressive education, democracy, and social justice such as Jane Addams's Hull-House (1889) and John Dewey's University of Chicago Laboratory School (1896).

Kerry James Marshall, *7am Sunday Morning*, 2003 (detail).

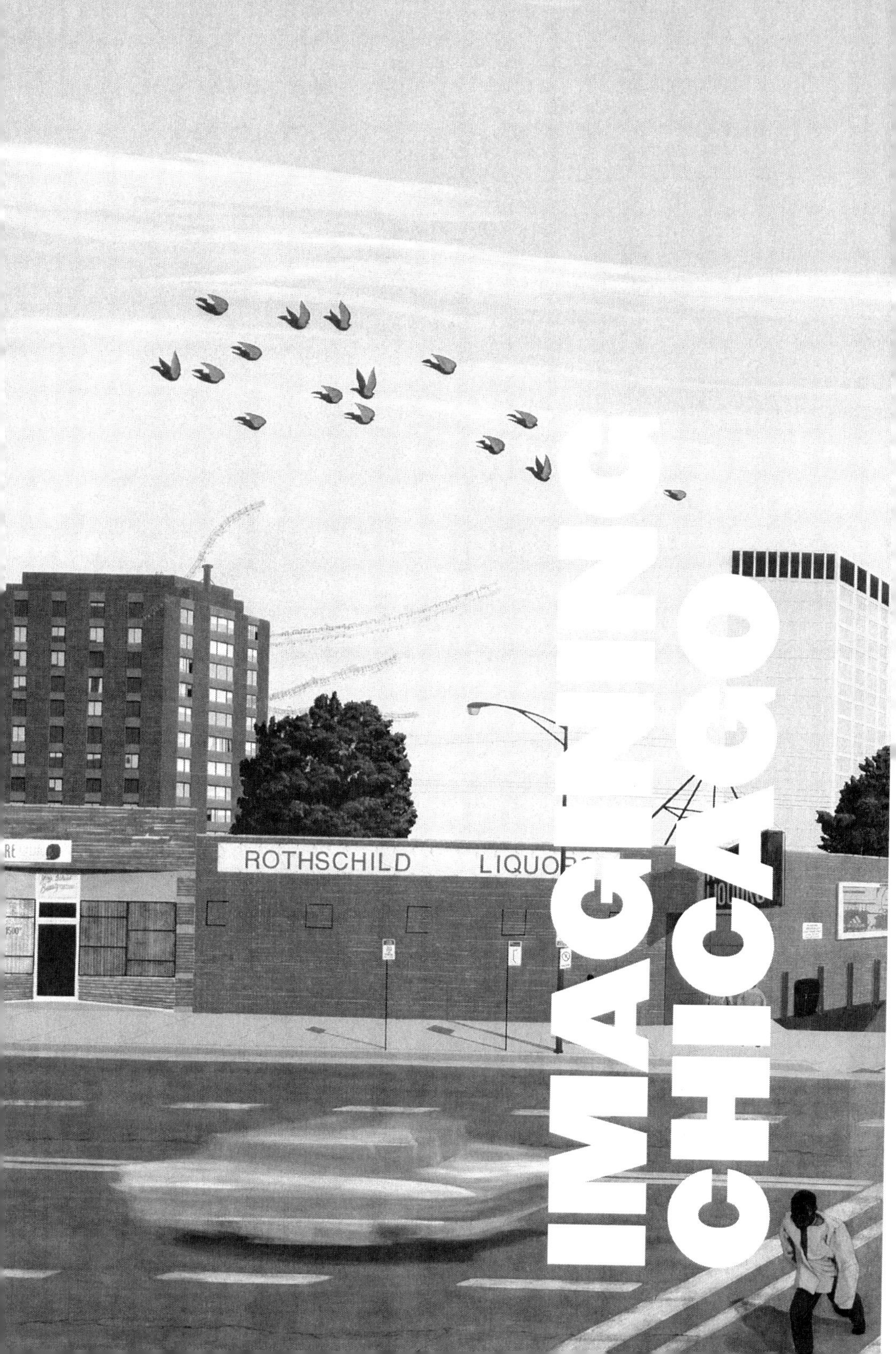

ROTHSCHILD LIQUORS
IMAGINING
CHICAGO

Bound for Glory

Studs Terkel

Bound for Glory (1920)
Away up in the northward,
Right on the borderline,
A great commercial city,
Chicago, you will find.
Her men are all like Abelard,
Her women like Heloise [rhymes with "noise"] —
All honest, virtuous people,
For they live in Elanoy.

So move your family westward,
Bring all your girls and boys,
And rise to wealth and honor
In the state of Elanoy.
          —A nineteenth-century folk song

When Abe Lincoln came out of the wilderness and loped off with the Republican nomination on that memorable May day, 1860, the Wigwam had been resonant with whispers. Behind cupped hands, lips imperceptibly moved: We just give Si Cameron Treasury, they give us Pennsylvania, Abe's got it wrapped up. OK wit'chu? A wink. A nod. Done. It was a classic deal, Chicago style.

As ten thousand spectators roared on cue, Seward didn't know what hit him. His delegates had badges but no seats. Who you? Dis seat's mine.

Possession's nine-tent's da law, ain't it?

Proud Seward, the overwhelming favorite, was a New Yorker who had assumed that civilization ended west of the Hudson. He knew nothing of the young city's spirit of I Will.

When, in 1920, Warren Gamaliel Harding was similarly touched by Destiny, there had been no such whisperings in the Coliseum. Just desultory summer mumblings (it was an unseasonably hot June: 100 degrees outside, 110 inside; bamboo fans of little use): Lowden, Wood, Johnson. Wood, Johnson, Lowden. Johnson, Lowden, Wood. Three frontrunnners and not a one catching fire. How long can this go on? Four ballots are enough. C'mon, it's too hot for a deadlock. Shall we pick straws?

But this wasn't just any conversation city. This was Chicago. Never mind the oratory. Yeah, yeah, we know about the Coliseum where, in 1896, the cry was Bryan, Bryan, Bryan as the Boy Orator thundered eloquently of crowns of thorns and crosses of gold. Nah, nah, let's settle this Chicago style.

A hotel room not far away.

The Blackstone, so often graced by Caruso and Galli-Curci during our city's lush opera season, was on this occasion beyond grace. Nah, nah, it's too hot. Maybe the Ohio Gang ran things that day, but with blowing curlicues heavenward from H. Upmann cigars in the smoke-filled room, the deal—Harding, OK?—was strictly My Kind of Town, Chicago Is.

As for my city, Chicago, yet, along came Jane Addams. Was it in 1889 that she founded Hull House? The lady was out of her depth, they said. Imagine. Trying to change a neighborhood of immigrants, scared and lost, where every other joint was a saloon and every street a cesspool. And there was John Powers, alderman of the Nineteenth Ward, running the turf in the fashion of his First Ward colleagues, Bathhouse John and Hinky Dink. Johnny Da Pow, the Italian immigrants called him. He was the Pooh-Bah, the high muckety-muck, the ultimate clout. Everything had to be cleared through Da Pow. Still, this lady with the curved spine, but a spine nonetheless, stuck it out. And something happened.

She told young Jessie Binford: Everything grows from the bottom up. This place belongs to everybody, not just Johnny Da Pow. And downtown. No, she told Jessie, I have no blueprint. We learn from life itself.

So many years later, years of small triumphs and large losses, Jessie Binford, ninety, is seated in a small Blackstone Hotel room. The Blackstone again, for God's sake? It isn't a smoke-filled room this time. My cigar, still wrapped in cellophane, is deep in my pocket. It's an H. Upmann—would you believe it? The old woman, looking not unlike Whistler's mother, is weary and in despair. The wrecking ball had just yesterday done away with Hull House and most of the neighborhood. Even the beloved elm beneath her window had been uprooted and removed.

The boys downtown tried to buy off Jessie Binford. You can live at the Blackstone as our guest for the rest of your life, they told her. Anything to keep her quiet. She and a young neighborhood housewife, Florence Scala, were making a big deal out of this. Sshhh. But they wouldn't shush, these two.

These two. Florence Scala, first-generation Italian-American. Her father, a tailor, was a romantic from Tuscany. He was a lover of opera, of course, especially Caruso records, even the scratchy ones. He had astronomy fever, too, though his longing to visit the Grand Canyon transcended his yen to visit the moon. He was to make neither voyage. The neighborhood was his world and that was enough.

For Florence, her father's daughter, the neighborhood reflected the universe, with its multicolors, its varied immigrant life, its circumambient passions.

Jessie Binford, of early Quaker-American stock. Her father, a merchant, trudging from Ohio to Iowa in the mid-nineteenth century, found what he was looking for. The house he built in 1874 "still stands as fundamentally strong as the day it was built," his daughter observed. At the turn of the century, she found what she was looking for: a mission, Hull House, and a place, Harrison-Halsted. She found the neighborhood.

For Florence Scala and Jessie Binford, Harrison-Halsted was Blake's little grain of sand.

They passed each other on early-morning strolls along these streets, not yet mean. They came to know each other and value each other, as they clasped hands to save these streets. They lost, of course. Betrayed right down the line. By our city's Most Respectable.

"I'm talking about the boards of trustees, the people who control the money. Downtown bankers, factory owners, architects, people in the stock market." Florence speaks softly, and that, if anything, accentuates the bitterness.

The jet set, too. The young people, grandchildren of the old-timers on the board, who were not like elders, if you know what I mean. They were not with us. There were also some very good people, those from the old days. But they didn't count any more.

This new crowd, these new tough kind of board members, who didn't mind being on the board for the prestige it gave them, dominated. These were the people closely aligned to the city government, in real estate and planning. And some very fine old Chicago families.

As Florence describes the antecedents of today's yuppies, she laughs ever so gently. "The nicest people in Chicago."

Miss Binford is leaving Chicago forever. She had come to Hull House in 1906. She is going home to die. Marshalltown, Iowa. The town her father helped found.

The blue of her eyes is dimmed through her spectacles. Her passion, undimmed. "Miss Addams understood why each person had become what he was. She didn't condemn because she understood what life does to people, to those of us who have everything and those of us who have nothing." It's been a rough day and her words, clearly offered, become somewhat slurry now. "Today we're getting further and further away from this eternal foundation on which community life must rest. I feel most sorry for our young people that are growing up at this time . . ." It's dusk and time to let her go. I press the STOP button of my Uher.

Our double-vision, double-standard, double-value, and double-cross have been patent ever since—at least, ever since the earliest of our city fathers took the Potawatomis for all they had. Poetically, these dispossessed natives dubbed this piece of turf "Chikagou." Some say it is Indian lingo for "City of the Wild Onion;" some say it really means "City of the Big Smell." "Big" is certainly the operative word around these parts.

Nelson Algren's classic *Chicago: City on the Make* is the late poet's single-hearted vision of his town's doubleness. "Chicago . . . forever keeps two faces, one for winners and one for losers; one for hustlers and one for squares . . . One face for Go-Getters and one for Go-Get-It-Yourselfers. One for poets and one for promoters . . . One for early risers, one for evening hiders."

It is the city of Jane Addams, settlement worker, and Al Capone, entrepreneur; of Clarence Darrow, lawyer, and Julius Hoffman, judge; of Louis Sullivan, architect, and Sam Insull, magnate; of John Altgeld, governor, and Paddy Bauler, alderman. (Paddy's the one who some years ago observed, "Chicago ain't ready for reform." It is echoed in our day by other, less paunchy aldermen.)

It is still the arena of those who dream of the City of Man and those who envision a City of Things. The battle appears to be forever joined. The armies, ignorant and enlightened, clash by day as well as by night. Chicago is America's dream, writ large. And flamboyantly.

Paradox: Today's council members opposing the younger Mayor Daley are more diffuse, less cohesive, of all color, affording the son of the old Buddha more power than his old man had.

It has—as they used to whisper of the town's fast women—a reputation.

Elsewhere in the world, anywhere, name the city, name the country, Chicago evokes one image above all others. Sure, architects and those interested in such matters mention Louis Sullivan, Frank Lloyd Wright, and Mies van der Rohe. Hardly anyone in his right mind questions this city as the architectural Athens. Others, literary critics among them, mention Dreiser, Norris, Lardner, Algren, Farrell, Bellow, and the other Wright, Richard. Sure, Mencken did say something to the effect that there is no American literature worth mentioning that didn't come out of the palatinate that is Chicago. Of course, a special kind of jazz and blues, acoustic rural and electrified urban, have been called "Chicago style." All this is indubitably true.

Still others, for whom history has stood still since the Democratic convention of 1968, murmur: Mayor Daley. (As Chicago's most perceptive chronicler, Mike Royko, pointed out, the name has become the eponym for "city chieftain"; thus, it is often one word, "mare-daley.") The tone, in distant quarters as well as here, is usually one of awe: you may interpret it any way you please. "Who's the mare-daley of your town?"

> Hog Butcher for the World, Tool Maker, Stacker of Wheat, Player
> with Railroads and the Nation's Freight Handler; Stormy, husky,
> brawling, City of the Big Shoulders...

Carl Sandburg, the white-haired old Swede with the wild cowlick, drawled out the brag in 1914. Today, he is regarded in more soft-spoken quarters as an old gaffer, out of fashion, more attuned to the street corner than the class in American studies. Unfortunately, there is some truth to the charge that his dug-out-of-the-mud city, sprung-out-of–the-fire-of-1871 Chicago, is no longer what it was when the Swede sang that song. It is no longer the slaughterhouse of the hang-from-the-hoof hogs. The stockyards have gone to feedlots in, say, Clovis, New Mexico, or Greeley, Colorado, or Logansport, Indiana. It is no longer the railroad center, when there were at least seven awesome depots where a thousand passenger trains refueled themselves each day; and it is no longer, since the Great Depression of the 1930s, the stacker of wheat.

During all these birth years of the twenty-first century, the unique landmarks of American cities have been replaced by Golden Arches, Red Lobsters, Pizza Huts, and Marriotts, so you can no longer tell one neon wilderness from another. As your plane lands, you no longer see old landmarks, old signatures. You have no idea where you may be. A few years ago, while I was on a wearisome book tour, I mumbled to the switchboard operator at the motel, "Please wake me at six a.m. I must be in Cleveland by noon."

Came the response: "Sir, you are in Cleveland." That Chicago, too, has so been affected is of small matter. It has been and always will be, in the memory of the nine-year-old boy arriving here, the archetypal American city.

One year after Warren G. Harding's anointment, almost to the day, the boy stepped off the coach at the La Salle Street depot. He had come from east of the Hudson and had been warned by the kids on the Bronx block to watch out for Indians. The Blackhawks. The boy felt not unlike Ruggles, the British butler, on his way to Red Gap. Envisioning painted faces and feathered war bonnets.

In Kiev, in 1963, I ran into kids who on hearing me say "Chicago" burst into laughter. They waved imaginary hockey sticks and howled out "Blackhawks!"

August 1921. The boy had sat up all night, but had never been more awake and exhilarated. At Buffalo, the vendors had passed through the aisles. A cheese sandwich and a half-pint carton of milk was all he had had during the twenty-hour ride. But on this morning of the great awakening, he wasn't hungry.

His older brother was there at the station. Grinning, gently jabbing at his shoulder. He twisted the boy's cap around. "Hey, Nick Altrock," the brother said. He knew the boy knew that this baseball clown with the turned-around cap had once been a great pitcher for the White Sox. The boy's head as well as his cap was awhirl.

There was expensive-looking luggage carried off the Pullmans. Those were the cars up front, a distant planet away from the day coaches. There were cool Palm Beach-suited men and even cooler, lightly clad women stepping down from these cars. Black men in red caps—all called George—were wheeling luggage carts toward the terminal. My God, all those bags for just two people. "Twentieth Century limited," the brother whispered. "Even got a barber – shop on that baby."

There were straw suitcases and bulky bundles borne elsewhere. There were all those other travelers, some lost, others excitable in heavy, unseasonable clothing. Their talk was broken English or a strange language or an American accent foreign to the boy. Where were the Indians?

This was Chicago, indubitably the center of the nation's railways, as the Swede from Galesburg had so often sung out. Chicago to Los Angeles. Chicago to Anywhere. All roads let to and from Chicago. No wonder the boy was bewitched.

Chicago has always been and still is the City of Hands. Horny, calloused hands. Yet, here they came: the French voyageurs; the Anglo traders; the German burghers, many of whom were the children of those dreamers who dared dream of better worlds. So it was that the Chicago Symphony Orchestra came into being; one of the world's most highly regarded. It was originally Teutonic in its repertoire; now it is universal.

They came, too, from Eastern Europe as hands. The Polish population of Chicago is second only to that of Warsaw. They came from the Mediterranean and from below the Rio Grande; and there was always the inner migration from Mississippi, Arkansas, Louisiana, and Tennessee. The African American journalist grandson of slaves spoke with a touch of nostalgia, memories of his hometown, Paris. That is, Paris, Tennessee. "Out in the fields, we'd hear the whistle of the Illinois Central engineer. OOOweee! There goes the IC to—Chica–a–ago!" It was even referred to in the gospel song "City Called Heaven."

The city called heaven, where there were good jobs in the mills and you did not have to get off the sidewalk when a white passed by. Jimmy Rushing sang the upbeat blues, "Goin' to Chicago, Baby, Sorry I Can't Take You."

It wasn't quite heaven. In 1919, an African American boy swam into a zone considered white and was stoned into the waves, setting off the riots of 1919.

Here I came in 1921, the nine-year-old, who for the next fifteen years lived and clerked at the rooming house, run by my mother, and the Wells-Grand Hotel. (My ailing father ran it for its first several years, and then my mother, a much tougher customer, took over.)

To me, it was simply referred to as the Grand, the Chicago prototype of the posh pre-Hitler Berlin Hotel. It was here I encountered our aristocrats as guests: the boomer firemen, who blazed our railroad engines; the seafarers who sailed the Great Lakes; the self-educated craftsmen, known as the Wobblies but whose proper name was the Industrial Workers of the World (IWW). Here in our lobby, they went head-to-head with their *bêtes noires*, the anti-union stalwarts, who tabbed "IWW" as the acronym for "I Won't Work."

Oh, those were wild, splendiferous debates, outdoing in decibel power the Lincoln–Douglas bouts. These were the Hands of Chicago making themselves heard loud and clear. It was the truly Grand Hotel, and I felt like the concierge of the Ritz of Paris.

There were labor battles, historic ones, where the fight for the eight-hour day had begun. It brought forth the song: "Eight hours we'd have for working, eight hours we'd have for play, eight hours for sleeping, in free Amerikay." It was in Chicago that the Haymarket Affair took place and four men were hanged in a farcical trial that earned our city the world's opprobrium. Yet it is to our city's honor that our governor, John Peter Altgeld, pardoned the three surviving defendants in one of the most eloquent documents ever issued on behalf of justice.

The simple truth is that our God, Chicago's God, is Janus, the two-faced one. One is that of Warner Brothers films with Jimmy Cagney and Edward

G. Robinson as our sociopathic icons. The other is that of Jane Addams, who introduced the idea of the Chicago Woman and world citizen.

It was Chicago that brought forth Louis Sullivan, whom Frank Lloyd Wright referred to as "Lieber Meister." Sullivan envisioned the skyscraper. It was here that he wanted to touch the heavens. Nor was it any accident that young Sullivan corresponded with the elderly Walt Whitman, because they both dreamed of democratic vistas, where Chicago was the City of Man rather than the City of Things. Though Sullivan died broke and neglected, it is his memory that glows as he is recalled by those who followed Wright.

What the nine-year-old boy felt about Chicago in 1921 is a bit more mellow and seared. He is aware of its carbuncles and warts, a place far from heaven, but it is his town, the only one he calls home.

Nelson Algren, Chicago's bard, said it best: "Like loving a woman with a broken nose, you may well find lovelier lovelies. But never a lovely so real."

This text was originally published in *Touch And Go: A Memoir* (New York: The New Press, 2007) 19-28. © 2007 Studs Terkel. Parts of the original text were excerpted from Terkel's book, *Chicago* (New York: Pantheon Books, 1985 and 1986). Reprinted here with permission of The New Press. www.thenewpress.com

City, School, and Image: The Chicago School of Sociology and the Image of Chicago

Terry Nichols Clark, Daniel A. Silver, and Stephen W. Sawyer

Saul Bellow wrote, "there were beautiful and moving things in Chicago, but culture was not one of them."[1] Yet by 2009, the Director of the National Endowment of the Arts could say: "Mayor Daley should be the No. 1 hero to everyone in this country who cares about art".[2] How do these old and new images of the arts interact with Chicago's social makeup? If the arts were not central to Chicagoans in the early twentieth century, arguably arts, leisure, and entertainment became key drivers of urban transformation by the end of the same century. The implications are broad as many changes are not unique to Chicago. The growth of twenty-five to thirty-four-year-olds in Chicago's three-mile downtown, relative to its suburbs, was larger than any other US city between 1990 and 2000. Many, especially civic and political leaders, felt that four months of summer entertainment, joined to more neighborhood festivals than any other US city, helped attract these new young persons.

The highly visible, city government–sponsored arts activities were a conscious effort to celebrate, extend, and transform Chicago's powerful ethnic traditions, rooted in its neighborhoods. They built on images of Chicago with long and deep histories, forged in no small part by the sociologists who became known by the name of their city, the Chicago School. Yet as the city has changed and grown more aesthetically sophisticated, so too have its sociologists, who continue to seek out ways to represent and imagine the local contexts in which contemporary social life unfolds, however globalized, networked, and digitized it has become.

Much has been written about the birth and influence of the Chicago School of Sociology. Less noted is the reciprocal relationship between the city, the style of social research, and the school that ultimately took its name. The city imprints its character on the school; the school produces a "Chicago way" of understanding cities. Distinctive representational and analytical techniques emerge, which feed back into the self-understanding of the city. We highlight key elements in this circuit of city, school, and urban imaginary, which persist to this day.

Several factors make Chicago distinct. These features played a strong role in forming Chicago social thinkers and their ways of analyzing cities. They continue to have resonance for understanding the urban culture, politics, and policies of the twentieth-first century, and in thinking about the continued legacy of the Chicago school of sociology.

Catholicism

Chicago remains the largest major US city with a strong tradition of Catholicism. As of 2006, the average Chicago zip code contained between two and four times as many Catholic churches as the average Los Angeles or New York zip code. White Protestants, on the other hand, were under 20 percent of the population throughout much of the twentieth century. This is not to say that Protestant elites and related reform movements have been absent—Chicago's Catholic tradition was drastically shaken, for example, in the 1984 mayoral election of Harold Washington, who led a coalition of Protestants (African American and white), Jews, and "Lakefront Liberals" against the Catholic establishment. Even so, Catholic culture and social practices have enjoyed a high level of legitimacy within Chicago, relative to most US cities.

Particularism

One of the key results of this Catholic legitimacy has been the emergence of a city built on strong neighborhood identities, woven together by personal relations. Obviously, the city has been rife with racial and ethnic segregation: in housing location and in politics, with ethnic slating of candidates, local parades, and jealously guarded neighborhood autonomy.

Aldermen classically made zoning decisions for their wards, granting or withholding building permits, sometimes indefinitely—unthinkable in a city with an at-large, good government ethos. The continual flow of immigrants from around the world has filled neighborhoods with new character, but ethnically and culturally distinct neighborhoods remain stronger and more politically legitimate in Chicago than in most US locales. Consider some distinctive Chicago slogans: Don't make no waves, don't back no losers; We don't want nobody nobody sent; Chicaga ain't ready for reform.[3]

Localism

Chicago has been home to consistent claims that the state and national governments are distant, alien, even irrelevant to what really matters, namely local respect, turf, and "juice." Within the city, Chicago politics builds on a microcosmic battle between fiercely independent wards and ward bosses and the centralizing tendencies of city hall. Though the myth of an autonomous local political sphere is belied by events as distant as Daley I's role in the Democratic Convention in 1968 or as recent as Rahm Emanuel's rapid transition from the White House to the mayor's office, the ideal of very local politics has maintained a powerful hold in Chicago's self-understanding. Indeed, seniority as a principle for political slating could lead to sixty-year olds being sent to Washington as freshmen congressmen. Likewise in Chicago, Rahm Emmanuel's decision to leave his federal position as Chief of Staff for a local mayoralty could count as "moving up in the world." This reverses the normal view that local government is secondary. To build legitimacy in the Chicago political scene, one must see the city as an end in itself.

Popular Cosmopolitanism

The main traditions in Chicago are not original, but hark back to such locations as County Cork, Puerto Rico, Krakow, or Mexico City. Restaurants and churches, neighborhood schools, bars and precinct captains have carried on these distinct traditions. A "big shouldered" acceptance of grit and crassness thus built on a snub-the-proper-folks attitude, and encouraged popular labels such as Hinky Dink Kenna, Bathhouse John, and Fast Eddy Vrdolyak—three powerful aldermen/bosses. The recent television series *The Boss* built its suspense around a vision of Chicago politics as a hard-hitting high-wire game between local ethnic, black, and other Catholic groups and a take-no-prisoners mayor. This attitude is epitomized in the speeches of Mayors Daley I and II. They were proud to speak Chicago Public School English, as are many CPS teachers. Hugh Heffner's Playboy empire exported Chicago's bawdy tradition globally. Still if "Chicaga" pronunciation was traditionally mainstream in at least Chicago politics, others still protested, like upscale *Chicago Magazine* which ran a profile on "Da Mayor," citing his diction and pronunciation as evidence that he was as corrupt as his father.[4]

The populist culture of beer and brats meant little focus on public art and aesthetics as public policy issues. This inattention was dramatically reversed in the mid-1990s, when public art and aesthetics were embraced with a dynamism impossible most elsewhere, at least in the United States. Drawing explicitly on the cultural planning traditions of European cities such as Paris, this embrace of culture and aesthetics by City Hall exploded onto the scene around 1995, after the blockbuster success of the Art Institute's Monet show, ostensibly the largest in the world. Flower gardens, wrought iron fences, arts districts, entertainment venues, and public art blossomed. Still, these innovations appropriated themes from Chicago's first *Cultural Plan*, developed as part of Harold Washington's initial agenda in 1986, which itself carried forward core Chicago ideas such as the strong charismatic individual artist who gives voice to local neighborhood cultures.[5] Even the fabulously post-modern Millennium Park bears the Chicago mark of local turf, divided up as it is into separate zones within which major donors controlled decisions about design and public art.[6]

Openness, Charisma, and Clientelism

The lack of an inherited early American elite and emergence of a frontier character pushed Chicago to sell itself, almost from the beginning, as a place where you could, and had to, make it on your own. Early boosters like John W. Wright insisted that it was Chicago that would make the East, not the other way around. In this context, new Chicago elites emerged quickly, borrowing from the East, but oftentimes leaving Venice and jumping over Manhattan to land directly in "plastic Chicago," as one of the great Boston Brahmins, Henry Adams, famously claimed in his chapter on Chicago.[7] With weak planning and minimal regulation, the best and worst architecture co-exist on the same block in Chicago. One of the great urban plans of the United States, Burnham's 1909 *Plan of Chicago*, rooted in the hierarchical principles of European urban planning, could be produced in the same city where Rudyard Kipling suggested: "There was no color in the street and no beauty—only a maze of wire ropes overhead and dirty flagging stones under foot."[8] Although non-governmental civic leaders long fought over the issues, individual ambition and personal charisma often trumped general planning and holistic aesthetics. Perhaps represented in recent years by

Trump Tower, greed and unbridled individualism were the labels of those who did not look more deeply—probed by Frank Norris's *The Pit*, Steffans' *The Shame of the Cities*, Brecht's *Saint Joan of the Stockyards*, Theodore Dreiser's *Sister Carrie*, or Saul Bellow's novels.

The huge political machine gave organizational form to this network of strong leaders. It fueled the ambitions of gangs, big corporations, real estate developers, options traders, and mayors to "make no little plans." Some international locations are similar to Chicago in this regard. Thus China today is a paradise for visionary architects and planners, who build unfettered by citizen protest and zoning found in Europe. In contrast, Chicago developer Sam Zell, visiting Israel, told the *Jerusalem Times* in 2004 that there was so much red tape that he refused to work in Israel.

Persistent Ethnic Politics

Ethnic politics have aligned in distinctive ways with class politics. In the heart of the Chicago Renaissance, a realist literary movement that would influence the Chicago School of Sociology, socialist Carl Sandburg penned poems in ethnic Chicago on "the dago shovel man." More recently, Barbara Ferman (1996) has explored the implication of this pattern by contrasting Chicago with Pittsburgh; all issues in Chicago from recycling to schools were (traditionally) redefined as questions of turf, power, and race/ethnicity.[9] The term "yuppie" was transformed in Chicago to label a new "ethnicity" invading the city. In Washington or even New York "yuppies" were part of the normal establishment. Not in Chicago. The idea that less articulate, blue-collar citizens held distinct values and preferences, that would not necessarily disappear with political reform, education, or Americanization, legitimated a distinct, explicit focus on ethnicity as interpenetrating all aspects of life and politics. No yuppies in my bar!

Pragmatic Relativism

This everyday acceptance of ethnic/national/cultural distinctiveness led to an anthropological cultural relativism and mutual tolerance—"You deliver your precinct, and I'll deliver mine"—that does not support the revolutionary moralistic aspirations of New England abolitionists, or David Dubinsky's Russian union organizers in New York City, or Caesar Chavez's Mexican farm workers in southern California. Still, this non-ideological, traditional style changed with Harold Washington after 1984. His implantation of reform from a black protestant/civil rights background brought the traditional machine to its knees. It redefined the core of Chicago politics and laid a foundation for new rules of the game. If Chicago politics traditionally was defined by non-ideological, personalistic, exchange, since Harold Washington, politics and policy have become more explicit and sometimes even ideological. But pragmatism remains a leitmotif: it is no accident that the pragmatist School of Philosophy, championed by Chicagoans such as John Dewey, G.H. Mead, and Jane Addams, took root in a city where practicality has long been a hallmark. Jane Addams specifically innovated by using general appeals to the public that invoked moral concerns to address new issues.

These features of the city strongly informed the Chicago style of social research. Robert Park's foundational *The City* is a seminal case in point. There is the strong emphasis on locality: for Park, the neighborhood, not the workplace, is the expression of the "common ties of humanity."[10] Similarly, for Park, in contrast to the Marxian tradition of class analysis, in the "last analysis" social organization rests on the "church, school, and family."[11] Numerous Chicago dissertations pursued these themes, which became key source documents for Cohen.[12] Chicago authors were equally fascinated by the rougher and popular sides of urban culture, examples of which the city offered in abundance: hobos, taxi-dance halls, gangs, ghettos, slums, and the like. The locality of social and cultural life was central to their vision: Park viewed the city as organized not only economically but also into "moral regions" where people with common temperaments and tastes congregate, whether for a "horse race or a grand opera."[13] Chicagoans, moreover, sensitive to a world of open possibility, did not conceive organizations as things and structures but as groups and processes, perpetually growing, ossifying, stagnating, adapting in conflict and cooperation with one another.[14] G.H. Mead's social psychology stressed interaction, play, improvisation, and the social cultivation of individuality. And Chicago authors, inspired by W.I. Thomas's classic *The Polish Peasant in Europe and America,* saw machine politics not as aberrant but as a natural response to the wrenching dislocations caused by mass migration from rural farms to megacity.

If Chicago social interpreters were concerned with Chicago topics, they were equally adept at developing analytic techniques to disclose the Chicago aspects of social life. Early Chicago social researchers made visual renderings of the city, especially maps, crucial to their work. Ernest Burgess's famous maps of concentric circles depicted the city as nested sets of geographically specific occupation and lifestyle zones. He also led in producing some of the first maps in the United States using census tract data. Burgess's concentric circles became iconic in their representation of ideal–typical spatial relationships pur-

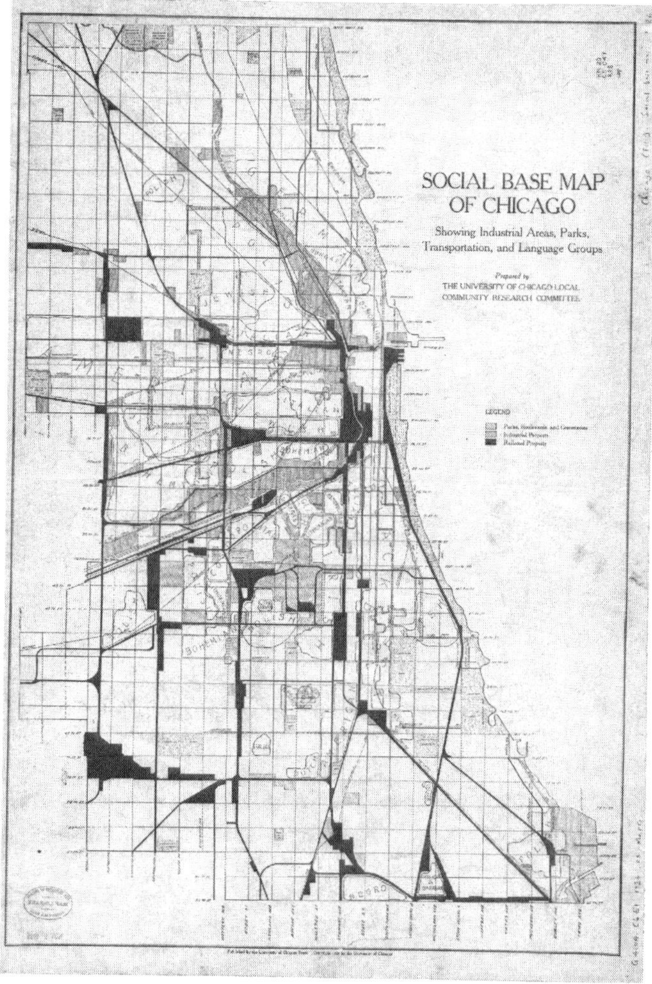

Social base map of Chicago showing industrial areas, parks, transportation, and language groups, prepared by the University of Chicago Local Community Research Committee. Courtesy of the University of Chicago Library, Map Collection.

portedly defining the ecology of all cities. Heavily criticized for their seeming determinism, exacerbated as the number of "anomalies" and divergent urban structures grew, these were not the only sorts of maps Chicago research produced. Another key type were community-area maps. These visualized the city as distinct cultural worlds, defined by the shared identity and self-understanding of community members, not by jurisdictional boundaries or ideal theory.[15]

Similarly, Chicago authors produced maps covered with dots representing the local incidence of different groups, organizations, and behaviors (hobos, ethnicities, dance halls, rooming houses, homicide, alcoholism, depression, divorce). These would often join specific organizations and individuals with the community-area maps to produce a more dynamic picture in which multiple groups and people flow across space, and local identity arises out of concrete interactions. For instance, Frederic Thrasher's 1927 study plotted more than 1300 gangs and their clubhouses across the city and mapped their local turfs. St. Clair Drake's 1940 *Churches and Voluntary Organizations in the Chicago Negro Community* went further, showing both the locations of individual churches and their members, within and beyond their neighborhoods. The "neighborhood" in these depictions emerged at once as a real source of identity and constraint on action but also a permeable boundary that did not fully determine the interests or contacts of its members.

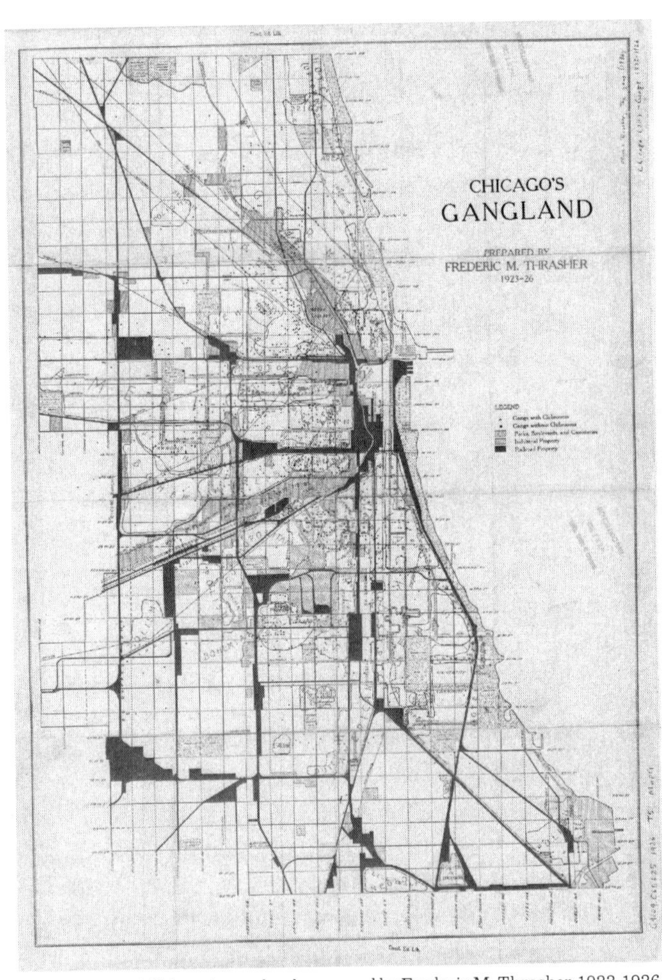

Map of Chicago's gangland, prepared by Frederic M. Thrasher, 1923-1926. Courtesy of the University of Chicago Library, Map Collection.

Likewise, as Chicago students fanned across the city, they refined the techniques of urban ethnography, enacting Park's dictum that the same "patient methods which anthropologists like Boas and Lowie have expended on the study of the life and manners of the North American Indian might be even more fruitfully employed ... in Little Italy on the lower North Side in Chicago."[16] Harvey Zorbaugh's *The Gold Coast and the Slum* perhaps realized this contextual and interactive Chicago approach to social process most fully. According to Abbott:

> The story of the Near North Side involves not only long-term processes like changes in economic structures and in the composition of the immigrant population, but also shorter-term ones like local succession in neighborhoods and even more rapid ones like the turnover of residents in rooming houses. Spatially, the interactional field involves not only the large-scale differentiation from and interdependence of this whole area on the city, but also shorter-range phenomena like the intermingling of church congregations produced by parishioner mobility and the economic interdependencies of the various subsections of the Near North Side itself.[17]

These various representational techniques sensitized the Chicago school and their readers to the locally textured and contextual character of life.

The "Chicago ways" of representing the city all have shaped urban perception in their own right. Richard Wright himself noted how deeply Chicago's sociologists inspired him. "It was not until I stumbled upon science that I discovered some of the meanings of the environment that battered and taunted me."[18] Literary critic Carla Cappetti suggests the connection extends to a "generation of writers in the 1930s." Through close readings of books by James Farrell, Nelson Algren, and Wright, she shows how "characters ... walk along the streets that the sociologists charted, join gangs that they studied, encounter problems that they explained, and come to the sorry ends they foretold."[19]

The influence of the community area maps has proven especially persistent, continuing to this day to shape Chicago policy and perception. Nearly a century later, the names Burgess and his collaborators gave to the seventy-five community areas they found are still the City of Chicago's official designations, and the boundaries they assigned continue to inform city policy and research. This example neatly illustrates the feedback loop between city, school, and image. Burgess and his students "saw" community areas around the city as self-created communities, social products of the Chicago ecology. Their maps gave those communities names and provided

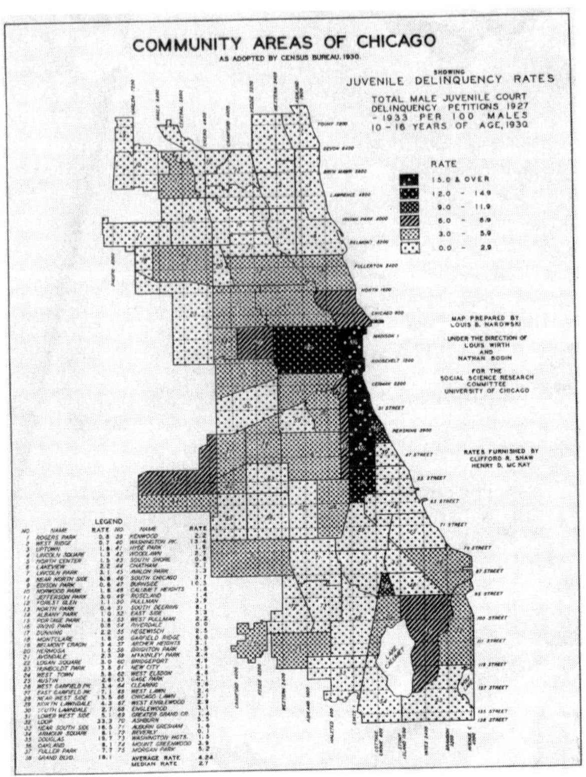

Community areas map of Chicago, as adopted by Census Bureau, 1930, showing juvenile delinquency rates. Map prepared by Louis B. Narowski under direction of Louis Wirth and Nathan Bodin for the Social Science Research Committee, University of Chicago. Courtesy of the University of Chicago Library, Map Collection.

means for representing them cognitively. Those representations and names in turn came to define many of the city's official policies and much of its on-the-ground self-understanding, as a patchwork of communities with distinct identities.

Despite, and perhaps because of, the continuing expansion of globalization, communication, and mobility, these Chicago styles and topics of thought endure. Evidence abounds that neighborhood, community, and local culture persist (sometimes in novel forms)—not to mention patronage and strong personalities—even amidst a chorus of claims about the death of distance, the demise of community, and the massification of life.[20] A steady stream of urban work continues to flow.

Our new Chicago approach, however, explicitly adds arts and culture and moves to higher levels of abstraction. It does so by decomposing local culture into symbolic dimensions of meaning (such as self-expression, glamour, tradition, or transgression) that combine in multiple scenes

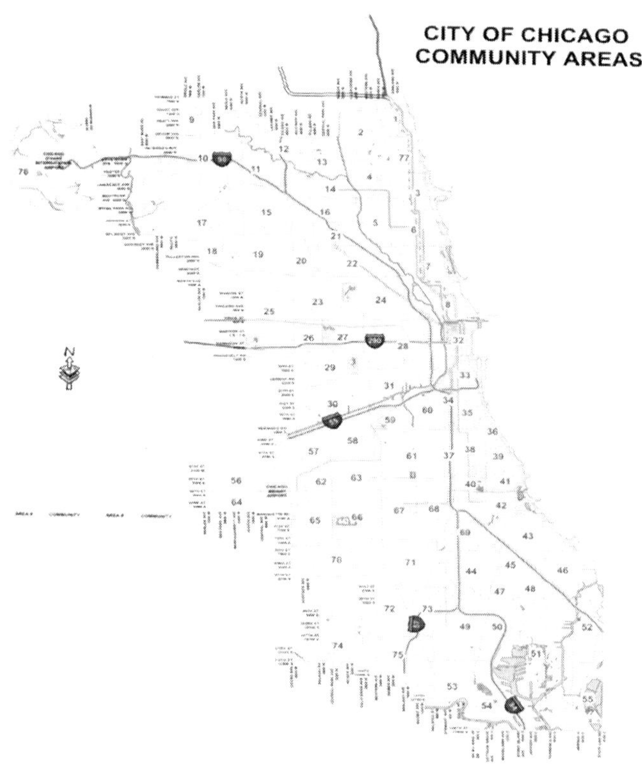

Community areas map of Chicago, 2010. © City of Chicago.
Courtesy of the Department of Planning and Development.

that harken back to classical literary and social theory concepts (such as Community and Urbanity), analyzed with local data across the United States, France, Spain, China, and beyond.[21] The study of race, class, gender, and ethnicity are enriched by adding cultural and aesthetic specifics like neighborliness and self-expression, measured with hundreds of specific amenities like Baptist Churches, community centers, art galleries, and tattoo parlors. The roots of these scenes of neighborliness on Chicago's South Side are shared with rural midwestern and southern areas of the United States, yet the analytical goal remains true to the Chicago spirit captured by Richard Wright's statement quoted above: to discern the city as an overlapping array of emotionally charged, value-laden environments, that can batter and taunt but also excite and elevate.

Scenes analysis explicitly seeks to overcome the under-emphasis on the arts by social scientists generally as well as in Chicago, by articulating how and where culture interpenetrates other processes like population and economic growth. Arts activities and their links to neighborhoods and politics are elaborated Silver and Clark's "Buzz as an Urban Resource."[22] Ethnographies such as Richard Lloyd's *Neo-Bohemia* (on Wicker Park) or Andrew Deener's *Venice* (on Venice, Los Angeles) document the ways of life that characterize iconic arts neighborhoods, subjecting them to the same close scrutiny that earlier researches had applied to Jewish quarters, the Gold Coast, or the slum. Such studies carry forward the Chicago focus on local collective processes but add that many contemporary neighborhoods encourage themes such as unique style, individual spontaneity, and personal expression, play key roles in artistic and cultural production chains, cultivate novel aesthetics such as "grit as glamour," and operate under newer principles of prestige, where coolness and "subcultural capital" are conditions for employment and crucial signs of status. Sampson's *Great American City* continues the more birds-eye tradition of mapping neighborhood concentrations of distinct groups and activities, showing how artist clusters track internet usage, and suggesting that new forms of "cosmopolitan" social engagement continue to be grounded in specific locations, even as communication technology connects people around the globe to one another. New Chicago research is multilevel and multicausal, situating individuals in neighborhoods, neighborhoods to one another and their surrounding cities, and to the wider world—all at once.

In these and other ways, urban social science still shows a Chicago impact. Perhaps more important than the specific topics, however, is the way of seeing. Thanks to the early Chicago-School circles, maps, and ethnographies, one can find the "Chicago dimension of life" in studies from Los Angeles to Nashville, from Bogota to Beijing. The School, that is to say, in assimilating Chicago into a mode of social scientific representation, both gave the city a way to cognize itself and produced portable techniques for extending that conception globally.

---

1 Saul Bellow, *Humboldt's Gift* (New York: Penguin, 1975), 69.

2 Chris Jones, "Daley's Chicago a model for nation, says NEA boss," *The Theater Loop* (blog), *Chicago Tribune*, October 22, 2009, http://leisureblogs.chicagotribune.com/the_theater_loop/2009/10/new-nea-chief-lauds-daley-arts-policy-says-model-for-nation.html#at.

3 The first two are titles of books by Milton Rakove published in 1975 and 1979; the third is a slogan shouted at political rallies, on the floor of City Hall, and emblazoned on t-shirts.

4 Jonathan Eig, "Da Rules," *Chicago* 48, no. 11 (November 1999): 115-17, 136-44.

5 Terry N. Clark and Daniel Silver, "Chicago from the political machine to the entertainment machine," in *The Politics of Urban Cultural Policy: Global Perspectives*, eds. Carl Grodach and Daniel Silver (New York: Routledge 2013), 28-41.

6 Timothy J. Gilfoyle, *Millennium Park: Creating a Chicago Landmark* (Chicago: University of Chicago Press, 2006).

7 Henry Adams, *The Education of Henry Adams: An Autobiography* (Cambridge, MA: The Riverside Press, 1918 [1906]), 340.

8 Rudyard Kipling, *American Notes* (New York: M.J. Ivers & Company, 1891).

9 Barbara Ferman, *Challenging the Growth Machine,* (Lawrence, KS: The University Press of Kansas, 1996).

10 Robert E. Park and Ernest W. Burgess, *The City* (Chicago: University of Chicago Press, 1984 [1925]), 14.

11 Ibid., 24.

12 Lizabeth Cohen, *Making a New Deal: Industrial Workers in Chicago, 1991-1939* (Cambridge: Cambridge University Press, 2008).

13 Park and Burgess, *The City*, 43.

14 Andrew Abbott, *Department and Discipline: Chicago Sociology at One Hundred* (Chicago: University of Chicago Press, 1999).

15 Robert B. Owens, "Mapping the City: Innovation and Continuity in the Chicago School of Sociology, 1920–1934," *American Sociologist* 43, no. 3 (2012): 264–293.

16 Park and Burgess, *The City*, 3.

17 Abbott, *Department and Discipline: Chicago Sociology at One Hundred*, 202.

18 St. Clair Drake and Horace R. Cayton, introduction to *Black Metropolis: A Study of Negro Life in a Northern City*, by Richard Wright, xvii-xviii (Chicago: University of Chicago Press, 1970 [1945]).

19 Carla Cappetti, *Writing Chicago: Modernism, Ethnography, and the Novel* (New York: Columbia University Press, 1993), 2.

20 Dennis R. Judd and Dick W. Simpson, eds., *The City, Revisited: Urban Theory from Chicago, Los Angeles, and New York* (Minneapolis, MN: University of Minnesota Press, 2011); Robert J. Sampson, *Great American City* (Chicago: University of Chicago Press, 2012).

21 Daniel Silver and Terry Nichols Clark, "The Power of Scenes: Quantities of amenities and qualities of places." *Cultural Studies* ahead-of-print (2014): 1-25; Stephen Sawyer and Terry Clark, "La politique culturelle et la démocratie métropolitaine à l'âge de la défiance," *Politiques culturelles 21: Débats et enjeux en Europe,* eds. Guy Saez et Jean-Pierre Saez (Paris: Editions de la découverte, 2012).

22 Daniel Silver and Terry Nichols Clark, "Buzz as an Urban Resource," *Canadian Journal of Sociology* 38, no. 1 (2013).

A Different Conversation,
A Different Kind of Work

Ronne Hartfield, Edward Maldonado, Robert Peters, and Hamza Walker
in conversation

Hamza Walker: I'm so touched that the three of you would come out for this conversation. This idea started when Stephanie Smith asked if I would consider writing about a history of social practice in Chicago, and I said, "Well, I definitely have some thoughts and recollections on practices that emerged in the 1980s, which could be said to have laid something of a groundwork for what we call social practices today."

I have been in Chicago for thirty years; I came here in 1984 for college. Bob Peters was one of my instructors. So, I think of myself as the product of a particular time and a particular place: Chicago, 1980s. Then there's the larger narrative of the 1980s as a paradigm shift, quite conscious of itself as a period distinct from the 1960s and 1970s. The 1980s was in part a disavowal of the 1960s. And I think there were some very important responses locally that reflect larger national values and concerns in the contemporary art field.

Chicago had been characterized at one point as largely a figurative town because of the Imagist tradition. That narrative/mythology, I would say, gained traction in the 1980s within the larger resurgence of figurative art. It took a while for me to not buy into that; it was probably decades before I could look back and say, no, Chicago is actually not a figurative town, per se, even though you could look at the Imagist and Monster Roster. Chicago is not at all reactionary. In fact, it seems like anything could take root, could sprout, here.

Looking back on having had you, Bob, as a professor, you would be my first example of that: someone who was not engaged with an Imagist or figurative tradition, but whose thoughts, concerns, and artistic engagement in the 1980s were something other. That gave me pause to think about a conceptual backdrop, set of social concerns, institutional critique, a way of approaching art that was well outside of painting or traditional concerns. So I am wondering if you could talk a little bit about your background that started in forestry and what were you doing when you got to Chicago? How would you characterize the town?

Robert Peters: I came here to teach at the School of the Art Institute of Chicago from California. I had this other history that you alluded to—these degrees and other work situations that had a lot to do with underpinnings in mathematics, statistics, and those kinds of things. So those were the structures that I brought to my art practice and being in an art school, that was my perspective: trying to absorb what that was and then trying to ask questions about it to see whether or not this vehicle, art, was a way for me to engage with the social reality that I was in. That's the way I thought about it, and that's what I brought with me to Chicago.

At that particular point in time in Chicago there really was no art community or else a very small one. Everything was happening on either coast and our communities, in general, were very small. There was a different scale of the operations. People were going to New York because, in effect, that's where the action was and where the audience was, and it simply wasn't here in Chicago at that point. It took some time for that to begin to develop.

And the School of the Art Institute was a very different place at that moment, also very small and very much dominated by Imagist folks. But there were all kinds of transitions going on there as well. A lot of young teachers had come in at the same time I did, and there was this whole movement to kind of transform the way in which the curriculum was directed, essentially open it up. It wasn't us against the Imagists but it was to ask, can we speak more broadly.

The term "social practice" doesn't mean much of anything to me. It seems to me that all art is social practice. In the West, I'd say, from the turn of the nineteenth century forward, there's been an awful lot of art that is about social reality and about trying to shift the social reality. It's gone through a lot of different mediums, a lot of different vehicles. Categorical distinctions don't make a lot of sense to me.

HW: As a former student of yours, I feel like you gave me a lot to think about in terms of conventions, questioning, challenging conventions, traditions—do things have to be the way that they are? If someone were to ask me, "Is Bob Peters a conceptual artist?" I would say, "I don't know how to describe what school Bob belongs to." Instead you are someone who always privileged the question more than the answer. I think that this is really key. I don't know if Dan Peterman was a student of yours. But I think you have a way, at least for me, of posing questions about art that were well outside of making pretty pictures—and this is before I would know anything about an Imagist tradition. In some sense I'm looking to you because I came to school bright-eyed and bushy-tailed at eighteen. Get out of the joint. And you were my port of call for Chicago. You were representative, at least for me at that time, of Chicago, which is very funny because this was not the typical characterization.

RP: It was a misrepresentation. *[Laughter]*

HW: Yes, I was sold a false bill of goods. But it proved important for my understanding of Chicago as pluralist in what it had to offer.

When you talk about the development of the scene and not much happening in one sense, you still had scenes going on here art-wise, like the Hyde Park Art Center. When you talk about the growth of other scenes, what are you referring to?

RP: I think there is a certain momentum with a younger group of people. The not-for-profits were really the key for a fairly long period of time—N.A.M.E. Gallery, Randolph Street Gallery, ARC, Artemisia. It's critical to the Chicago art scene, because one is not looking to either coast, yearning to move there, but saying this is a place to be.

HW: When you think about those spaces, I'm often taken by the term "alternative" as alternative to something. Now the term has lost something of its bearing, whereas it used to be quite clear then as being artist-run organizations that presented themselves as an alternative to a commercial art scene. So in terms of their ethos and being important for the development of a kind of self-sustaining ecology, how important were such organizations in terms of helping develop a kind of pluralist set of activities here in Chicago that included performance, conceptual work, post-minimal work?

RP: When you talk about it that way, it strikes me that they were the venues for those explorations. There was opportunity because Chicago had these institutional structures that supported those kinds of investigations. The gallery scene at that point didn't support that kind of stuff, didn't take those kinds of risks. Lots of the work that was done was problematic and that's great.

As things got much larger, it became much more tightly knit and the barriers got stronger. The boundaries are stronger now; they're not as permeable. So those are some of the good things about that time. Of course part of the downside was that there was a small group of people participating. You knew everybody. You probably went to school with them.

Ronne Hartfield: But it allowed for a whole non-profit movement, much of which involved cooperative galleries, that enabled a really large number of people who never would have had an opportunity to exhibit but who could exhibit in the gallery because they worked there. You'd give an afternoon or two a week and you didn't have to pay. I knew tons of women who would never have had a career without that opening, really, and the range of work was huge, from conceptual to portraits or whatever.

Edward Maldonado: I'm thinking about some of the projects that were done in those alternative spaces by people who were the outliers at some point. Institutions eventually absorbed all of that activity, and it redefined both institutional behaviors and educational processes. A lot of work today has its antecedents in the early processes of creating non-profits, inventing new spaces.

HW: Are there moments, events, or exhibitions that stand out for you as being confrontational, radical, or representing some kind of challenge to existing paradigms?

RH: There was an exhibition at ARC of text and painting; artists chose text to go with their visual images. There were many really fabulous discussions because it extended the relationship between the printed word and what you put on the walls. The outstanding thing for me was just the range of options.

Back then people had to invent their own idea of an exhibition. Three or four people would get together and say, let's have an exhibition on this, and they'd work on it and do it, and draw real, live audiences. Having one night a month as an opening gallery night, with everyone going out on the streets, also helped to create an arts community too.

HW: As far as participation in the scene, I didn't come aboard Randolph Street Gallery's exhibitions committee until 1992, and that was thanks to you, Ed. You and Mary Murphy said to me one day at the Cultural Center, "You talk a lot. Why don't you come over to this place? Do you know Randolph Street Gallery?" I said, "Yeah, I've been there before." "Well, come to this meeting."

EM: People contributed to the collective effort, and we all walked away with something as well. I wound up working at the Cultural Center; Hamza, you're at the Renaissance Society; Peter Taub, who was deeply involved with Randolph Street, is at the Museum of Contemporary Art. As a collective effort or a collective group of people who were all working artists at the time, we had a vision. We knew what was happening in the world of art; we were well-read, really smart (or smartass) kind of people. We wanted to see certain things happen and give exposure to them.

Guerrilla Girls, which became a phenomenon, is one example that comes to mind. We forget now, but AIDS was a real big issue at the time. And Guerrilla Girls did this piece where you could get a key chain with a condom that said, "Break in case of emergency." It was sort of a flippant but astute of way of dealing both humorously and seriously with a real problem of transmitting AIDS. So these galleries became a vehicle at certain points

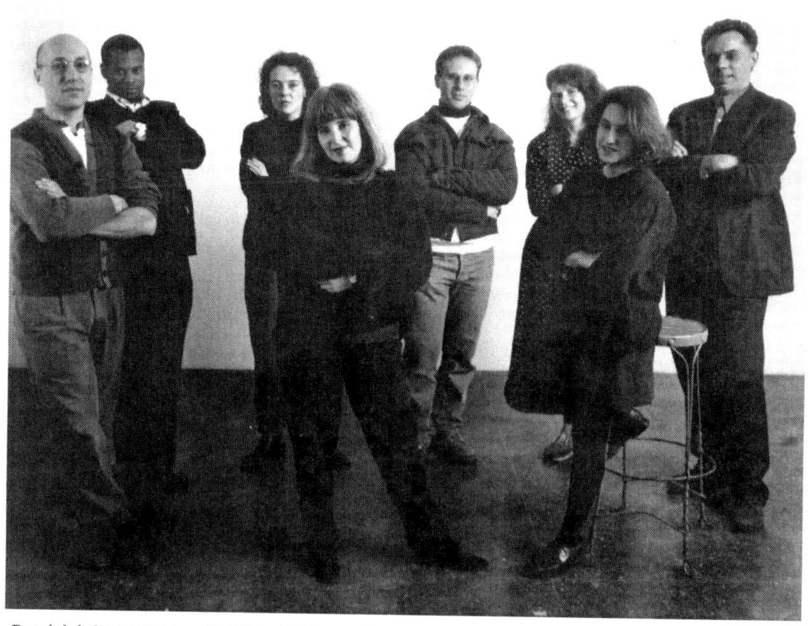

Randolph Street Gallery Staff. Back, left to right: Peter Taub, Hamza Walker, Mary Murphy, Ted Stux, Jane Smith, Edward Maldonado; front, left to right: Lynne Brown, Julie Ruskin. Photo © Liz Chilsen.

for social engagement and that kind of thinking or practice. We weren't all thinking, "I'm going to make a political statement" but it was part of the milieu of things of that period.

Meanwhile women's collectives were very important to dealing with what were then feminist issues, such as inviting Susan Sontag, who I saw at one of these alternative spaces. *Against Interpretation* had been published. These collectives or groups of people getting together were important, not just to create a venue for artists, though that was one important facet, but also as an intellectual place to go and get a read on the culture of the time because criticism itself had become a practice of the arts, by which I mean, the idea of social engagement and critical thinking.

HW: And that was a shift from the 1960s, which was itself a paradigm shift out of the 1950s, and by the 1970s and 1980s artists were taking matters into their own hands and starting to write and that also became theory.

EM: Well, don't forget the *New Art Examiner*.

HW: A local voice.

RH: Powerful.

EM: And one that took a very clear political stand on a lot of issues.

HW: Yes. We talk about that period as a precursor to social practices, and whether it was AIDS, sexuality, gender, homelessness, class, race, the issue of representation that made the 1980s. So what kind of pressure points was art under at that time?

EM: It was a funny time. The 1960s were not really over until the 1990s, partly because that whole generation of people were still pumping blood and walking around. This whole Occupy Wall Street. I'm like, Occupy Wall Street? Burn it down. There's a 1960s radicalism that's gotten kind of watered down today.

And Chicago, just to share with you, it wasn't a pretty place then. So the art crowd really did operate in the cracks in a lot of ways. Nobody was paying attention to us because there were other things going on apart from the art community, and the art community engaged in those practices with other agencies.

RH: Well, that's very important—the cross discourse between the arts community and other agencies and other people was much richer at that time. That is a definite fallout from the 1960s that was still going on.

Did any of you go to Bill Walker's funeral? I have to write a piece about it because it was an amazing gathering of people; it was so from the 1980s. William Walker was a black artist who had spent some time in Africa, Europe, and Mexico. He lived on the South Side and had initiated the *Wall of Respect*. But it was not a separatist movement. That's what you need to know. He worked with all the Mexican muralists at Casa Aztlan. A lot of them were old Communists, Chavez people. And there they all were in constant conversation with the Black Arts Movement. Then there were the people from the School of the Art Institute, because the school at the time was very close to both of those communities. The Black Harvest Film Festival started at the School.

What struck me when I went to Bill Walker's funeral was the representation of so many different arts communities that I had not seen in Chicago in years. These people no longer talk to one another. There they were, old lefties, Mexican avant-garde, the black community, and students and faculty all together. We used to all talk to each other. We used to go to openings together, and everybody was in a certain kind of fertile conversation. But what happened in the 1990s is that this broke up into little fiefdoms where people had their own power groups. So the 1980s—I loved what you said about the 1960s going on to the 1990s because they did. And it's over. The 1960s are finally over. You will never see another funeral like that, except maybe mine.

RP: Too bad.

HW: Ronne when I thought about inviting you, it was in regard to the rhetoric of multiculturalism. I started in 1999 at Urban Gateways, and it was a beautiful experience in terms of getting to know Chicago. I was a secretary in the development office, raising money with Steve [Lovey] who was great just because he was so totally brazen and up front about everything. He said,

"I need somebody black to work in this office because I need them to act as a liaison. I can't have everybody in the fundraising office be white. I need somebody who's going to act as a liaison between the rest of the office and what goes on in here." And I said, "Great, that's perfectly fine. You've got your reasons, I've got mine, and we'll work together."

I didn't realize what I was signing on for. I got to know Chicago through its philanthropic community, all the names that are etched in stone at the Art Institute. This was also the heyday of multiculturalism, and Urban Gateways, as far as being a center for arts and education, interfaced with the larger community. I'm wondering if you could talk a little bit about multiculturalism in the 1980s here in Chicago. I'm thinking about the annual *Black Creativity* exhibitions at the Museum of Science and Industry that came about through a national call to black artists. How did it come to be hosted by that museum?

RH: *Black Creativity* was an unprecedented showcase for black artists and was enabled because of the innovation of one black trustee and an open-minded museum president. Together, they located a good group of people, insisted on high quality for the curatorial end of it, and moved forward from their prior focus on the sciences. A large gala event attached to the opening brought in a lot of money for the museum, which helped to ensure its continuation—and it is still going on.

This was a very interesting moment for us at Urban Gateways because we were very committed to the rhetoric of multiculturalism and to making that a reality. Thus, the fact that Steve, our development director (and one of the best fundraisers I've ever known), said, "I've got to have somebody black working in my office," was the way it was and we were quite open about that—that we had to have black staff and white staff. We had to hire black artists, white artists, Latino artists, if we wanted to be multicultural. It wasn't affirmative action in the sense that we were just filling a racial slot; it was a concerted effort to find the very best people that we could within those kinds of ethnic categories. For the ten years I was there, we had pretty much 50 percent black and Latino, and occasionally Asian, and 50 percent white. But if we hadn't been conscious about that it wouldn't have happened, if we hadn't been absolutely affirmative. And that was a big factor in helping us to become the largest arts education program of its type in the country. The reason is that this incredible mix of people brought to their work their networks of people. They represented other social and cultural contexts, adding richness and more opportunities for interesting collaborations. This was not inclusiveness for rhetorical reasons. These were successful efforts to broaden the conversation and the range of ideas about definitions of art, across the board.

It was a great asset to have staff with such connections. We had this huge cadre of people who had their fingers in every pie in Chicago, so it allowed us to find artists. I can't walk the streets of Chicago now without seeing an Urban Gateways artist. And it was a great gig for them because they could work during the day and go work or perform at night. The key to it was quality, it really was.

Later, I went to work for the Art Institute of Chicago, and obviously there were very few black curatorial people around. I was very determined to find somebody for the Education Department that I directed at the time. I must have interviewed twenty-five or thirty people to find a black lecturer of the quality and scope I was seeking. Eighty percent of them knew nothing about art except African American; they'd been pigeonholed early and that's what they knew about. I was running a department in a museum that specialized in Impressionism, so I wanted someone black who knew about Impressionism. I had to work to find that.

HW: I'm wondering if you can talk about the role of culturally specific organizations here in the 1980s, like DuSable and the Mexican Fine Arts Center Museum [now National Museum of Mexican Art].

RH: It's changed so profoundly that it's hard to even imagine those organizations the way they were in the 1980s. I think a lot of what was happening at the time responded to complicated and gradual perspectival shifts, inflected by changes in the art world nationally. Decisions being made by their leadership seemed to make good sense at the time, but were later revised in positive ways.

The DuSable Museum in those days was very culturally specific, insisting on black programming under black leadership. They didn't even partner with Urban Gateways because we had too much "otherness" going on. Now look at the amazing changes that Carol Adams put in place; they've grown exponentially because they partner with everybody, but they do it on their own terms. They did a great partnership with the Mexican Museum on blacks in Mexico. I looked at that and I thought, neither of these two organizations would have done that ten years ago. Neither of them.

The Mexican Fine Arts Museum was so culturally specific then that the entire staff and board were Mexican. Carlos [Tortolero] and I talked about this, from different perspectives, mine reflecting my Urban Gateways experience, and his anchored in his passionate commitment to the Mexican community. Now this has become radically different. In the long run, both museums did respond to the forces of change.

When I was working at the Art Institute, there were barriers to partnerships, too. I did one with the DuSable Museum, and due to many staffing changes and a certain amount of ensuing chaos, that was a disaster. But the one that we did with the Mexican Museum turned out to be fabulous. Yet my staff refused to go to the Mexican Museum because of the neighborhood. They said they'd have to come down to the Art Institute to meet with us so that we can make this work. My position was, you can't make it work unless you go there. So I had to hire a van, a little bus, to take my staff out there.

There are barriers and none of this was something easy or something that happened overnight. We were putting black artists at Urban Gateways in white suburban schools, and some of the teachers were terrified. They didn't know any black artists. They didn't know what they might say, what they might do; they didn't know how they might look, how they might talk. We had to do a vast amount of preparation that was really a cultural education in order to get people ready. Then they would spend $100,000 buying a year's worth of programs from us. But it was work and it was cultural work. We couldn't have done it if our whole staff was black, and we couldn't have done it if our whole staff was white.

Time changes people, and I think part of the change is very practical. When you talk about cultural or social practice, people realize at a certain point, how can I grow? How can my organization grow? And they realize that if you keep to such radical ethnic specificity, it's just not going to happen. But they've changed and I think it's good for the city.

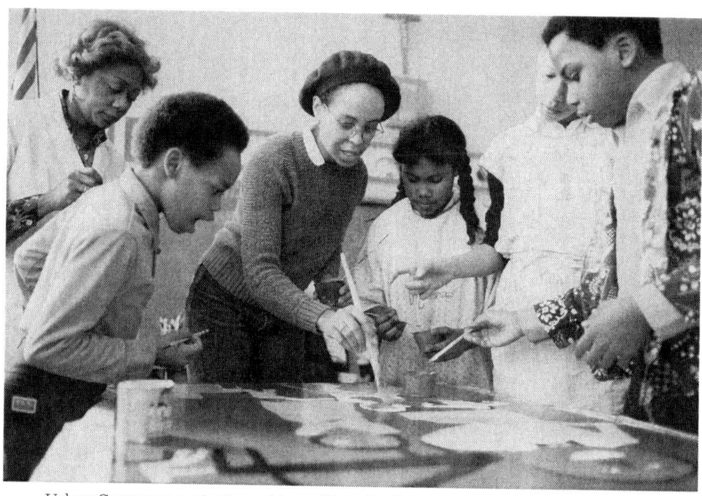

Urban Gateways artist in residence Dorothy Carter working with elementary school children, 1982. Courtesy of Urban Gateways.

HW: That was a beautiful reflection on Urban Gateways. Now I want to go forward. If we were going to talk about the 1960s as going all the way up until 1990, I want to think about the 1980s as continuing into the early part of the 1990s. If I were going to think about the 1993 Whitney Biennial or the Rodney King riots in Los Angeles that year, those things were a sort of zenith, events that marked that time socially.

HW: When I went on to the Exhibitions Committee at Randolph Street Gallery in the early 1990s, there was a sense of social urgency around putting together exhibitions. They were responding to something; we didn't do a single artist show. I still carry that with me from that period. While I was volunteering there, I was also at the Department of Cultural Affairs in the Public Art Division, working on a series of branch libraries.

Ed, I was wondering if you could talk about your reflections on the late 1980s and early 1990s period at Randolph Street Gallery. We did a really big show with the Mad Housers back then. The first exhibition I worked on was with Mary Murphy on the 1992 election when Clinton came into office. The AIDS epidemic was going full tilt in terms of our artistic responses to it. What was your sense of those times?

EM: Nothing happens in a vacuum and a lot of things were happening simultaneously. Randolph Street operated from the point of view of artistic engagement. There was not an overtly political side but a kind of politicization that occurred by virtue of the people who were volunteering there and thinking about different kinds of artistic practices.

Conceptual art had in one way led us towards that because it allowed us to think about politics in a different way. Before, you were trying to make paintings, including myself, to come up with some kind of image that meant something, not making political points.

But the world at the time was very complicated for all of us. In the mid-to-late 1980s, we had just come out of a total economic collapse by virtue of the fact that industry in the United States had completely shut down. We think this is new today, given current economies, but this is like the second or third time around that I've gone through a period....

HW: The crash of 1987.

EM: Right. I was at Randolph Street; I had a new baby; I had no full-time job. I was working as a carpenter, a teacher, a plumber, an electrician. I had just ended my job as a part-time CTA bus driver. I needed to get out of that clutter. I needed to find a real job, and I found a job at the Cultural Center. It was just serendipity. I had been working as a part-time carpenter there, too.

One important thing that happened was the Shakman Decree in 1983 that dismantled the patronage system, the practice of hiring and firing government workers on the basis of political loyalty. City employees had to conform or face retribution. Shakman made it unlawful to take any political factor into account in hiring public employees. That for me was a very transformative moment because those of us at the time remember that city government was essentially a giant employment agency for unions. And while the Shakman Decree was something very specific, the outcomes were that people like myself got hired, actually, because of being Puerto Rican, Latino....

Plus Harold Washington was becoming mayor, and that was for me a transformative moment in Chicago, too, because suddenly that opened up a whole series of doors that included the arts.

When Richard M. Daley came into power in 1989 he brought Lois Weisberg in as Commissioner of Cultural Affairs to recreate the Department of Cultural Affairs, basically given the Cultural Center, which was the Central Public Library, to rethink this white elephant at the front door of the city. She called her little minions, including myself, and said, "Do something." At that moment the Cultural Center was this vast building with stacks of library books everywhere, many of which are now in my personal collection.

I had a union card as a carpenter, so I could fight with the unions, which Lois loved because then she didn't have to do it. And I had the experience of Randolph Street helping organize exhibitions. So I brought that experience with me. Along with others, I could help transform that building. The carpenters would leave at five and I would show up at five-thirty and work until midnight. Gradually the Cultural Center changed physically and institutionally from one kind of civic space, a library, into a cultural art institution that was still different from the mainstream Art Institute. I always saw it as being in that position—between public space and institutional space—so that when we started to reprogram it, we shaped it in a way that reflected an alternative space. It had multiple spaces within it where we could do different shows, all the time with the grandiose patina of a *beaux-arts* building.

HW: By virtue of it being a city institution, did you feel as though the Cultural Center had a particular mandate in terms of who it was accountable to?

EM: Chicago being Chicago politics, the beauty was that Lois Weisberg was a kind of buffer between City Hall and the Cultural Center. Maybe only those of us who worked for her can appreciate how much the political machine would have overtaken and destroyed us in a heartbeat had she not been there. But Lois gave us all the tools and opportunities to recreate a kind of public artistic space from which public art became a real important aspect of the city. And by that I mean everything from Millennium Park to music festivals. They are all an outgrowth of her kind of thinking.

And so the Cultural Center as a venue kind of existed in this funny realm of being part government, part alternative space, part institutional space. And those of us who worked there tried to measure up to the institutional rigors of museums, while at the same time have the flexibility to work with artists in a give-and-take kind of way.

We could do installation art, responding to people who were in Chicago doing that kind of work, including artists like Bob Peters. So in that period we went from wall-hung work or plop artwork, as we used to call

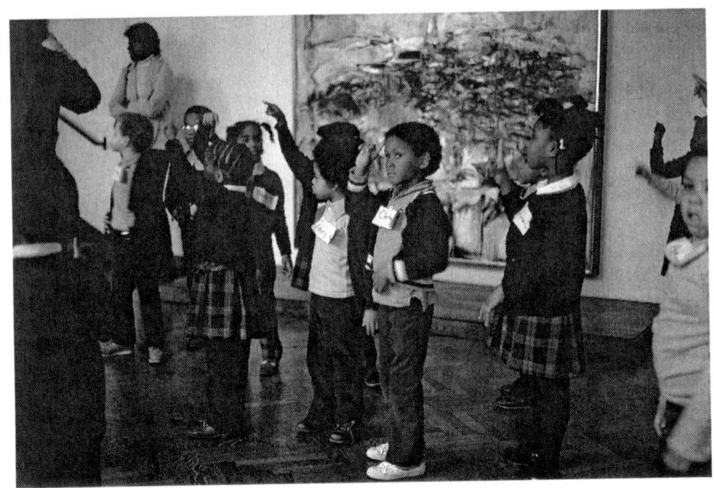

Urban Gateways programming at the Art Institute of Chicago, 1982.
Courtesy of Urban Gateways.

sculpture, to a more elastic understanding of what art had become but that maybe the general public was not used to at the time. It looks easy now, but this kind of work in that venue at the time would have really been a challenging statement to the sensibilities of the public. But it helped create a consciousness about art. When you go down Michigan Avenue or State Street now, the School of the Art Institute and Columbia College dominate these places... but they weren't there back then.

RP: I think one of the things that's interesting about the Cultural Center that the history you outline shows, is its use, its place in the public's consciousness, that it's free, and that we have a totally different audience that goes there. It's not just the audience; it's an ideal audience, in a sense, because people who would never walk into the door of the Art Institute come in contact with things that might be somewhat alien, but bringing whatever experience or baggage they have with them. People feel like they own that space. I think that's a critical difference between that space and more conventional venues in the city—and I hope it never loses that character.

HW: Now it's becoming clear what you were saying earlier: that there's alignment in terms of ethos with the alternative venues, but not that the Cultural Center is an alternative venue. But it is an alternative venue in another sense, in relationship to big museums.

RP: Even more than that, I think most alternative spaces we speak about still are very balkanized and isolated with small audiences specific to them. The Cultural Center has the potential for people to bump into things that they weren't even thinking about and all of a sudden recognize that maybe there's a kind of contemporary practice we happen to call art that has meaning for them and is useful. It seems to me that that's an ideal space or condition in which you can put artistic practice and get out of the framework that artists constantly have in which they're speaking to themselves.

EM: On the one hand we're sometimes out there creating art that has no economic value in and of itself. It has no intrinsic economic value. So it goes like this: I make paintings and I try to sell paintings, but I'm doing that because I want to make this other art that doesn't necessarily have a market. So I'm trying to fund my projects. I have to live in a certain economy. Then there's this other practice that I want to get to where, if I'm lucky, maybe I'll get a show at the Cultural Center or at the MCA [Museum of Contemporary Art] someday. Or, maybe I'm too old for that. In other words, you're faced with a certain kind of economics that is very problematic. Another way to look at it is if you're a theorist and you're writing papers, you don't make money off of that. You may have huge influence, profound influence, but you know you'll make no money out of it.

So we're stuck with the economies of where we are. These quasi-institutional spaces or projects, like Urban Gateways, apart from the fact that it is an educational vehicle, is in itself a kind of model space in which this seemingly useless activity we call art—but that is absolutely the lifeblood of our souls— can function. We've got to preserve these spaces. Maybe our failure was that we didn't figure out a way to make alternative spaces institutional. Take the MCA. Some people very astutely decided a few decades ago that these should become our cathedrals, a rarified place where ideas have to reside because we don't have another place for them. Places like the Chicago Cultural Center are in-between places. I wish there were more non-profit spaces still around, allowing for experimentation.

HW: Thinking about your comment on the economics of the situation, it hits me how you're a kind of funny jack-of-all-trades. I kind of feel the same way, especially in spanning the arts and education scene. I was part of different discussions about where to place that line.

As to the non-balkanization, there was a time—and this sounds nostalgic—when there was a like... there was a finer line between community-based arts organizations, whether they were arts and education, and alternative art spaces, not a division. You could have friends in both; it was the same community.

RP: So the membranes of the institutions were much more permeable.

HW: Right, arts and education teachers, mural painters, artists showing at galleries, who were all still sort of...

EM: You're talking about having a real community. That's been fragmented in so many ways. We were much closer as a community thirty years ago or so. We knew each other if not by name, then by face.

HW: At the time, we couldn't have talked about social practice as a rarified thing, as something else, as something outside?

RP: It's like with performance art. One of the reasons to do it at that particular point in time was because there wasn't that history around it; there wasn't that structure. There was open space in which you could operate. As soon as it's codified—it's a thing that you do in the institutional structure—possibilities are cut off. That doesn't mean they don't also generate other things. But it's different from those kinds of spaces in which the categorical structures are not so rigid and in which there is the idea that one thing can permeate the other, and in which there is a scale of connections, so that conversations between disciplines can happen. That space is very rare at this point.

EM: We used to think of artistic practice as a vocation, not a profession. Like a priest, it was a calling. And that was a real piece of the puzzle that has disappeared. The job of the artist was not a job but it was a vocation. That part is gone.

RH: That's huge, though, what you're saying.

EM: I think there were a lot of things that happened. We all became very smart in the 1980s. Suddenly we all needed a Ph.D. to teach our history. My best art history teacher at the time was a painter and his knowledge base and depth of understanding was profound. And then suddenly the institution itself kind of got smarter and smarter, partly due to that damn conceptual art you guys started.

It's always a two-way street. On the one hand, Chicago artists became very hip, very intelligent, very smart, very cutting edge. On the other, for the educational systems, the museum, suddenly you had to produce a dissertation in order to justify your existence as an artist. I don't know when that happened, but somewhere in the 1980s we got very smart, but we also got very stupid.

RP: Well, I think art practice in that respect has become academized. In other words, you can't find a gallery unless you have an MFA, and that an MFA is delivered by institutions like this which have, then, their structures which focus you into ways to be successful to get that, except the conversation is totally different when that's the structure in which you're operating. It's a different conversation, it's a different kind of work.

EM: It's actually transformed the whole landscape.

This conversation occurred on December 20, 2014 in Chicago.

South Side Story: A European Curator's Adventures in Chicago

Dieter Roelstraete

The world promised by the leaders of the October Revolution was not merely supposed to be a more just one or one that would provide greater economic security, but it was also and in perhaps even greater measure meant to be beautiful.

—Boris Groys[1]

My first ever visit to Chicago dates back to the cold and dreary spring of 2011 and took place on my way back from an extended curatorial research trip to Rio de Janeiro. I had arranged for my return flight to Europe, where I was living and working at the time (in Berlin and Antwerp respectively), to pass through Chicago with the intention of visiting Kerry James Marshall, one of the city's most celebrated artists, in his studio on the South Side. (I traveled to Chicago hoping to talk to Marshall about doing an exhibition at M HKA, the museum of contemporary art in Antwerp where I was working at the time. I admittedly knew very little about the city's flourishing art scene, and I probably wasn't the first European curator who associated the city primarily with the leading African American painter of his generation, i.e. with a contemporary incarnation, if you will, of the "Black Arts Movement." My encounter with Marshall's work inevitably colored—no pun intended—my subsequent experience of Chicago's cultural life, in particular its communitarian inclinations.) I ended up spending little more than forty-eight hours in all in the

Windy City—blissfully unaware that a little more than nine months later this would become my new home—and most of that time was whiled away in a part of town whose fraught yet undeniably rich history I knew very little about; indeed, I hardly knew what the "South Side" really meant, in the particular context of this American city. (In Rio de Janeiro, the Brazilian metropolis whose art scene I had been researching, the so-called Zona Sul, symbolizes wealth, luxury, and the tourist fantasy of *a cidade maravilhosa*— the barrios of Copacabana, Ipanema, Lagoa, and Leblon. A marked contrast, in other words, with what I came to learn the South Side generally connotes in the context of Chicago: a tangle of impoverished, predominantly African American neighborhoods, many with tremendous histories of their own, comparable to Rio de Janeiro's Zona Norte.) I liked it, however, found many parts of the area beautiful, and, for a variety of other reasons—much to the surprise, occasional astonishment, and sometimes even sheer disbelief of many—ended up living in this part of town when I moved to Chicago in February 2012 to take up the position of senior curator at the Museum of Contemporary Art Chicago.

As it so happened, my wife and I moved on February 14, just in time to attend the opening of a major group exhibition at the Smart Museum of Art at the University of Chicago titled *Feast: Radical Hospitality in Contemporary Art*. (Full disclosure: said exhibition was put together by the editor of the present volume, Stephanie Smith; she also happens to be our oldest friend in Chicago.) "Presenting the work of more than thirty artists and artist groups who have transformed the shared meal into a compelling artistic medium"—though it should be said here that the exhibition and the many events that accompanied it did much more than merely focus on food and "the shared meal" as platforms for experimentation in creative sociality—*Feast* certainly made a lasting impression on the both of us, casting our festive entry into the Chicago art world in the distinctive light of a particular emerging tangle of artistic concerns and practices (most pointedly 'social' ones) that would soon prove to be central to the current *hausse* of cultural activity across Chicago's reviving South Side. (I am referring here to the recent opening of the Reva and David Logan Center for the Arts in Hyde Park and the Arts Incubator in Washington Park, both affiliated with the University of Chicago, as well as to the ever-expanding reach of artist-entrepreneur, social activist, and South Side renaissance man Theaster Gates's various community arts initiatives in Grand Crossing, a neighborhood adjacent to Woodlawn.) Indeed, it is from the entwined perspective of the above anecdotes, chronicling the experience of my move from Europe to the United States, from the M HKA in Antwerp, to the Museum of Contemporary Art Chicago, from the Berlin district of Friedrichshain to the Chicago neighborhood of Woodlawn, that I have attempted to theorize my rudimentary insights into what I believe to be certain key aspects of the Chicago art ecology.

As a newcomer, I naturally sought to familiarize myself as soon and as much as possible with the Chicago arts community—and quickly found it to be one of the most hospitable (or social) environments I have ever had the pleasure of working in. (There could not have been a better-cast welcoming committee than the crowd assembled at the opening of an exhibition devoted to "radical hospitality.") As an outsider, I soon arrived at certain findings concerning what I believe to be the constitutive characteristics and determining traits of the local artistic landscape, informed in part by my rudimentary knowledge of both the Chicago arts ecosystem and the city proper before I moved here. Among these features, in my mind, two attributes in particular continue to stand out. To begin with, the city hosts a truly massive population of art students (i.e., aspiring artists) and art teachers (i.e., actual, practicing artists) scattered across half a dozen art schools and university art departments, making for an understanding of art that is at least minimally anchored in a knowledge and research economy as well as in an ecology of *learning*. Combined with a relatively weak commercial sector, this results in the singular yearly spectacle of literally hundreds of graduates trying to figure out what to do with the early days, weeks, months, and years of their artist life in the relative absence of a market infrastructure whose powers of conditioning and defining would otherwise most probably lead to an inevitable streamlining and narrowing of art production to the manufacture, first and foremost, of commodities. (There is some irony to be gleaned from the fact that Chicago, as a hub of socially engaged art practice—that is to say, art which one may rightfully expect to be critical of the forces of free-market-thinking that, in the neoliberal era, have come to dominate and permeate all facets of human behavior and society—is also the birthplace of the economic theory that laid the groundwork for neoliberalism's global conquest: the ideology underpinning the commodification of everything. Irony, yes—but a coincidence, no.) The answer to the question of what to do with the early days, weeks, months, years of their lives as artists is instead being given in a myriad anti- and/or para-institutions, artist-run spaces, artist-curator initiatives, and apartment galleries—social spaces of all stripes. In terms of particular (more or less historically sanctioned) traditions of art-making as well, I relatively quickly discerned a couple of dominant *local* trends—mirror images, in some ways, of the qualities of the ecosystem outlined above: one being a continued dedication to the idiosyncratic tangle of artistic motifs and concerns called painting (abstraction, expression, gesture, imaging, métier-facture and manufacture), the other revolving around a very different, indeed almost opposite, set of preoccupations called *social practice*—the corollary, in part, of the peculiar nature of Chicago's art world (one characterized by the aforementioned "myriad anti- and/or para-institutions, artist-run spaces, and artist-curator initiatives") as an intensely *social* system.

The notion of what is commonly referred to, in the American institutional art field, as social practice doubtlessly constitutes one of the more important discoveries I have made during my first year as a curator working in the Midwest—and as I already pointed out, it has also been a crucial factor in the South Side renaissance I have been so fortunate to witness up close.[2] This paradigm, once perhaps a more self-consciously marginal artistic phenomenon and roughly equivalent with what we Europeans have come to identify as relational aesthetics, has now become so well established that even *The New York Times*, not usually known for its forward-looking or wide-ranging taste in art, dedicated an in-depth feature to the trend in question, noting how "its practitioners freely blur the lines among object making, performance, political activism, community organizing, environmentalism and investigative journalism, creating a deeply participatory art that often flourishes outside the gallery and museum system."[3] Flourishing *outside* of the gallery and museum system that I am part of, yet ultimately dependent, in so many cases, on that selfsame system—or at least certain key parts of it—for its enshrinement in a critical art history: art-as-social-practice and social-practice-as-art present as many challenges to art as they do to the realm of social interaction as such— indeed, to the point that one may perhaps think of these sets of challenges, aimed at both art and the realm of social interaction as institutionalizing forces, as the very essence of social practice. (Enter the ghost of Joseph Beuys's *Sozialplastik*: an art of provocations as much as of propositions.) Some of these challenges structure my own doubt-ridden curatorial interest in the resultant expanded field of artistic practice—an art "movement" that involves countless essentially un-artistic activities such as cooking and talking, education and exchange, hosting and healing, sleepovers and workshops, and a myriad of experiments with related alternative economies and lifestyles that essentially anchor it in the long tradition of the avant-garde's transgressive dream of dissolving the boundaries between art and life. (Curiously enough, it seems somewhat incongruous to think of social practice as an avant-garde strategy, its peculiar, pragmatic philosophy of time somewhat at odds with the traditionally futurist impulses of all vanguardism.) What are some of these challenges? First and foremost, it is of course notoriously difficult to assess or even discuss the merits of many social practice projects as art, and it is equally difficult to assess or even discuss their value as actual social projects *outside* of the validating context of art—a cultural context that is predicated on a highly distinctive brand of institutional sociality (one organizing principle of which concerns the *autonomy* of the work of art—its being art and nothing else). The vital point, in part, of many social practice projects is to question the very nature of art's separation from society—as embodied by the reigning ideology of the white cube and the autonomous art object contained within it—as well as the techniques of estimation and valuation that are part of this separation. These challenges and interrogations are obviously especially topical in the context of the American art system, where the market, whose smooth functioning is so structurally reliant on the circulation of discreet, i.e., 'autonomous' art objects—many of which end up in the private collections of individuals whose generosity and wealth make possible the smooth functioning of privately funded public art institutions such as the one I now find myself working in—quite simply wields much more power. (This is precisely where my initial observations concerning Chicago's recent art history fold into each other: the local flowering of social practice is clearly made possible in part by the relative weakness of the local commercial ecosystem. Correspondingly, New York City, with its three hundred commercial galleries crammed together in a dozen city blocks, hardly counts as a hub of social practice–styled art production today. Chelsea is where social practice goes to die, so to speak, although it would obviously be utterly naïve, woefully misguided even, to disregard the commercial potential of certain social practice projects, or to diametrically oppose commerce to social impact more generally speaking. The emblematic success story of Theaster Gates is a case in point here, and one could argue that the singular power of Gates's project is located in his refusal, precisely, to reproduce the undialectical opposition of commercial: impact (for lack of a better term, *for now*) and social impact under the aegis of art. His being featured in a twelve-page *New Yorker* profile, however ("The Real-Estate Artist," January 20, 2014), may well serve to confirm his standing as the triumphant kind of exception that the status quo, both within and without the art world, can afford itself rather than an emerging new rule, both in terms of art-market clout and larger socio-economic muscle. The willfully ambiguous relationship of Gates's project to the dominant economic framework is an issue far too complicated to be disentangled within the confines of this essay, but his defining, genre-defying contribution to the expanding field of social practice—which does remain, thankfully, an *art* project first and foremost—has certainly helped to complicate the standard narrative of the paradigm's occasionally questionable humanitarianism, especially with regards to its undeniably paternalistic impulses.

From the perspective of my previous curatorial experience at a publicly funded public art institution in Europe—where mainstream museum culture's structural dependence on *everyone's* taxes means that the art shown and collected in these museums is much more literally *everyone's* business, i.e., an integrating form of social practice by the art world's very economic definition—it is perhaps inevitable that I should occasionally question the soundness of social practice's well-intended therapeutic and philanthropic impulses as well as its grand ambitions and the effectiveness of its posing as art: under its lofty banner, I see artists propose and do things that I rather expect (or, more importantly, *want*) others to do and propose (such as, most pointedly, the *state*). Indeed, is it really art's role (or the art world's) to care, heal, nourish, and shelter—to serve and protect? (The notion of service is key here, begging the question, or rather matter, of economy, of the pragmatics of efficiency. Hence the telling distinction between social *practice* and relational *aesthetics*—gestures versus deeds.) More fundamentally still, should art be expected to assume a role at all? And if it does, and if this role is so emphatically social, should art's relationship to the social fabric be such a monolithically affirmative one—one mired, a tad too often perhaps, in the bureaucratic language of duty and responsibility, reform and support?

Of course, if the social fabric is as broken and battered as it so often appears to be today—especially so in a city like Chicago, especially so on Chicago's South Side—the answer to these last questions should probably be an unreservedly affirmative one, no matter how much we may naturally be inclined to cling to progressive art's historical affiliation with the powers of negation, with saying no rather than yes. Indeed, under the current circumstances of an unrepentant suicidal neoliberalism—one that truly did not fail to "let a serious crisis go to waste"[4]—it may seem insultingly insidious and positively preposterous to argue for a return to art's putative essence as (*pace* Adorno and so many other long-dead paladins of puritanical modernism) *asocial* practice. For it is a certain brand of asocial practice, that is to say a certain *economic* interpretation of asociality, that got us—in the art world that is part and parcel of the neoliberal world order, if not, much more troublingly, its leading creative paradigm—in this mess in the first place, and it is only laudable that a growing number of artists are interested in reformatting and reinventing their respective practices as so many potential ways out of said mess—and not just rhetorically or symbolically so, as mere *promesses de bonheur*, but in the real-time terms of actually lived social experience. Against the asocial practices of contemporary casino capitalism—many of the philosophical precepts of which were hatched out, we should once again remind ourselves, on Chicago's South Side, at the University of Chicago's economics department, of the solidary practices of art's newfound social consciousness seek to reestablish a connection with the aging avant-garde adage of producing difference, imagining otherness, and making another world possible—of "making a difference." Yet such a difference, however, can only truly be made when art (in this case, social practice) once again clarifies its object, that is to say, specifies who deserves or needs caring, healing, nourishing, and sheltering, and who, just as importantly, does not—that is to say, when and where art must remain its original asocial self; when and where the (not merely symbolic) distinction between friend and enemy, which Carl Schmitt famously singled out as the fundamental principle of the political, must be drawn, if you will. (In other words: *selective* embraces, distinctions—with Adornian rigor now concentrated in the process of selecting the objects of these embraces, in identifying social practice's so-called *causes*, and in theorizing the historical conditions of these causes' emergence. Overall, in fact, one could wage that social *practice* needs more social *theory*.) Art as social practice, yes, but only up to a point, then—and only in acknowledging these exact limitations (i.e., in knowing both what it cannot do and should not do, and *why*) can art become political, as opposed to merely social, again. For this, I believe, may well be the greatest weakness in many artistic projects associated with social practice: their lack of political imagination, if not outright refusal to be identified as essentially (or necessarily) political undertakings. As both a newcomer and outsider, I certainly continue to be surprised by how *unpolitical* the social in "social practice" can sometimes be, and how *cosmetic*, therefore, its interventions, tending to the battered social fabric without fully questioning the political conditions that produced the state of this fabric in the first place—the exact type of depoliticization, one could argue, that is one of the neoliberal gospel's most vicious victories.

Perhaps I should conclude this brief reflection, this close-up view from afar, by returning to the work of the artist who brought me to Chicago in the first place—Kerry James Marshall. Shortly after meeting Kerry in his adopted hometown with the aim of inviting him to do an exhibition at M HKA, I quit my job there to start working at the MCA Chicago instead (where, as it happens, I am currently preparing a retrospective of Marshall's work planned to open its doors in the spring of 2016).

I was fortunate enough, however, to be able to witness the unfolding of Kerry's European exhibition project—after its debut in Antwerp—*Kerry James Marshall: Paintings and Other Stuff* traveled to Copenhagen, Barcelona, and Madrid—up close, and in every European city, the same set of questions made themselves heard: what does it mean to show the work of an artist whose conceptual concerns are so intimately bound up with American, and even more specifically African American, history in a cultural context where those histories are not particularly well known, if they

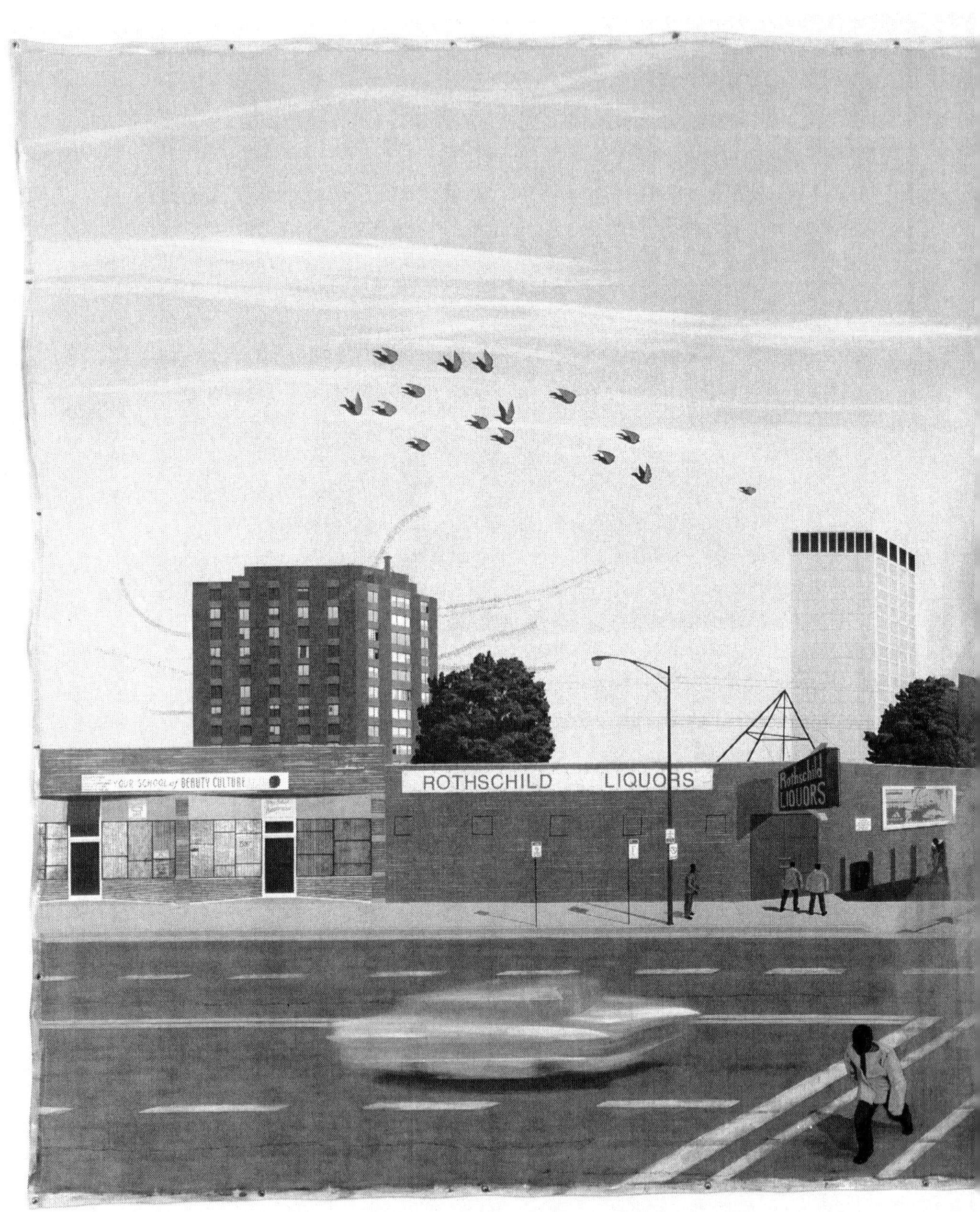
YOUR SCHOOL of BEAUTY CULTURE
ROTHSCHILD   LIQUORS
Rothschild
LIQUORS

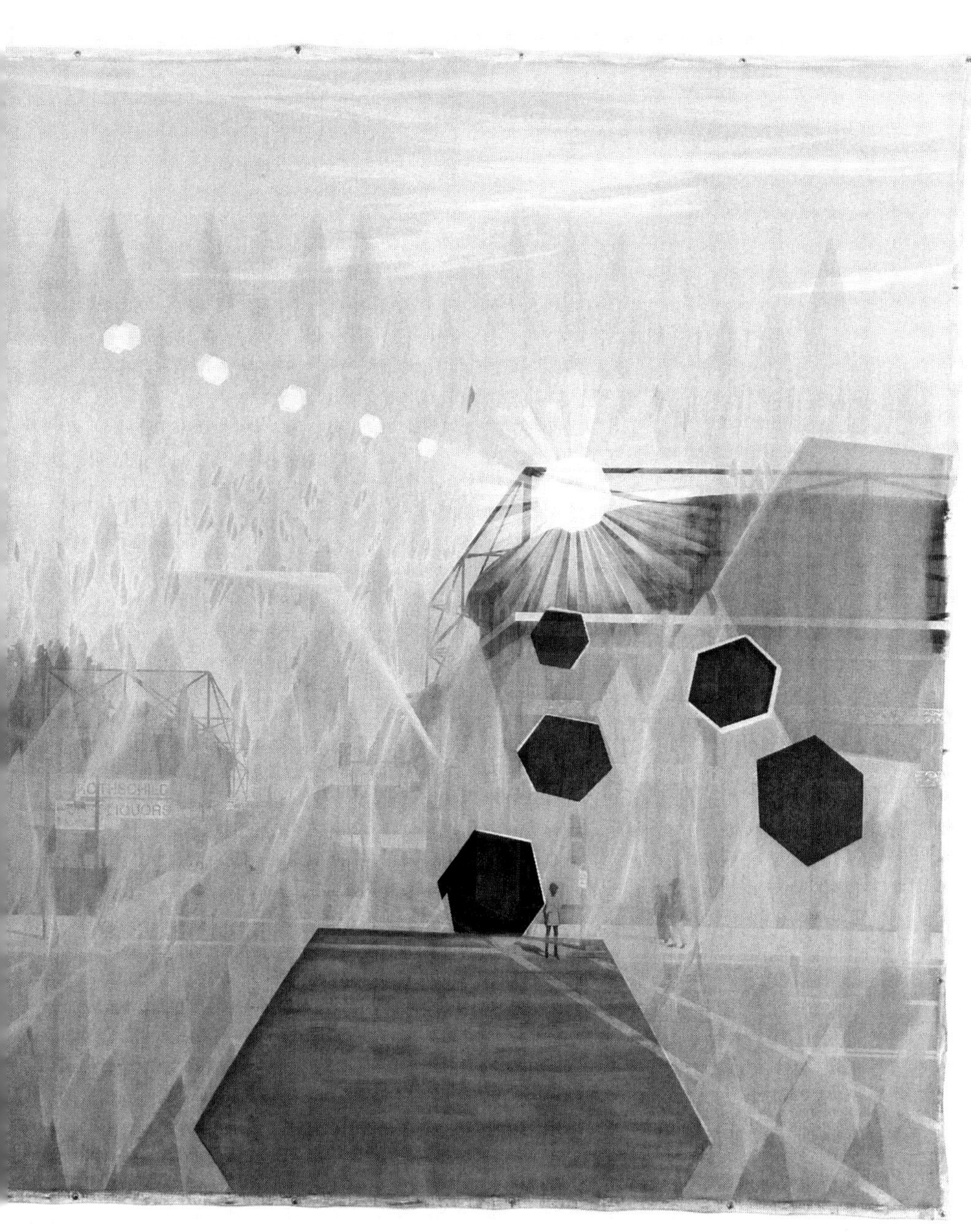

Kerry James Marshall, *7am Sunday Morning*, 2003. © Museum of Contemporary Art, Chicago. Photo: Michal Raz-Russo.

are known at all? Although answering that question in full would proba-bly lead us too far, one possible set of answers, I believe, would be related to the aforementioned distinction between *social* practice and *political* prac-tice—not so much between social art and political art, but between making art socially (which may or may not entail an *asocial* practice rather than a *social* one) and making art politically. (Another element touched upon ear-lier that comes into play here concerns Marshall's singular devotion to the grand tradition of painting as the highest and most hallowed of all arts, and therefore perhaps the one art form that, in all its philosophical purity, is the furthest removed from the promiscuous hybridizations of social practice. Of course, it is also the one art form that continues to command the high-est prices on the global art market, and will probably continue to do so for ages to come—definitely a factor worth keeping in mind when making lofty political claims on painting's behalf.) Kerry James Marshall's practice is undoubtedly a *social* one, but only insofar as it is, first and foremost, a *polit-ical* one—a project whose questioning of the politics of imaging may have much more far-reaching social consequences, perhaps, than many so-called social practice projects. Both in and through his work—this much I have been able to assess following his paintings' odyssey through the European institutional landscape—a difference is certainly being made: an inter-vention in the *political* realm (that of a certain 'ocular' regime) with *social* consequences.

As a critic and curator living in the unlikely locale of Woodlawn, it is of course inevitable that my conclusive musings should pause, however briefly, to ponder the marvel of Theaster Gates's *Sozialplastik* on an urban scale. In a city whose art scene is already well known internationally for "blurring the lines among object making, performance, political activism, community organizing, environmentalism, and investigative journalism," to rehearse the basic ingredients of the social practice phenomenon, Gates has proven to be something of a game-changer (to put it modestly) to the extent that questioning the effects and effectiveness of his various projects may seem positively academic (and this is obviously even more the case for any appre-hensions that may exist concerning the intrinsic value of these projects as artworks, as forms of artistic practice—who, in the end, cares?). A truly social practice indeed, and one wielding formidable transformative power for sure—hence the challenges awaiting anyone out to engage with these projects on the tired terms of art criticism: what have *you* done for the world lately?—but is this practice also a sufficiently political one? (The distinction between those two registers may not be as academic as it seems: divorcing the social from the political is a deeply political deed in any case, as we have noted in passing before—it *depoliticizes* all social questions.) The ultimate horizon of art's potential for transformation—that tried and tested yardstick of avant-garde ideology—is a question that should probably be asked, at this point in time, in revolutionary *political* terms as much as in predominantly reformist *social* ones. And here's one way of posing that question: how about some *socialist* practice, for a change?

---

1 Boris Groys, *The Total Art of Stalinism: Avant-Garde, Aesthetic Dictatorship, and Beyond* (London and New York: Verso Books, 2011), 3.

2 "Social practice" evidently means many different things to many different people (or, more pointedly, when fielded within different institutional contexts); for the purpose of the current account, it is perhaps helpful to point out some of the different contexts in which I was confronted, early on, with said paradigm: the Smart Museum of Art at the University of Chicago; the Jane Addams Hull-House Museum at the University of Illinois at Chicago; Theaster Gates' Dorchester Projects; Tricia Van Eck's 6018 North, a self-declared "intersection of art, community, and sustainable ideas"; Michael Rakowitz's *Enemy Kitchen*; and Dan Peterman's Experimental Station.

3 Randy Kennedy, "Outside the Citadel, Social Practice Art Is Intended to Nurture," *The New York Times*, March 20, 2013.

4 Cfr. Philip Mirowski, *Never Let a Serious Crisis Go to Waste: How Neoliberalism Survived the Financial Meltdown* (London and New York: Verso, 2013).

Students on the grounds of the Laboratory School (detail).

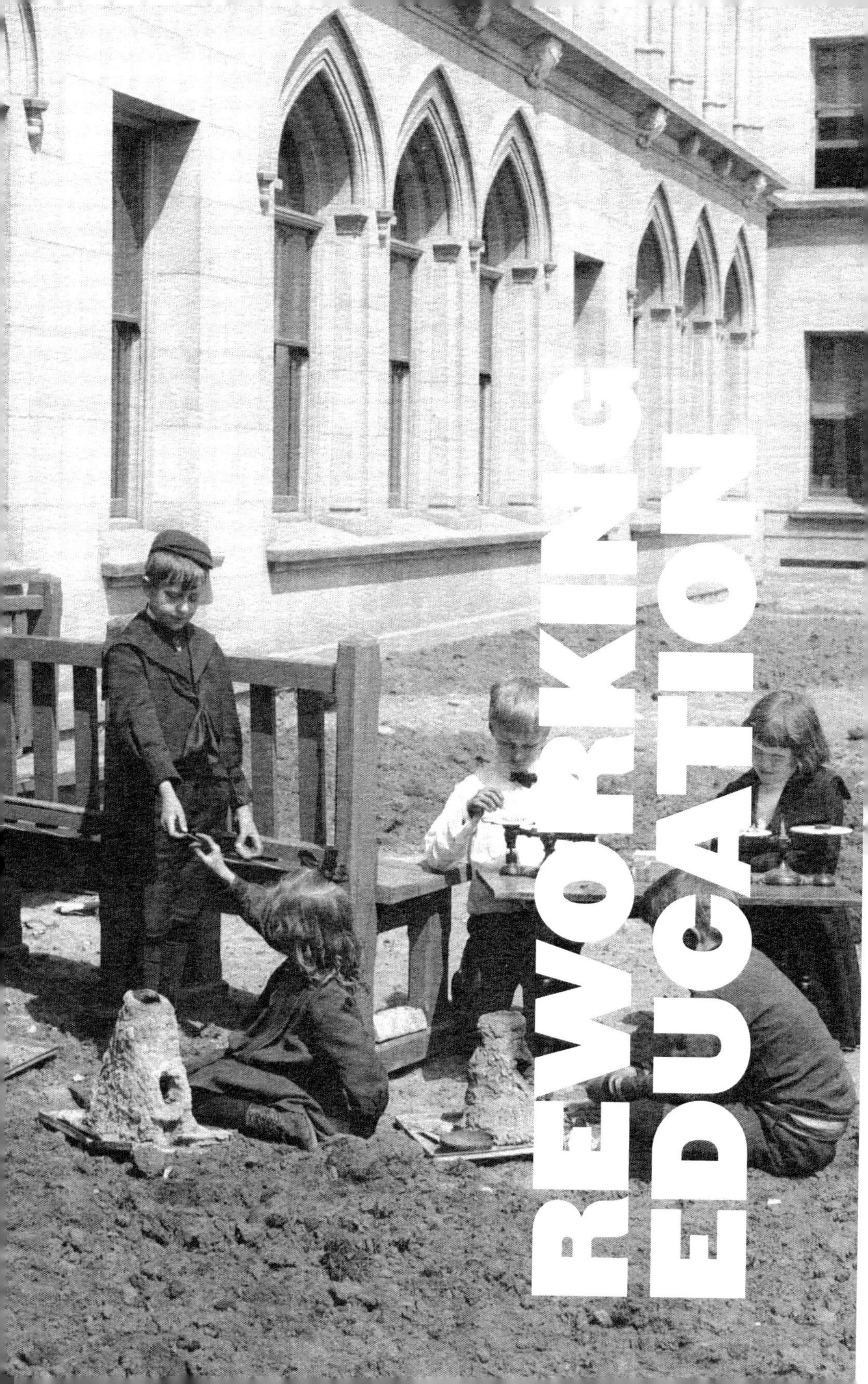

REWORKING
EDUCATION

Reworking Education

Through their dynamic thought and action, two nineteenth-century luminaries—the philosopher John Dewey and the social reformer Jane Addams—inspired generations of global progressives including practitioners of socially engaged art. Addams lived in Chicago for most of her life; Dewey for a briefer period. Each profoundly shaped Chicago's social practice imaginary, not only through their ideas, but also through their work as founders of pivotal institutions. Beyond the continuing influence of beloved texts like *Art and Experience*, Dewey's legacy includes his work as founder of the University of Chicago's Laboratory Schools (1896). There Dewey pioneered hands-on, collaborative, experiential methods of inquiry aimed at forming self-actualized and critically minded citizens. Addams had already pursued equally democratic ideals at the legendary Hull-House, the settlement house that she co-founded in 1889 with Ellen Gates Starr. Their work with poor and immigrant communities was grounded in mutual respect and a desire to learn from, as well as aid those living there and coming from many different backgrounds.

Some texts in this section address these legacies directly and creatively, drawing on the past as ballast and cultural capital as inspiration to challenge current institutional educational conditions. Education theorist and Weather Underground cofounder Bill Ayers is even willing to take on the complex and floundering Chicago Public School system. In an essay that is both lament and a call to action, he addresses the lost legacy of Dewey's ideas within public education. Carol Becker's text, "The Social Responsibility of the Artist," written while she was dean of the School of the Art Institute of Chicago, issues a direct call to artists to take up the ethical responsibility of active social engagement.

Other texts address the importance of teaching as a means of shaping an intellectual and creative culture within the city of Chicago as well as a key forum for the exchange of knowledge among different generations of socially engaged artists. Writer and cultural administrator Abigail Satinsky considers the current resonance of writer, artist, and educator Gregory Sholette's Extreme Arts Administration course at the School of the Art Institute: an attempt in the early 2000s to loosely codify and teach an experimental approach to arts administration that drew on the work of activist and politically engaged artists from the 1980s and 1990s.

Schools are not the only institutions to play a role in reworking education. Public historian and educator Lisa Junkin Lopez discusses a sex-positive public programming series at the Jane Addams Hull-House Museum. She positions the series within a long-term process of reanimating this house museum by linking its specific histories to present concerns and by drawing on Addams's inclusive spirit to open up this institution in a deeply reciprocal way to the range of communities around her in Chicago.

Writer and educator Scott Sikkema brings together both the role of the school and the responsibility of the artist in a conversation with a group of socially engaged artist-educators who embed their practices within schools. Projects in which schools are the sites for a meaningful co-practice can transform the experience of students K–12 and their perception of the societies in which they live. Meanwhile art historian Rebecca Zorach presents a selection of ephemera from the Free University Movement of the 1960s, which in Chicago offered radical alternatives to mainstream forms of higher education.

Today, as in recent decades, Chicago's art schools and universities have been central sites for social practice in this city. And though they may be at times targets of critique, they provide venues for discussion, debate, and the development of projects. Moreover, they support the practices of many teaching artists who have been critical to socially engaged practice here and who work outside or at the edges of the market. Perhaps most of all, they allow for the transmission of knowledge among generations, making this way of working live in Chicago.

—SS

John Dewey, Democracy, and Education: A Lost Legacy

Bill Ayers

Nelson Algren once described Chicago—rightly, I think—as a beautiful woman with a broken nose. In *Chicago: City on the Make,* his wonderful book-length love song to his hometown, Algren highlighted a metropolis characterized by conflict and contradiction:

> Not that there's been any lack of honest men and women sweating out Jane Addams' hopes here—but they get only two outs to the inning while the hustlers are taking four. When Big Bill Thompson put in the fix for Capone he tied the town to the rackets for keeps...
>
> The best any mayor can do with the city since is just keep it in repair.
>
> Yet the Do-Gooders still go doggedly forward, making the hustlers struggle for their gold week in and week out, year after year, once or twice a decade tossing an unholy fright into the boys. And since it's a ninth-inning town, the ballgame never being over till the last man is out, it remains Jane Addams' town as well as Big Bill's. The ball game isn't over yet.[1]

Carl Sandburg who was famously Chicago-identified—"Halsted Street Car," "They Will Say," and most spectacularly, "Chicago," "city of the big shoulders"—had moved from Milwaukee where he'd served as secretary to that city's first socialist mayor. Milwaukee had the longest run of socialist mayors in American history, and one of them, Daniel Webster Hoan, had met Albert Parsons, the Chicago anarchist, as a five-year old child in 1886 when Parsons was on the run from the Chicago police hiding out in the Waukesha home of Daniel's socialist parents.

Parsons was from Texas and had fought with the Confederacy during the Civil War, went through an essential American transformation during which he renounced white supremacy—a dazzling, life-altering choice available to everyone, then and now—became a leading voice for workers' rights and the eight-hour day, and married Lucy Parsons, a former slave who outlived him by half a century and was herself called "more dangerous than a thousand rioters" in the 1920s by the Chicago police.

Albert Parsons was hanged in 1887 after a quick show trial for his role in the famous Haymarket demonstrations that had turned into a police riot and massacre; the three surviving Haymarket defendants were pardoned in 1893 by Governor John Peter Altgeld, at one time my favorite Illinois governor now replaced by George Ryan, a corrupt right-wing Republican who declared himself an abolitionist and cleared death row in 2003 of 163 men and four women just hours before he left office and two years before going to prison himself—for fraud, corruption, quiet money, the whole banal three-step program for Illinois politicians.

In 1889, two years after the hanging, Jane Addams established Hull-House, the first settlement house in America, and with an intrepid group of crusading women went on to create the first juvenile court in the world, which freed children from adult prisons and poorhouses, the first playground in a city park, put an end to child labor, and a thousand other projects and reforms. She argued that building communities of care and compassion required more than "doing good," more than volunteerism, more than the beneficent but ultimately controlling stance of a Lady Bountiful. It required, rather, a radical oneness with others in distress, an identity of purpose with the wretched of the earth—she labored *in solidarity with*, rather than *in service to*, the people.

Five years after the Haymarket hangings, Eugene Debs was jailed outside Chicago for six months for violating an injunction against supporting the Pullman Strike—a tumultuous labor conflict that threw the city into turmoil and drew Jane Addams into the fray as a mediator—and one hundred thousand people gathered in the rain to greet him upon his release. He linked the cause of labor to the aspirations of the revolutionaries of 1776 and famously said, "I would not lead you into this promised land if I could, because if I could lead you in, someone else would lead you out."[2]

In that same year, a young philosopher named John Dewey took a teaching position at the University of Chicago and wrote to his wife back in New York that "Chicago is the place to make you appreciate at every turn the absolute opportunity which chaos affords."

Chaos and opportunity; conflict and contradiction; hope and history—and it's all still true.

John Dewey's Vision

John Dewey was the preeminent American philosopher of the twentieth century, and his voluminous writings over many decades plunge deeply into questions of psychology, ethics and aesthetics, art and logic, experience and education, democracy and social theory. He was a steadily engaged intellectual, founder, for example, of the Laboratory Schools at the University of Chicago, co-founder of The New School for Social Research in New York, president of the League for Industrial Democracy, board member of Hull-House in Chicago and of Goddard College in Vermont. Dewey believed that education was the essential means of social progress, and his works on education in a free and democratic society remain classics: *The School and Society* (1900), *The Child and the Curriculum* (1902), *Democracy and Education* (1916), and *Experience and Education* (1938).

In 1897, Dewey published an article in *The School Journal* called "My Pedagogic Creed," and it is perhaps the best brief ever issued on the principles of progressive education. His later work would elaborate and extend these ideas in a thousand directions, but, remarkably, the structure and design for a revolution in education are all there from the beginning.

Dewey argued that the starting point of education must be the child's own instincts and powers and not some external standard or goal or competency or reward. The child's inherent desire to live, to grow and make sense, to develop and to become competent and powerful in the social world was the proper beginning—with family at first, then in larger and larger contexts and communities as life advanced. He believed learning and living were essentially the same thing: if one lives, one learns; if one is learning, one is living.

Think of a new mother—after hours and hours of pain and labor her first child is born, bursting into the world, triumphant and noisy, quickly swaddled and placed in his mother's arms. Exhausted and exhilarated, ecstatic and awed, she puts her son to her breast—she had reflected on this moment for months, listened to the advice of peers and elders, read books and articles, and joined La Leche League—and begins to teach the baby to nurse. She holds his head and guides his mouth, and he pushes back a bit, readjusts, and begins to tell her things about nursing she apparently had not gotten from books or friends. And he's only minutes old! She pays rapt attention, and together they negotiate the moment, she teaching him how to nurse, and, yes, he teaching her how nursing works best as well. The first dialogue has begun, each participant a conscientious student, and each an engaged, committed teacher. This is profoundly human and powerful learning—innate, natural, self-directed, authentic, discursive, vital, multidimensional, and ongoing. So it begins.

Learning and living—they are each half of an inseparable whole; they are in fact *one* in a critical sense. Baby and mother are driven by an essential desire for life—so simple and yet so profound—and no other motivation is necessary. The learning they are each experiencing and that they share between themselves is situated fundamentally in trust, respect, and care—each of them is confident in the expectation that the other is reliable and responsible, and that the developing faith in the other and in oneself is steady. The mother day-by-day is gaining self-assurance in her own capability, and the baby is becoming more secure as well, increasingly certain of being heard and understood. The belief that they can know or discover their own deepest needs becomes self-fulfilling and begins to accelerate, leading rapidly onward—they listen more carefully to each other as well as to their own minds, bodies, spirits, and interior emotions as critical guides to future learning.

Dewey believed that education proceeds from the psychological to the sociological, from the emotional to the logical, and that neither the psychological nor the sociological aspects of the process can be subordinated or ignored without damaging the whole; each is necessary. He wrote that if we ignore "the social factor from the child we are left only with an abstraction;" if we ignore "the individual factor from society, we are left only with an inert and lifeless mass."[3]

He thought that "school is primarily a social institution," a "form of community life [geared toward] bringing the child to share in the inherited resources of the race, and to use his own powers for social ends."[4] A central tenet held that education should never be a prescribed preparation for future life, but must be based, rather, on the dynamic process of living life itself. Dewey pointed out that no one knows what society will be like even twenty years ahead, and it is therefore impossible to prepare the young "for any precise set of conditions."[5] He believed that the young should focus on developing the power to have command of themselves as moral actors and socially responsible individuals with a strong sense of their own agency. Starting with the child, aware that each individual is a complex social being, conscious of education as life itself, the school becomes a site of constructive and expressive activities including cooking, building, composing, manual training, performing, and more—and all of this has, like life itself, a "scientific aspect, an aspect of art and culture, and an aspect of communication."[6]

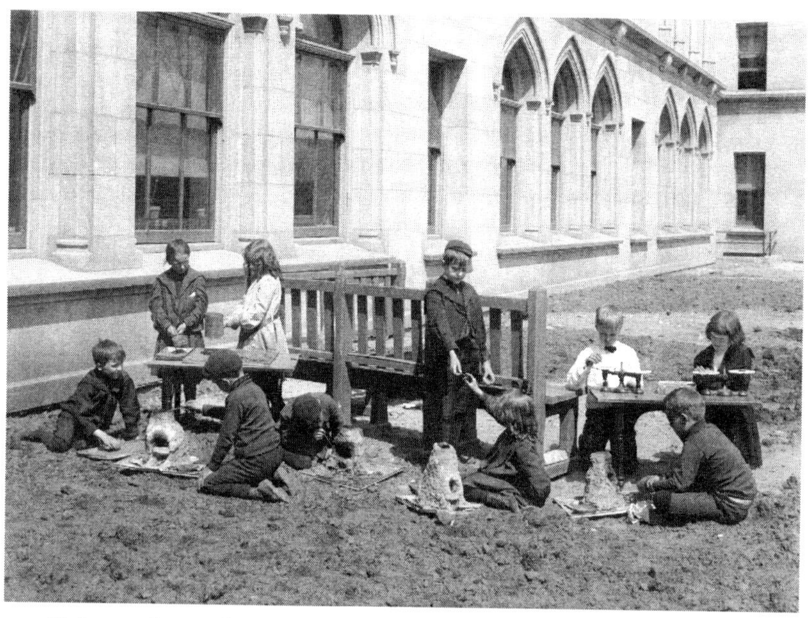

Students on the grounds of the Laboratory School. Courtesy of the University of Chicago Library, Special Collections Research Center.

Dewey's fundamental critique of the existing schools was that they failed utterly to understand the dialectic of the individual in society—the school as a form of community life—and failed as well to recognize that the motor force for growth and development was internal to each human being. Much of education was unsuccessful because it "conceives the school as a place where certain information is to be given, where certain lessons are to be learned [and t]he value of these is conceived as lying largely in the remote future; the child must do these things for the sake of something else he is to do; they are mere preparation. As a result they do not become a part of the life experience of the child and so are not truly educative."[7] Schools too often turn wildly diverse and dynamic sparks of meaning-making energy into passive receptacles of the ideas of others, and this in turn means the child is "not permitted to follow the law of his nature; the result is friction and waste."[8] And worse, they impart a sense of failure or incapacity, insecurity and a longing for external affirmation, fear and embarrassment in many young people.

John Dewey's Visit with the Utopians

Many years ago my friend and colleague William Schubert, a curriculum scholar and John Dewey authority, showed me a short speech by Dewey called "Utopian Schools" that had appeared as an op-ed in the *New York Times* in 1933—thirty-six years after "My Pedagogic Creed." In this piece, Dewey condenses his ideas dramatically and still the essence is dazzlingly clear as he imagines himself magically transported to a Utopian society and discovers to his surprise that, "The most Utopian thing in Utopia is that there are no schools at all."[9]

Looking more deeply into that peculiar detail, Dewey notices a range of differences between schools as he knows them and the places in Utopia where children and youth "gathered together in association with older and more mature people who direct their activity." The Utopian assemblies are small—no more than two hundred people—so that relations can be close and personal and intimate; these places have gardens, orchards, and a collection of studios, museums, workshops, and active laboratories all around, and everyone interacts more or less like members of a family rather than a formal institution; the adults are "carrying on some line of action" at their own level—scientific inquiry, maintenance, construction, painting, music—and the young are part of that purposeful activity, doing projects, making things; no sign of competition for rewards is evident in these assemblies, and no emphasis on personal acquisition or private possession—of skill, of knowledge—is deemed worthwhile; there is no indication that learning is a bitter pill that must be forced on the young, or that the joy of living and creating must be deferred to a phase of life sometime in the future.[10]

To do and to make, to know you are valuable and valued: here is progressive education set into motion; here is where the essential building blocks for a lifetime of productive and powerful learning is secured; here is where education toward freedom and agency, autonomy as well as social responsibility, begins to take hold.

In Dewey we become aware of learning as an unpredictable and volatile energy force propelled from within and intent on exploration and growth, unhooked from convention or any linear expectations whatsoever. We notice a central paradox: teaching is most difficult precisely because it requires teachers to let go, to get out of the way and to *let learn*. This is the first of many contradictions and paradoxes that characterize teaching and learning from start to finish.

Look at a toddler negotiating her apartment or a nearby park or the beach—all five senses are fully engaged, every discovery considered and touched and smelled and—oops!—into the mouth for a taste! Soon she is imagining stories and inventing words, putting her handprints on everything, sorting and building, drawing on paper or painting at the easel if the materials are at hand; that is, if the adults are ready for her. Did they put red, yellow, and blue paint at the easel so that one day she can exclaim to her surprise: "Look! Red and blue makes purple!"? This is different from knowing what primary and secondary colors are; this is constructing a world. Teachers can create the dense and layered environments that will elicit discovery and surprise, construction and rethinking. Every kid, after all, comes to school a question mark and an exclamation point—her work after all is the assembling not only of a life, but of an entire world.

Every school, every classroom, and every teacher could choose to support and aid in that construction, to help unbolt the vitality of the world, to provide opportunities for students to do and to make. Diving into that energy is not exactly smooth but it is learning—letting go, yielding, being here now, and stepping onto shaky ground not knowing what the result might be. Every school and each teacher must decide whether—and then *how,* in the hard-edged spaces we often inhabit—to keep the questions and the passions alive—creating environments for exploration, for doing and making, for experimenting and hypothesizing and falling down and getting up—or to hammer the children into shape so that they leave her classroom, no longer vital question marks or exclamation points, but as dull periods.

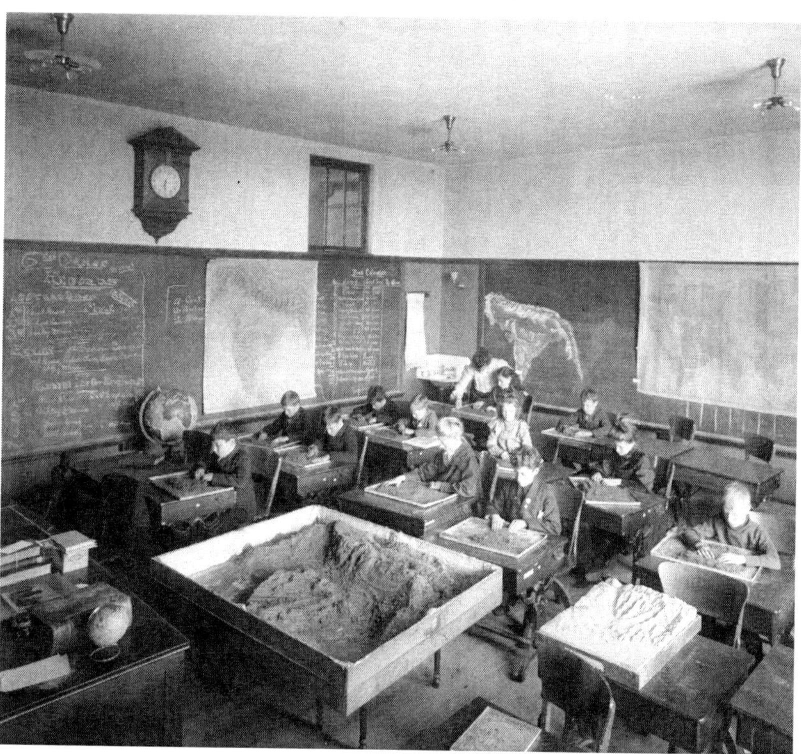

Elementary geography class at the Laboratory School. Courtesy of the University of Chicago Library, Special Collections Research Center.

Schooling based on the insight that learning is for all intents and purposes living would move us away from an obsessive focus on externally developed or teacher-directed approaches, and would foreground the foundational qualities that promote trust and confidence, curiosity and imagination, self-direction and internal motivation. After all without any bribes or stars or grades whatsoever, most kids most of the time learn to nurse and to eat, to creep and crawl and walk, to babble and talk as we engage with and respond to their jabbering, and to engage in a thousand other complex skills and undertakings. Long before we arrive at the schoolhouse door we are motivated by enthusiasms that spring from within, the deep innate human yearning to learn and to live. There is no valid reason—if constant growth and permanent development are our goals—that school should throw all of this away in favor of a regime of external and distant stimulations. Educators can choose to build on what's already there—in natural abundance.

When we respect a child or a student and support her or him in the work of unfolding what is within and creating a unique and specific identity, the signals of what to do and how to respond come from specific encounters with unique persons—complex, culturally informed, dynamic, ambiguous, twisty and wiggly—and not some disembodied, one-size-fits-all rule or principle. This reality inspires an ethic of care and a sense of reverence and awe in teachers.

Each of us is the one and only who will ever walk the earth, each lives life in unique ways. Teachers who acknowledge this evident fact build flexibility and openness into the work, allowing for authentic curiosity, deep creativity, and wild diversity to hatch and flourish. The project then becomes to unleash the human mind and spirit rather than to search for techniques that will cast us as circumscribed predictors of what cannot be predicted, or authorities who enforce obedience and conformity through top-down directives.

Picture the schools we might have had today if the country had created a massive pedagogical experiment based on Dewey's ideas over a century ago, or simply the experiences of Dewey with the Utopians eighty years ago. Imagine the kind of social and economic system that would have been required to maintain those schools.

Students would become authors of their own scripts, stars in their own dramas, sculptors of their own identities. They would resist the objectification they suffered in society or in the boot camps they knew as school before. They would engage in naming the circumstances of their lives, identifying obstacles to their full humanity and the humanity of others, and planning ways to overcome those obstacles—paradoxically they would experience freedom as never before through becoming aware of its limits, and they would understand in unique ways their agency by fighting the forces of un-freedom.

They might begin with an engagement with fundamental questions: What does it mean to be human? Who in the world am I? How did I get here and where am I going? What in the world are my choices and my chances? What does it mean to be educated? What did I learn that the teacher didn't know? What's my story, and how is it like or unlike the stories of others? What is my responsibility to those others?

A spirit of open communication, interchange, and analysis would become commonplace. There would, of course, be a certain natural disorder, some anarchy and chaos, as there is in any busy workshop. But there would also be a sense of joy, and a deeper discipline at work, the discipline of getting things done and learning with one another and through life. We would see clearly that education at its best is generative—in a way that training, for example, never can be—and that offering knowledge and learning and education to others diminishes nothing for oneself. An educational experience where questioning, researching, and undertaking active work in the community is the order of the day, helping others would no longer be a form of charity, an act that, intentionally or not, impoverishes both recipient and benefactor.

Freedom Schools Now!

We have in our recent experience an example of progressive education in action—Freedom Schools sprang up all over Mississippi in 1964 as a strategy to revitalize the flagging civil rights work there. While the black youth of the South were denied many things—decent school facilities, honest and forward-looking curriculum, fully qualified teachers—the Freedom Schools were a way to address the fundamental injury: "a complete absence of academic freedom and students are forced to live in an environment that is geared to squashing intellectual curiosity, and different thinking."[11] The classrooms of Mississippi were "intellectual wastelands," and the Freedom Schools were designed "to fill an intellectual and creative vacuum in the lives of young Negro Mississippi, and to get them to articulate their own desires, demands and questions."[12] Their own desires, their own demands, and their own questions—for African Americans living in semi-feudal bondage, managed and contained through a system of law and custom as well as outright terror, this was a revolutionary proposal.

Andrew Goodman, James Chaney, and Mickey Schwerner were all volunteers engaged in the Freedom Schools. They had been investigating the arson bombing of a church that hosted one of the schools when they were arrested and jailed in June 1964; they were released into the dark of night and then kidnapped and brutally lynched by the Ku Klux Klan near Philadelphia, Mississippi. The revolutionary meaning and potential of the Freedom Schools was apparently not lost on the rulers of Mississippi; it was understood by the barbarians and their terrorist enforcers as well.

The world-shaking significance of the Freedom Schools—their potential, legacy, and cost—should not be lost on us either. Begin by focusing on the young folks who have been written off and marginalized by the powerful and the mainstream society. They are the descendants of formerly enslaved people or recent immigrants or First Nations people; they're from working-class families—people who survive by selling their labor power, and even then frequently in the informal economy; they've attended schools of poverty, and many have participated in a sort of general strike and run away from those schools; they have endured institutions—not only schools, but police and courts, hospitals, La Migra—that routinely disregard their humanity and their full personhood.

And now to restate: the youth of South Central Los Angeles or Detroit or Philadelphia or New Orleans or the West Side of Chicago are denied many things—decent school facilities, honest and forward-looking curriculum, fully qualified teachers to work with them—but the fundamental injury is a complete absence of academic freedom with students forced to live in an environment that is geared to squashing intellectual curiosity and different thinking. What would it mean and how would it look to help them to articulate their own desires, their own demands, and their own questions? I think the world would crack open—as it did in Mississippi—and in the best possible way.

And I think that all schools and all educational encounters could improve if they began there: creating the conditions where all students could articulate their own desires, their own demands, and their own questions.

As young people discover and develop their own sense of agency, they can start to see themselves as actors in the world, and not merely adjuncts in society. No longer objects—instructed by people who tell them where they may or may not go, when they may or may not speak, what propositions they may or may not cross-examine, which books they may or may not read, when they may or may not pee or shit, what time they may or may not eat, what materials they may or may not study—they begin to question the nature of the schooling they're offered and the schools of poverty they're required to attend. In interrogating the real conditions of their lives they step out of subjugation and into history as subjects themselves. They realize as free and full human beings that they are inherently (and not contingently) valuable, that they are in-motion swirling through a vibrant living history, that both they and the world they inherit are works-in-progress and still under construction, that as humans they are paradoxically completely unique and simultaneously the same as all others—we are all born into a human culture, we all experience pain, we all die—and finally that *they don't need anyone's permission to interrogate the world.*

Free People in a Free Society

Dewey believed education and democracy are linked: a strong participatory democracy requires a thoughtful, engaged, and active citizenry, and an education that encourages critical thought, reception and resistance and empowerment, pushes toward a more vital and inclusive democracy.

Democracy is based on a fragile and particularly precious ideal: every human being is of irreducible and incalculable value. In a robust and functional participatory democracy we build schools that reflect that principle and its corollary: the fullest development of all is the necessary condition for the full development of each, and conversely, the fullest development of each is necessary for the full development of all.

This is why experiments and experiences in progressive education—for all their good intentions and high ideals and invested energy—eventually crash: the progressive ideal cannot thrive in a system designed to create a few winners and many more losers, a system that encourages predation, vicious competition, unchecked acquisition, and greed.

John Dewey argued that in a democracy whatever the wisest and most privileged parents want for their children must serve as a minimum standard for what the community wants for all of its children. Arne Duncan as well as Barack and Michelle Obama sent their children to the "Dewey School," the University of Chicago Laboratory Schools (as my wife and I did) where they found small classes, abundant resources, and opportunities to experiment and explore, to ask questions and pursue answers to the far limits. Oh, and a respected and unionized teacher corps as well. Good enough for the Obamas and the Duncans, good enough for the children of privilege, good enough for the kids in public schools everywhere. Any other ideal for our schools, in the words of John Dewey, is "narrow and unlovely; acted upon it destroys our democracy."[13]

---

1 Nelson Algren, *Chicago: City on the Make* (Chicago: University of Chicago Press, 2001 [1951]), 14.

2 Eugene Victor Debs, *Debs: His Life, Writings and Speeches*, eds. Stephen Marion Reynolds and Bruce Rogers (Chicago: Press of Geo. G. Rennkker Co., 1908), 71.

3 John Dewey, *My Pedagogic Creed* (New York and Chicago: E. L. Kellogg, 1897), 6.

4 Ibid., 7.

5 Ibid., 6.

6 Ibid., 12.

7 Ibid., 8.

8 Ibid., 14.

9 John Dewey, "Dewey Outlines Utopian Schools," *New York Times*, April 23, 1933, http://www.yorku.ca/rsheese2/3410/utopia.htm.

10 Ibid.

11 Charles Cobb, "Prospectus for a Summer Freedom School Program," *Radical Teacher* (Fall, 1991): 6.

12 Ibid., 36.

13 John Dewey, "The School and Social Progress," *The School and Society: Being Three Lectures* (Chicago: University of Chicago Press, 1899), 19.

Social Responsibility and the Place of the Artist in Society

Carol Becker

Art is the individual's way back to the collective.

—Ernst Fischer, *The Necessity of Art*[1]

This has been an amazing period for the art world. After the Harold Washington painting; the Scott Tyler flag installation; the Mapplethorpe, Serrano, and Artists Space exhibitions, artists and art students have been forced to rethink their position in relationship to the art world, to each other, and to society as a whole. Together we have watched in horror as serious work has been taken out of context, held up like pornographic smut on the floor of the Senate, defamed by the media. And we have seen congressional representatives—not the most art-literate authorities—make decisions concerning the fate of arts funding in the U.S. based on literal, Neanderthal, reactionary reading of the work.

In another context, at another time, I would discuss these actions as attempts to reify the prototypical American as a white, male, heterosexual patriot. I would rant about increasing repression, the attempt to squelch diversity and to punish those who choose to project an opinion about American society and the nature of daily life different from that which Jesse Helms finds comfortable and comforting. And I would address, probably exclusively, the responsibility of society to create a supportive environment for the artist, while making reference to countries like the Netherlands, which for many years subsidized visual artists in the hope that they actually would challenge society. But here I want to confront a different and, for the art world, definitely more controversial, aspect of the problem—the artist's responsibility to society.

This is a sensitive issue, one that many in the art world systematically attempt to avoid because it makes everyone ill at ease, defensive, and insecure. But I believe the unwillingness of American artists to debate this question is only in part the result of a kind of laissez-faire elitism and actually has more to do with fear: fear of accusations of those both inside and outside the art world who might label the work in question narcissistic, sexist, racist, classist, elitist, indulgent, hermetic, or at worst, naïve and unpolitical. Instead of attempting to clarify the meaning of art in society, to validate the work they do, to struggle with the complex issue of the place of the artist in society, many artists simply refuse to address the issue—as if artists alone did not have the obligation to ask themselves how their work fits into the broader social framework of which they are a part.

I saw this pattern occur most blatantly around the Harold Washington painting incident, where it seemed impossible to address the complexity of the episode without discussing the content of the work; yet the art world focused primarily on the outrageous tactics of the aldermen. One was forced to choose: for or against the painting, for or against Nelson. That was, for the most part, the extent of the discussion. But this put many artists, especially many African American and Hispanic artists, in a bind.

Why couldn't we all, as an art community that believes in freedom of expression, insist on David Nelson's right to make the painting while also insisting that we talk openly among ourselves about the issues of racism, homophobia, and accountability provoked by the image? Why couldn't we deconstruct the image in an attempt to understand, and thus perhaps ultimately to assuage its effect on, race relations in Chicago?

The silence among white artists around the content of David Nelson's painting disturbed me and continues to disturb me. Implicit in this silence was, and is, an unconscious complicity. In our reluctance to ask *how* work engages within the larger social context, we are attempting to protect art and the artist from censorship. In practice, however, we are participating in the bourgeois notion of the isolation of the artist from society and of so-called high culture from the debates about representation and plurality current in popular culture. Instead of healing the split between the flatness of mass media and the complexity of the art world, we are allowing the split to become an abyss. In our refusal to contextualize the work historically—not art-historically, but world historically—we contribute to the relegation of art to the sphere of entertainment and commodification. In our resistance to confronting the content of a work and the emotions such work generates, we make it easier for the work to be rendered impotent and vulnerable by the voices of congressional representatives who would turn the process of evaluating art into McCarthy-like witch-hunts—the goal of the hunt not to ferret out communists but rather all those whose ideas might be considered deviant, subversive, or just down-right "unAmerican." To fight these battles we must not fear the more difficult debates.

As a writer, educator, and art administrator, I have thought a great deal about these issues and have tried to analyze the problem in various essays I have written. In these works I have explored the elements of the art education process itself and have attempted to understand why the art world, as reflected in the art school environment, has not developed a stronger methodology and discourse for addressing issues of social responsibility and accountability.

I have observed, for example, that although we talk endlessly about postmodernism and now about post-postmodernism, in fact the way in which we educate our students is better suited to a romantic paradigm. We continue to envision the artist as a marginalized figure, cut off from the mainstream of society—operating out of what Freud calls the Pleasure Principle while the rest of us struggle within the Reality Principle, or within its present manifestation, the Performance Principle. Even though this model never did, and certainly now no longer does, fit the actual lived lives of artists, we nonetheless unconsciously expect creative, intuitive people to be ill-equipped to function in the adult world. We even tend to be suspicious, as Arthur Danto notes, of those artists who survive too well within the "straight world." We wonder about their creative credentials. We tend to train people as we ourselves were trained and so the myth tends to lag behind the actuality. We do not, for example, add to this category of the childlike artist the new invention—the artist-businessman. Like Jeff Koons, stockbroker become artist, this artist stands in a postmodern parody of his own dilemma, a charlatan reflecting, with every work and every posturing, the lack of distinction between himself and the money-making world of art collecting that sustains him. Even in this era, when all categories have been thrown up for grabs, we continue to reinforce certain archaic dichotomies. For example, we separate the aesthetic acumen developed in the studio from the more linear intelligence cultivated in the classroom. We divide the physical space of the school and the credit hours in accordance with this division. At the undergraduate level a great deal of time is taken up developing technical skills. Students are trained to work in many media and technologies without equivalent time or guidance in determining what to make work about. It is assumed that students already have many of the intellectual tools they need to think through the dilemmas in the content of their work. Or that they will look inside themselves and find imagery already articulated or that the process of physically making the work will reveal its inherent contradictions. We relegate a proportionally small percentage of educational time to those courses that actually teach students how to think about their work. We rarely analyze to what extent we are all the sociological products of our individual upbringing as it converges with the collective condition. In the same vein, we do not force our students to challenge rigorously their ethnocentrism or to recognize that a historicity—the tendency to deny history—is endemic to this society. One need only listen to Chicago's ten-o'clock news to understand how on one night a fire in Joliet, Illinois, will be given more time and coverage than the overthrow of governments in Eastern Europe. The media, reflecting and creating the society, focuses on what seems to affect us, the so-called American people, directly. The result, as it trickles down, is that American art students, like most American college students, tend not to be trained to think globally or politically about their own position.

This inexperience in dealing with broader societal issues becomes particularly apparent when students choose to make overtly political work. Because of this general isolation of art students from society, such work often takes its definition of "political" from what the art world defines as political, responding to ideas once removed from their societal framework. This work can therefore be naïvely informed, dogmatic, one-dimensional, dependent on shock and on art world references, which means that it becomes difficult for those outside the art world to respond to it sympathetically.

This issue of accessibility, which might in itself be a subject of political debate, is often not addressed as such within the art school environment. This is because art students, like other anthropological sub-groups, together share knowledge of the hidden signifiers—the references to which the work alludes—and rarely notice that these signifiers are unknown to those on the outside. Added to these difficulties, student artists often are not taught carefully enough how to research their subject matter thoroughly so that, when appropriate, they can integrate what may be a sincere outrage at the world in which they live with the objective facts that might infuse their critique with meaning and credibility. The work may therefore have a confrontational or heavy-handed feeling that assaults the viewer with its lack of subtlety and generosity to the audience it supposedly wishes to influence. Hence, the examples of political art many students encounter further convince them that work that is socially motivated is destined to be narrow, limited, literal, and defensive.

But perhaps the most dramatic, and at time disastrous, extension of the difficulties posed by educating artists within the romantic paradigm is that they often develop a very naïve sense of artistic freedom, one which permeates the entire art world. Students become unable to separate the need to express and explore freely the entire range of ideas, fantasies, and creations within their studios from the decisive editing process necessary for artists to choose what they will show and how they will show it. They come to perceive *all* serious queries about the effect or potential social impact of their work as an impingement on freedom of expression—hence the resistance to real discussion around the Harold Washington painting; hence the limited analysis and narrowly defined debate in relation to the recent art-censorship events. Freedom for the artist thus comes to signify the right to do whatever one wants, however one wants, whenever, and wherever one wants, without consideration of consequence. This does not leave the artist alone, free to do whatever he or she imagines possible, but inevitably lonely, without an ongoing dialogue with a world larger than the art community.

By this definition of freedom, artists have been categorized, along with children and emotionally impaired adults, as the only members of society not held responsible for their actions. The historical result of such thinking is that it perpetuates an infantilized notion of the artist, keeping student artists at an arrested stage of development. Such polarizations also foster the notion that most people must relinquish the pleasure principle in order to enter the adult world, while the artist alone remains in a state of unobstructed childhood. But the fact of such an imagined condition of innocence disenfranchises the artist, who then becomes a blank screen upon which the rest of society projects its desire for a lost narcissism. The implication for the culture as a whole is that works of art, relegated to the world of culture, become objects of sentimental longing, intellectual curiosity, or that which may be consumed for economic gain. The implications for the art school are that it is forced into the role of permissive parent, while its students play out their respective parts as precocious and at times unruly children.

At this point we can begin to see the complicity of art education in this infantilization, and the consequences of relegating the artist and the art world to a position as "other," "different," or "exotic." These categories, which artists themselves often reinforce in their attempt to find self-definition, only further isolate the artist and his or her work from the society as a whole.

When Jesse Helms held up the Mapplethorpe and the Serrano and asked good god-fearing Americans if they wanted their tax dollars to fund such work, he was capitalizing on the myth of the artist and the artist's bohemian lifestyle to unnerve his audience. But however grotesque his manipulations may have been, they have forced the art world to ask some serious questions, the most significant to this discussion being: What *is* the place of art in American society? What *is* the place of the artist?

In the nineteenth century, American writers Walt Whitman, Melville, and others, had a dream that the artist in America would be the voice of democracy, integral to the daily life of a pluralistic society, representing diverse, hidden, necessary points of view. But there have been only a few times when this vision actually became a reality, as in the 1930s when the economy collapsed and artists aligned with workers and intellectuals to form a strong progressive movement—not unlike what we are now seeing in Eastern Europe. But modern art, as we know it in this country, has often existed outside the lives of many Americans. Although it does reflect the ontological changes of daily life, most find the forms employed by the art world to be incomprehensible and obscure because these forms are often dependent for effect on knowledge of the art-historical precedents that are removed from the recognized iconography of many people's daily lives. In other words: most people simply don't have the information or training that would allow them to "get it." When postmodernists attempt to use popular imagery to break down the distinction between high and low culture and to adopt forms already popularized by the mass media, they are in a bind, because many outside the art world see such work as a joke, a scam, perpetrated on them by artists. People outside the art world rarely understand the seriousness with which even humorous, parodic art is executed. And artists have often remained silent, unwilling or unable to explain their work to a popular audience—hence the hostility people feel to the art world that excludes them and that they fear deceives and mocks them as well. While all this is going on, artists themselves often feel alienated, misunderstood, and unsupported by mainstream society.

At this moment the art world and the general populace, although actually closer than ever in their shared postmodern dilemma, are nonetheless at a standoff. Into this historical mess walks Jesse Helms, ready to make his name and build his career by furthering this confusion and aggravating this tension. But ironically, at the same time that artists in this country are personae non-gratae, fighting to be heard and understood, artists around the world are much in demand, asked to assume, of all things, politically useful positions.

Right now, while students, artists, poets, philosophers, and workers have made a revolution in Romania, and intellectuals are influencing the reunification of Germany and the transformation of Poland, Vaclav Havel, the playwright, has become the transitional president of Czechoslovakia. The only president in history, as the *Village Voice* proclaimed, "who can quote John Lennon, Samuel Beckett, and Immanuel Kant." Havel has spent decades of his life in and out of prison opposing the governing ideology. But at this moment he is in the Prague palace as the voice of Civic Forum—a movement which brings together artists, intellectuals, students, and workers—a coalition of diverse groups that is inconceivable at present in the U.S. Imagine, if you can, a person of creativity, morality, integrity, and vision—

imagine an artist—who could also have enough mass support and backing to become President of the United States. Imagine if that person were a leading playwright. Imagine Sam Shepard, for example. He might one day run for President. It's possible, but if he were elected it would not be because he makes serious work, has an artistic vision, a critique of American society, or a level of intelligence respected by his peers, but rather because he is a glamorous movie star, who has appeared on the pages of *People* magazine—many times. Art in this society, like politics in this society, has been relegated to the realm of entertainment. The rest of the world understands this about the United States and felt it perfectly fitting, poetic justice that Ronald Reagan, a Hollywood actor, a bad actor, actually became President.

But the art world itself has been corrupted by this laughable, but infinitely, globally, dangerous capitalist system that can chew up, spit out, sell, and commodify controversy at will. The art world has been corrupted by the market's inflated prices and by the dream artists and art students alike have of "making it big" (whatever *it* is), like Jeff Koons, like Julian Schnabel, like Jenny Holzer. The market has taken the edge off the art world. The individualism, romanticism, and competitiveness of the art world has played right into the hands of the investors. The result is that even art that begins as a critique of society often becomes depoliticized, objectified, institutionalized, consumable by those who have the money. Often it is work that somehow can be assimilated because at its core it does not threaten the prevailing ideology. It does not unmask the basic contradictions. Often it is work that challenges the art world itself, but which stays safely within that arena, often devoid of emotion, uncritically embracing new technologies, obscure in form, incomprehensible to many outside, and finally comfortable within the existing social system.

What might the position of artists be were work not assimilated by the marketplace? If there were no marketplace? For twenty years, the work of five hundred Czech writers, Milan Kundera and Vaclav Havel among them, officially were banned. They were still stars, however. They mimeographed their manuscripts or smuggled them out of Czechoslovakia, printed them in the West, and smuggled them back into Prague and other cities where there were Czech readers. They voiced the dreams and courage of the people. These writers were forced underground because they refused to infuse their work with the "obligatory optimism" demanded by the party in power. There was no comfort in their work, and there was no comfort in the life of the artist. There was no money to be made. There was no quantifiable success to be had. Success was measured by the strength of the work in conveying the complexity and absurdity of the Czech situation—poetically. Most writers went into exile, or to jail. Those out of jail, formally banned from any established positions, were forced to work as waiters, waitresses, janitors, and furnace stokers, for low wages. When Joseph Papp tried to get Havel out of jail and to bring him to the Public Theater as a dramaturgist, Havel agreed to go, but only if the Czech government also released all his co-defendants. The result: Havel did not go to New York. He spent the next years working in a prison foundry, where he almost died of pneumonia. The point is that these artists stayed true to a personal political vision that kept their spirits alive—kept them in touch with all those, in all areas of Czech life who shared this vision. They appeared to be repressed and silenced, but in fact they were neither. They were preparing for history to take an inevitable turn, at which time they would be ready—intellectually and philosophically ready—to seize the moment and assume real political power.

Now, twenty years later, those with whom they aligned, who were in fact the majority all along (albeit seemingly silenced), have made Havel interim President. This will mean, as he acknowledges, that inevitably his writing will cease for a time, until the interregnum has passed. And he has said, he will miss the writing. Havel is reluctant to be a political leader, but, as he says, "history has overtaken me." His first identity is as a "citizen," and as a citizen he has assumed the challenge of a desperate economy and a country in chaos.

Why do I go on about Havel and make this seemingly obscure analogy with Czech society? Because these dramatic changes are living proof that the role of the artist is an historical, social construction. It is not an eternal fixed role. It is not only romantic. It is not without context. It changes, evolves, grows, diminishes, dictates, and is dictated to, and by, history and the market economy. And as such, the creative vision of an artist can be utilized both to construct art and to construct a new society, because these goals each depend on bringing into creation that which does not as yet exist.

In many societies in Europe, Latin America, Africa, Asia, and here, artists use their voices to struggle against the master text, to create alternative narratives in visual imagery, dance, in music, in theater. They interweave all that is silenced, repressed, feared, hidden, and attempt to make it known. The difference between these countries and ours is that here there is no overt recognition of the importance of art to daily life.

The recent "A Day Without Art: A National Day of Action and Mourning" was a brilliant, powerful, and successful attempt to make people recognize the place of art and artists in society, and the loss of both as a result of the AIDS epidemic. But imagine a day that was truly without art, not just a day with paintings covered in museums and galleries but one without architecture, interior design, graphic design, fashion, film, photography, video, theater, music, dance, magazines, books. Imagine every place where these would be, shrouded in black, and you can understand the power artists actually do have. They fill the void, give meaning to the tedium of everyday life, and make society civilization. We do not feel that collective power in the United States because art has been either placed on a pedestal, removed from daily life, or pushed to the peripheries of the society, manipulated by politicians or used as a means for rich people to become richer. And although artists in this country can produce what they want (as long as no public funding is involved), art actually has little direct societal impact. I believe we are beginning to see that in the nineties this will change and that the goals of the art world will change as well. I think we will be hearing more from those who may not have received visibility in the eighties but who have a great deal to say—those who cross over, move between cultures; those who have struggled to raise serious issues of gender, class, and race; those who understand the process of self-definition to be a political act; those who refuse to allow the imagination to be colonized. I think these artists will find ways to seize visibility and to control the means of distribution. I think the more superficial aspects of postmodernism will die a natural death, and from the best of this movement will evolve a new form, one which will attempt to reach out to an audience greater than just the art world and will not see it as enough to mirror the fragmentation, banality, and destructiveness in this society and its physical environment, without also offering some vision for developing a less alienated future.

Artists in this country now appear to be refusing the place of isolation and marginality they have been given and which they themselves romantically have often confused with freedom. It is time for artists to challenge what they cannot live with and to bring into view what they refuse to live without. This task of confronting contradictions in all forms, at all levels, and of crossing beyond the parameters of the art world to do so, is not the work all artists will have the inclination to choose. It need not be understood so much as a responsibility—any more than the responsibility we all must assume for securing the survival of this planet—but rather as a possibility that I hope many will embrace.

This text was originally published in *Zones of Contention: Essays on Art, Institutions, Gender, and Anxiety* (New York: State University of New York Press, 1996), 27-36. © Carol Becker.

1 Ernst Fischer, *The Necessity of Art* (New York: Penguin, 1963), 45.

Extreme Arts Administration

Gregory Sholette interviewed by Abigail Satinsky

Abigail Satinsky: *Greg, I initiated this conversation to talk with you about your time in Chicago from 1999 to 2004, while you were faculty in the Art Administration and Policy program at the School of the Art Institute of Chicago (SAIC). I attended the same program as a graduate student in 2006, shortly after you left. While at the School, fellow students and I started InCUBATE, a research group that produced a series of projects and experiments addressing art administrative structures and art economies to imagine new support systems for socially and politically engaged art.[1] Your artwork and teaching, operating as it did between administration and art practice, created space for us to begin our own set of investigations, though we didn't experience it firsthand. Thus, given that you were based in New York working as an artist and activist during the 1980s and 1990s, what drew you to Chicago and an institutional position at SAIC?*

Gregory Sholette: Fifteen years ago, scholar and curator Rachel Weiss invited me to co-chair SAIC's Master of Arts in Arts Administration program with her. Rachel had pretty much reinvented this department just a few years earlier, and she was looking for someone a bit unconventional to serve as the only other full-time faculty in the program at that time. I suppose what interested her was my combined experience with formal and informal forms of cultural administration. I had been involved in do-it-yourself organizing with such artists' collectives as REPOhistory (1989–2000) and Political Art Documentation/Distribution (PAD/D, 1980–1988), but I also had worked at non-profits, such as Public Art Fund and the New Museum during the 1990s. So in the fall of 1999 I packed up my books and left New York, where I had lived more or less continuously since 1977, and moved into the fifty-ninth floor of Chicago's Hancock Tower where I had a one-year apartment-sitting situation, just enough time for me to get acquainted with this new city. Ultimately I lived in four different Chicago neighborhoods before returning to New York in 2004.

AS: *What was Chicago like at that time? Did you feel like there was a particularly vibrant community for critical art practice and how did that affect your own work?*

GS: Other than finding myself living an odd, perpendicular existence in a self-contained vertical city, the first extraordinary Chicago cultural encounter I remember was visiting Dan Peterman's space at 6100 Blackstone Street on the South Side, also known then as The Building and today as Experimental Station. Dan's center immediately blew me away. No refined white space or antiseptic academic venue, 6100 Blackstone was housed in a former recycling center. Its irregular brick walls were surrounded by organic gardens and piles of compost. The setting was a challenged, urban, semi-residential area abutting the University of Chicago campus. Inside this industrial artifact was a bustling hive filled with enterprises including Dan's studio and a few temporary studio spaces for other artists, a bicycle repair shop, a carpenter, an auto mechanic, and the offices of a brilliant little oppositional literary magazine called *The Baffler*. At the center of everything stood an open-plan kitchen where I found Dan stirring an enormous pot of pasta. Nearby Connie Spreen—Dan's wife at the time and collaborator in developing The Building—and their two kids entertained a large white dog. Guests filtered in for the event.

What struck me most was how alive the scene was and how different it seemed from 1990s New York where alternatives to the art world had either vanished or become ossified. A decade earlier New York still harbored the possibility of generating counter-institutions. Projects like the *Real Estate Show*, PAD/D, Carnival Knowledge, World War Three Illustrated, Paper Tiger, Group Material, or later Gran Fury, Guerrilla Girls, Critical Art Ensemble, Bullet Space, and REPOhistory were organized around decidedly anti-market ideals. And even if at times this avowed resistance proved to be more fantasy than reality in practice, a certain widespread delusional energy had generated a stream of antiestablishment art experiments throughout the 1980s. The decade that followed was different, dare I say less delusional? New York had taken a revanchist turn: the late progressive geographer Neil Smith's term for an ascendant urban gentry intent on extracting retribution from the city's losers, including the homeless and working poor. Artists who typically were cast in the Judas role soon found themselves outcasts as well, becoming familiar with ever more distant stops on the L train. Even once proudly defiant institutions like the New Museum and PS1 underwent makeovers, affirming their place within what sociologist Richard Lloyd calls an ersatz Neo-Bohemia, where a sign of dissent is always preferred to acts of real opposition.

Against that backdrop, my encounter in Chicago's South Side reminded me just how necessary it was to reimagine organizational models for artists. In turn, this realization fed directly into to my newly minted role as earnest teacher of arts administration. The tone was set for my entire Chicago experience. Not long after this I came across other Chicago-based practices like Temporary Services, Lumpen/Version Fest, Stockyard Institute, and so forth.

AS: *How did you think about teaching administration at SAIC, in light of your background as an artist and an activist? What were the challenges of negotiating institutionality?*

GS: One outcome to my epiphany at The Building was the development of a class entitled Extreme Arts Administration or XAA. It was structured as a seminar in which, as the class syllabus read, we would investigate new, as well as some older, overlooked ways of "organizing cooperative, cultural spaces; interactive, public-art projects; art actions for political demonstrations; as well as even community gardens and recycling centers." We did readings about anti-institutional activism and organizational tactics from the Art Workers Coalition (late 1960s) to the Barbie Liberation Organization or BLO (early 1990s). I also promised students they would travel to "the edge of the known organizational universe where art, politics, and institutional planning converge." I am not sure we actually went that far, but one exercise involved creating your own how-to management procedures in which students transformed normal into aberrant forms of administration. The final result was perverse versions of those little self-help business books, like *The 7-Minute Manager*, rendered in the form of a booklet, presentation, or video. The final class was described as "Wrapping it up/just getting started..."

The XAA class coincided with the *Critical Mass* exhibition at the University of Chicago's Smart Museum of Art, which I was invited to be a part of by Stephanie Smith and Jacqueline Terrassa, and which also included projects by A. Laurie Palmer (and one project she made with Wendy Jacob), Robert Peters, and Temporary Services. I proposed that my XAA students get involved in some way, and both Stephanie and Jackie enthusiastically agreed. Perhaps they did not know what they were getting into, because over the course of the opening my students turned up and carried out interventions that in most cases I knew nothing about beforehand. Perhaps the most memorable was an action organized by Dara Greenwald who devised a "pop-up" wrestling match to take place on opening night. I remember a moment when a very crowded museum floor was suddenly parted and a quadrangle of benches installed. Out of some unseen corner came Dara and a half dozen others wrestlers; each was wearing a unique sports jersey with a name written across it in collegiate lettering. The group split into pairs to face of and recreate historic ideological battles: Karl Marx vs. Mikhail Bakunin, Pat Califa vs. Adrea Dworkin, and apropos of the post-Seattle protest moment, "The Black Bloc" vs. Medea Benjamin. What followed were seemingly spontaneous scuffles between communism and anarchism, and pacifism and violence that went on for some time, although I do not believe either side managed to pin the other down long enough to call the match closed.

Such experiences in Chicago were significant and impossible to summarize, except to say that they directly and substantially contributed to my 2010 book *Dark Matter: Art and Politics in the Age of Enterprise Culture*. Among other lessons I learned was that how we organize may seem independent of any given economic or social reality, but it is in fact far more representative of the range of possibilities and limitations available at any given cultural juncture, in any specific city or location. (And who knows, perhaps this suggests that Dara actually won in the end?)

AS: *What do you think about how art institutions now welcome these critical and activist art practices? Where do you see extreme arts administration happening now, if at all?*

GS: Extreme Arts Administration was more like an ideal target that I knew I would never hit. It emerged out of a frustration with the largely academic discourse about cultural institutions in the 1990s. For instance, it seemed that negation as a tactic of countering existing administrative structures was ultimately ineffective at a time when institutional critique was not only mainstream academic parlance, but also when museums themselves were experimenting with it. I imagined XAA to be like an operating manual for outsider arts organizers: a radically de-centered management program that was, by definition, not manageable. The danger in this, of course, is that the cutting edge of real-world management theory was already borrowing heavily from the way artists work to reinvent corporate business models. Overturning hierarchies and thinking outside the box have become norms for management, especially in the so-called creative industries.[2]

Therefore, the difficulty moving forward, was neatly expressed in a panel that Oliver Ressler and I put together for Gallery 400 at the University of Illinois at Chicago in conjunction with our exhibition *It's The Political Economy, Stupid* in November 2013. Brian Holmes, who was on the panel, outlined his idea of autonomous politics that peels away from both mainstream of capitalism as well as such traditional Left notions of class identity and party building. From the audience, historian Blake Stimson's comment that Holmes's notion of autonomy curiously paralleled the rise of neoliberal enterprise culture insofar as it celebrates self-determination at the expense of a broader investment in social solidarity including class-consciousness. What they both hold in common, however, is a strong sense that we are way beyond tweaking the system and the very notion of society is in ruin. Some attempt at rebuilding it is necessary, if only for purposes of survival. Perhaps the students involved in Occupy Berkeley several years before the Zuccotti Park occupation put it most dramatically when they labeled current conditions the "necrosocial": "It is November 2009. For an end to the values of social death we need ruptures and self-propelled, unmanaged movements of wild bodies. We need, we desire occupations. We are an antagonistic dead."[3] (Perhaps it's not a coincidence that we are obsessed today with the zombies, vampires, and the paranormal?)

So I suppose the question is: what do you do with a dead society? One answer is the way some artists have invented ways of mimicking its function. I think you can see this in the rise of what I call "mockstitutions," whose satirical names imply a form of necromancy at work: Institute for Applied Autonomy (IAA), Church of Shop Dropping, Temporary Services, Mess Hall, The Yes Men, Baltimore Development Cooperative, Bruce High Quality Foundation, and so forth. And perhaps their ironic gestures also harbor a small inner hope that through an act of sly imitation social institutions can be brought back to life even better than before? The question is not all that different from: whatever happened to the avant-garde? In other words, how do you radically disrupt a world in which, as Marx put it so well so long ago, everything solid is always melting into air? How can you create a vanguard art or radical art organizational theory when the mainstream that you despise is busy adopting some of your most extreme ideas, metaphors, and techniques? I mean, do you attempt to re-establish certain forms of pre-capitalist or non-market social relations, such as consensus politics, discussion groups, and bartering systems, like InCUBATE, Occupy Wall Street, 16 Beaver Group? Do you attempt to ride the wave of deconstructive capital itself, all the while using policy and activism to steer it in more egalitarian directions, like Laurie Jo Reynolds's Tamms Year Ten, Rick Lowe, The Laundromat Project? Or do you simply acknowledge that there is a degree of aesthetic pleasure within this dissonant process of destruction and reconstruction, as well as an inherent paradox that leads the system into crisis and, therefore, also into an opportunity for critically intervening, as do Critical Art Ensemble and Tactical Media in general? One thing that remains constant is the need to learn ways of successfully organizing as a response to a global social and economic crisis that is far from over. And as a matter of fact, I have been reworking the whole XAA class in order to present a version of it at Home Workspace in Beirut in 2015.

AS: *What do you think is lost, if anything at all, by teaching social practice as a discipline? On one hand, strategies and histories become available to a wider swath of people, while on the other, there is a danger that the politics of place and connection to actual communities can be overlooked or ignored, so that the discipline is only judged by its success as art in art spaces. Do you have specific thoughts as someone who has been involved with teaching this constellation of subjects for the last twenty years?*

GS: I would go even further and say that the roots of this emerging discipline that a growing consensus now calls social practice art (an inevitable outcome of the push and pull between a lost social, and the phenomenon of social networking), threads its way back as far as the protest movements of the 1960s, or even further to the organized Left culture of the 1920s and 1930s.[4] The notion of achieving critical mass—an especially suggestive and perhaps intentionally subversive term given that the first sustained nuclear chain reaction using a critical mass of uranium took place at the University of Chicago—is also important to consider with this proviso: organic communities and original principles can also be fetishized in a negative way. Think of Tea Party "foundationalism" today. For as significant as it is to know one's history and to experience what I have described as the dense, inert missing mass of shadow practices, artists, collectives, events, frustrations, and desires, it is equally important to forget, not in a simple way, but as Nietzsche proposed, in an active way, in order to address possibilities that would be foreclosed by what Marx (an unlikely partner) called the burden of history that "weighs like a nightmare on the brain of the living." OK, that is a bit abstract, but it points not only to the necessity of learning to think with contradictions—something artists are or should be very good at—but also the necessity of acting in the world even if such contradictions cannot necessarily be resolved. For example, returning to the question of social practice means grasping the historical significance of this emerging field, without letting that past dictate the direction of one's project.

In that sense, Chicago during the years 1999 to 2004 when I was there, was a place as much ahead of us as it is behind us. This is to say, by documenting and learning from the history of that particular time and place we avoid such traps as nostalgia and resignation only if we attempt to conceive of the past as a means of actively disturbing the present as well as the future: only if we approach history as an archive of unrealized possibilities waiting to be brought to life through our imagination. In that sense Chicago is always tomorrow.

This interview was conducted between November and December 2013 as an email exchange.

1 InCUBATE was a collaborative project of Abigail Satinsky, Ben Schaafsma, and Roman Petruniak, and later with Bryce Dwyer and Matthew Joynt (not a student in the SAIC program). The organization's initiatives took the form of a project space and residency program, exhibitions, and experiments in alternative fundraising, including Sunday Soup, a community meal which raised money for creative projects.

2 For example, since XAA first ran back in 2002, dozens of books have appeared with titles like *Management and Creativity: From Creative Industries to Creative Management*, *Ideas Are Free: How the Idea Revolution Is Liberating People and Transforming Organizations*, *The Creative Enterprise: Managing Innovative Organizations and People* (three volumes!), or perhaps most apropos *Innovation Management by Promoting the Informal: Artistic, Experience-based, Playful Action* (though its probably a bad translation from German). But also from within academia Luc Boltanski and Eve Chiapello published *The New Spirit of Capitalism*, which explicitly theorized that neoliberal enterprise culture's managerial zeitgeist models itself on a rejection of workplace discipline and authority borrowed from artists.

3 See *The Necrosocial*, "Anti-Capital Projects," November 18, 2009. http://anticapitalprojects. wordpress.com/2009/11/19/the-necrosocial/.

4 See Lucy R. Lippard, *Get the Message*, or Andrew Hemingway's important study *Artists On The Left: American Artists and the Communist Movement, 1926–1956* (New Haven: Yale University Press, 2002). Lippard's out-of-print book and a chapter from Hemingway's book are available on the Dark Matter Archives site: *http://www.darkmatterarchives.net/?page_id=1020.*

Sex in the Museum: Building Relationships and Pushing Boundaries at Jane Addams's Hull-House

Lisa Junkin Lopez

We go to social gatherings, hoping that somehow, with somebody, we can have the real intercourse of mind with mind.

—Jane Addams

We've really done it this time. We brought pornography into the nineteenth-century historic house museum. Not nineteenth-century pornography, though of course, we're fans of that as well. No, this time we brought the real thing, hardcore: dildos, whips, vulvas, cocks of every shape, size, and color, and put it on the big screen for the public to view. Call it the dream of a mischievous museum worker. Or, call it a successful outreach plan.

From 2009 to 2012 the Jane Addams Hull-House Museum (JAHHM), a National Historic Landmark, hosted the Sex Positive Documentary Film Series (referred to as our SEX+++). We screened documentaries, often graphic and sometimes pornographic, followed by lively discussions. The series strived to be radically inclusive, incorporating pro-sex, pro-queer, and pro-kink films and highlighting marginalized communities. It became one of the most popular programs in the museum's history and provoked the JAHHM staff to reframe our understanding of the relationship between historic house museums and the public. While the content of the film series at times felt radical for the museum, the community collaboration became a best practice.

The film series arose from the sex positive movement, a liberation movement rooted in pro-sex feminism, queer theory, and the work of other pro-sex activists such as BDSM[1] practitioners and polyamorous groups. The sex positive community seeks to discourage harmful laws, stigmas, and stereotypes around sexual behavior and identity including bisexuality, sex work, masturbation, transsexuality, BDSM, etc. The movement aims to bring diverse communities into conversation and collective action to ensure that all people have "the freedom and resources to pursue a fulfilling and empowering sex life."[2] When I developed the film series in conjunction with activist and sex positive writer Clarisse Thorn, we originally did not consider asking my employer, JAHHM, to host the program. As it turned out, the museum was the right fit for many reasons.

Out of the Closet and into the Public Sphere

While known for its far-reaching progressive work on numerous social issues, Hull-House has not always been identified with issues of sexuality. Jane Addams, who is best known as America's first woman to win the Nobel Peace Prize in 1931, founded the Hull-House Settlement in 1889 as a place where immigrants of diverse communities gathered with American-born citizens to socialize, learn, advocate for their rights, and co-create a thriving, democratic public sphere. The settlement grew to serve more than 10,000 immigrants per week by 1910 and became known as a leading site in Chicago for discussion and action on women's rights, immigration, labor rights, public education, the arts, and more. The Hull-House Museum, located on the campus of the University of Illinois at Chicago, preserves and interprets the history of a community that helped expand the meaning and benefits of democracy to include immigrants, women, and people of color.

In 2007, JAHHM director Lisa Yun Lee invited a public examination of sexuality at Hull-House by foregrounding Jane Addams's relationship with reformer Mary Rozet Smith. Lee and the staff created three labels for a portrait of Addams's long-term partner, each providing frameworks for understanding the relationship, and asked visitors to respond to the labels by choosing the one they preferred. While none of the labels directly named the relationship as lesbian or queer (a source of disagreement among scholars and activists given the modern origins of the terms), this Alternative Labeling Project pushed visitors to consider how historical narratives are produced and proliferated. What do we gain when private (and non-heteronormative) aspects of our national heroes' lives are revealed? What is lost when they are obscured? The museum's spotlight on sexuality and the effective outing of Addams's same sex partnership led Therese Quinn, a queer educator and activist, to call Hull-House "one of Chicago's queerest sites," opening the door for SEX+++ and the continued exploration of sexuality at Hull-House.

The SEX+++ film series motivated us to continue our research of sexuality at Hull-House, which exposed an impressive but largely unexamined history. One story that had never been interpreted in the museum was that of Hull-House resident Rachelle Slobodinsky Yarros, M.D., a Ukranian immigrant and pioneering sex educator. Yarros fought to make contraception more widely available, to eliminate sexually transmitted disease, and for the acceptance of female sexual pleasure. With the support of birth control activist Margaret Sanger, Yarros helped to found Chicago's first family limitation center, or birth control clinic, in 1922. Yarros argued that women were "unwilling to be subjected to involuntary motherhood" and felt they ought to have "the power of choice."[3] She advocated for immigrant women to have better access to sex education and health care while staunchly rejecting the eugenics movement, which sought to limit the reproductive rights of immigrants and people of color. Yarros helped to found the American Social Hygiene Association and titled a book published in 1933 *Modern Woman and Sex: A Feminist Physician Speaks.*

At SEX+++ screenings I shared bits of this history with our audience, a truly diverse group of LGBTQIA advocates, students, sex workers, feminists, transgender, and kinky folks, and other curious attendees.[4] At its height, over 140 people attended the series each month and at least 95% of this audience had not visited the museum prior to the screenings. Many people told me not only how surprised they were to learn about Hull-House's history around sex education, but also how they were impressed to see a museum become an ally for the sex positive community. With film titles like *When Two Won't Do* (on polyamory), *The Sacred Prostitute*, and *Private Dicks: Men Exposed*, everyone expected some amount of resistance, either from the university or the public. It never came. By leveraging its institutional privilege and cultural capital, the Hull-House Museum was able to support the sex positive movement, providing resources, public attention, and a space for dialogue.

Counterpublics and Museum Audiences

Due to changing values within museums, museum professionals no longer talk of the public as if there is only one. We now recognize multiple publics—diverse audiences with different needs, interests, and stakes in the museum. In his book *Publics and Counterpublics*, social theorist Michael Warner expands this understanding to include counterpublics, or groups that have been excluded from the public sphere and are left to create their own spaces, norms, and realities, largely within the private sphere.[5] Examples of counterpublics might include documented and undocumented immigrants, the incarcerated, youth, the differently-abled, or those with divergent sexual identities or practices such as transgendered or polyamorous people. Counterpublics are rarely considered to be legitimate audiences by museums and other institutions, and so their needs largely go ignored. This means that museums, as so-called "neutral" institutions and agents of "truth" are often complicit in marginalizing the very publics they should be serving.[6]

In *Making Museums Matter*, Steven Weil writes, "In a dozen different contexts, identity and interest groups of every kind insist that the mainstream museum is neither empowered nor qualified to speak on their behalf."[7] Though some of these groups have rightly formed their own museums and institutions, there is yet opportunity for mainstream museums to stop ignoring marginalized counterpublics. Museums must represent new voices and commit to examine and rethink dominant narratives in history, science, civics, and the arts. As institutions of authority, museums offer needed amplification to these stories. Including counterpublics is not the same thing as attempting to transform counterpublics into normative audiences, but rather, encourages these groups to maintain politics identities that resist normativity. Significantly, Jane Addams was never afraid of working with stigmatized publics and communities deemed threatening. She encouraged political radicals—communists, socialists, and anarchists, who were also often immigrants—to meet at Hull-House, though she did not ascribe to their beliefs. This decision contributed to her becoming a target of the FBI in the 1920s, when she became known as the most dangerous woman in America. Addams never backed down from her commitment to free speech, dialogue, and allowing dissenting voice to be heard, and likewise, the Hull-House Museum seeks to cultivate this sort of dangerousness.[8]

Warner along with queer theorist Lauren Berlant have written about the oppression created by heteronormativity, demanding for queer counterpublics to be given space and legitimacy. In their essay, "Sex in Public," they call for society to "support forms of affective, erotic, and personal living that are public in the sense of accessible, available to memory, and sustained through collective activity."[9] Museums, particularly historic house museums, are an ideal place for this to happen. Where better to explore topics of sexuality than spaces that are already adept at negotiating the boundaries between public and private life? The SEX+++ audience must agree, for it chose to remain at JAHHM long after other queer venues became available. Resoundingly, the SEX+++ audience wanted to locate the film series

SEX +++
pro-SEX, pro-QUEER, pro-KINK

April 28

"It's Still Elementary" (2008)

Examines the incredible impact of the 1996 film "It's Elementary", which aimed to teach kids about LGBTQ issues. Follows up with teachers and students featured in the first film to see how those lessons changed their lives.

May 12

"Private Dicks: Men Exposed" (1999)

Interspersed with clips from vintage sex education films and humorous cartoons, men—young and old, gay and straight, large and small, virgin and porn star—offer personal revelations that are honest, humorous and often poignant. Discussion ranges over puberty, power, impotence, circumcision, sexuality, myths and perceptions, growing old, and, of course, size.

May 26

"The Aggressives" (2005)

Butcher than butch, these dykes of color have coined a new term to define their identity: Aggressive. Identifying as women, but looking and acting like men, from their haircuts to their suits to their swaggering behavior, the Aggressives have powerful personalities that buck traditional societal restrictions on women's roles.

June 9

"Boy I Am" (2006)

A look at the experiences of three young Female-to-Male transpeople addresses the way conversations about trans issues can run into resistance from the many queer women who view transitioning as a "trend" or as an anti-feminist act that taps into male privilege.

June 23

"On The Downlow" (2007)

Creates a portrait of Cleveland's underground black gay scene including coming out to one's parents; black homophobia; and the persisting rumor that only gay people spread AIDS.

July 14

"Filming Desire" (2000)

Female directors talk about the reality of an explicit women's point of view, the desire in their films to 'fantasize and dream a new image of themselves', and how their depictions of sexuality and relationships are correctives.

A FREE documentary film series for people who like sex

Curated by Clarisse Thorn

http://groups.google.com/group/sexplusplusplus

Jane Addams Hull-House, 800 S. Halsted, (312) 413-5353

http://www.hullhousemuseum.org

2nd & 4th Tuesdays of the month at 7PM

Delicious snacks provided

Positive sexuality. Alternative sexuality. Sexual identity.
We want YOU to come to these screenings — whether you're a free speech advocate, an AIDS worker, a progressive pastor, a sexuality activist, a radical feminist, a sex worker, a pornographer, a student, not at all studious, or just someone who likes talking about sex, all are welcome. Sexy PRIZES will be given for regular attendance!

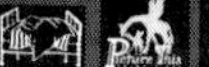

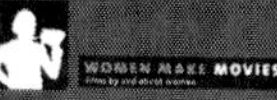
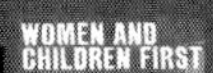
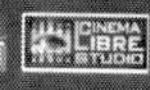
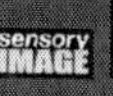
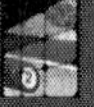
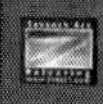
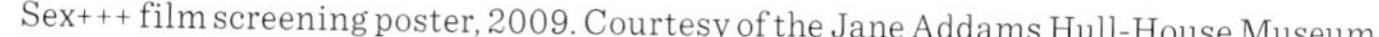

Sex+++ film screening poster, 2009. Courtesy of the Jane Addams Hull-House Museum.

at the Hull-House Museum, which they perceived as a mainstream location, in order to better challenge heteronormative and sex negative discourses.

Negotiating Boundaries

As a pro-peace, -immigration, and -women's rights museum, JAHHM often centers its values within the history of our site. With SEX+++, however, this is not entirely the case. Although Rachelle Yarros took a decidedly progressive stance on sexuality, Addams herself did not. This is especially clear in regard to Addams's view of prostitution, which stands in direct conflict with the sex positive movement's general acceptance of sex work as a valid option for both work and the fulfillment of desire. In *A New Conscience and an Ancient Evil*, Addams rails against sex trafficking and prostitution, positioning women as moral guardians of sexual purity and sexuality as proper only within a traditional marital structure.[10, 11] SEX+++ therefore offers us an opportunity to use our site's history as a counterpoint and opportunity for dialogue, rather than as a replication of Addams's values.

As with any new relationship, JAHHM's work with the sex positive community has raised unexpected challenges; for example, should the museum allow our community curators to have full control over the series, even when a chosen film depicts graphic violence that challenges our understanding of consensual behavior? Can or should we seek funding from Playboy when doing so may be unacceptable to our university? And how, exactly, should the museum respond when two audience members take the call for sexual freedom literally… in the darkened theater during one of our screenings?

In my search for answers, I take direction from what is perhaps the most poetic tenet of the sex positive movement: that the negotiation of boundaries is a constant process. Consent is never a one-time decision, but must occur actively and enthusiastically as individuals explore their desires and limitations together over time. In this way, the Hull-House Museum struggles with sex positivity as we move toward it. Perhaps the most radical aspect of the film series, then, was not the content, but our willingness to re-examine the traditional values of our site.

Midwifery and the Business of Museums

Could the sex positive notion of active consent offer a new framework for how institutions might develop programs and institutional values in partnership with their constituents? Museums and other institutions often seek to avoid conflict, dissent, and differences, but great insight can be found within those tensions and the ability of institutions to be responsive to them. Addams often brushed up against similar questions of the function of the settlement house in relation to its community. One example follows:

In her book *My Friend Julia Lathrop*, Addams writes that she and fellow resident Julia Lathrop were brought to a nearby tenement house where a young woman was beginning to go into labor. The young woman could not afford a doctor and her neighbors would not help deliver the baby because it would be born out of wedlock. Addams and Lathrop successfully delivered the baby, but on their return to Hull-House, Addams began to question their decision, saying, "This doing things that we don't know how to do is going too far. Why did we let ourselves be rushed into midwifery?" Lathrop replied, "If we have to begin to hew down the line of our ignorance, for goodness' sake don't let us begin at the humanitarian end. To refuse to respond to a poor girl in the throes of childbirth would be a disgrace to us forever more. If Hull-House does not have its roots in human kindness, it is no good at all."[12]

The story represents an important lesson learned by the Hull-House residents, that the services of the institution should be shaped by needs of the communities surrounding it, rather than by an abstract vision of the role of institutions in society. Elaine Heumann Gurian has made a similar argument for museums in a piece titled, "Museum or Soup Kitchen." She argues that museums can meet concrete needs of their constituents, particularly in economically unstable times:

> What I am proposing is not "business as usual"—museums cloaked in the name of social good, justifying their pent-up need—but rather transforming currently less-than-useful local institutions into dynamic and community-focused "clubhouses" for building social cohesion, and incorporating social services usually delivered elsewhere, such as job retraining, educational enhancements, and public discourse—in addition to their classic role of collections care, interpretation, and exhibitions. [13]

I believe this vision for a more responsive museum will not only meet the needs of the community, but will also transform museums' traditional business of collections care, interpretations, and exhibitions. Once again, it is a lesson Addams learned herself: as she devoted herself to the work of the settlement, she fully expected that she and the upper-middle-class residents of Hull-House, would be *as transformed* as their immigrant neighbors.

By engaging in an authentic partnership with the sex positive community, JAHHM was motivated to develop new museum content around sexuality, and later, to create a gender and sexuality tour. The story of Rachelle

Yarros and her groundbreaking work in sex education has been added to the permanent exhibition for the first time. Addams's sexuality has moved from margin to center in the museum by interpreting her relationship with Rozet Smith. Never before shown love poems and letters, photographs of the two sharing their lives, and the material residue of their deep commitment are now displayed in Addams's bedroom alongside her most intimate possessions, honoring this relationship as central to Addams's life and a critical part of what sustained and motivated her work.

In her defense of settlement work, Addams wrote, "the only thing to be dreaded in the Settlement is that it loses its flexibility, its power of quick adaptation, its readiness to change its methods as its environment may demand. It must be open to conviction and must have a deep and abiding sense of tolerance. It must be hospitable and ready for experiment."[14] According to this mischievous museum worker, the Hull-House Museum's collaboration and willingness to engage with the sex positive community has resulted in a more inclusive, more relevant and just museum. It is an institution of which, I believe, Addams would be proud.

This text was originally published in *The Radical Museum: Democracy, Dialogue and Debate*, ed. Gregory Chamberlain (United Kingdom: Collections Trust, 2011), and as an excerpt in *AREA Chicago*, 10 (2010). It is reprinted here with minor revisions.

1 BDSM is the practice of consensual role-play using power and pain for erotic tension and fulfillment. The acronym is overlapping abbreviation of Bondage and Discipline (BD), Dominance and Submission (DS), Sadism and Masochism (SM).

2 Center for Sex Positive Culture, Seattle Washington. See www.sexpositiveculture.org.

3 "Some Practical Aspects of Birth Control," *Surgery, Gynecology, and Obstetrics* (August 1916): 189.

4 LGBTQIA refers collectively to Lesbian, Gay, Bisexual, Transgender, Queer or Questioning, Intersex, and Allied people.

5 Michael Warner, *Publics and Counterpublics* (New York: Zone Books, 2002).

6 I would argue that this is also true of the State, which does not meet the needs of many counterpublics regarding social services, accessibility, and in certain cases, civil rights.

7 Stephen E. Weil, "The Museum and the Public." *Making Museums Matter* (Washington, D.C.: Smithsonian Institution, 2002).

8 Lisa Yun Lee, "Museums as 'Dangerous' Sites" in *Handbook of Public Pedagogy: Education and Learning Beyond Schooling*, ed. Jennifer A. Sandlin, Brian D. Schultz, Jake Burdick (New York: Routledge, 2009), 291-8.

9 Lauren Berlant and Michael Warner, "Sex in Public" *Critical Inquiry*, 24, no. 2 (Winter 1998): 547-566.

10 In Addams's personal life, scholars have noted her admiration of platonic love over physical intimacy and belief in the selfish nature of sexual desire. (See essays by Victoria Bissel Brown and Louise Knight in Hamington, Maurice, ed. *Feminist Interpretations of Jane Addams.* Penn State Press, 2010.) Addams thought the "sex impulse" should be controlled and, when redirected toward nobler pursuits, could offer "an inspiration to the loftiest devotions and sacrifices" and become "a fundamental factor in social progress." (*A New Conscience*) Though she often shared a bed with Smith, there is no indication of physical intimacy between them.

11 Jane Addams, *A New Conscience and an Ancient Evil* (New York: Macmillan, 1912).

12 Jane Addams, *My Friend Julia Lathrop* (New York: Macmillan, 1935), 53.

13 Elaine Heumann Gurian, "Museum as Soup Kitchen," *Curator: The Museum Journal* 53 (January 2010): 5.

14 Jane Addams, "The Subjective Necessity for Social Settlements," *Philanthropy and Social Progress* (New York: Thomas Y. Crowell & Co., 1893), 1-26.

Engaged Education and the Schools

Phil Cotton, Jim Duignan, Jorge Lucero, and Scott Sikkema in conversation

Scott Sikkema: To work as an artist in a school is to understand that a social arts practice is a co-created practice, not just at the end, but also from the beginning. In schools, social arts practice should be unfolded equally by artists and students and teachers; the art, and the learning, never really has one author. In thinking about social arts practice and my work at Chicago Arts Partnerships in Education (CAPE), I turn first to the notion of practitioners as researchers. Framing both the artist as researcher and the arts organization as researcher enables the CAPE program staff and myself to perceive school as site. As sites, schools have parameters, flows of knowledge and language, hierarchies, and modes of existing and acting within time and space. In our work as facilitators for arts-education programming in the schools, we act as an external element, consciously entering into this site and encountering all these components in a mutually investigative relationship, in order to then generate a place where everyone can pull back and ask questions. What is school? What roles are we playing, and why? How can we develop from and towards questioning? How do we conceive and energize spaces for learning inside and outside of school? How do we use time in school—can we instead use it deliberatively? Slow it down? Let it unfold? Inquiries like this forge a classroom/studio where the roles of teacher, artist, and student shift in meaningful ways.

Jim, one of Stockyard Institute's works from 2009 was called the *Cafeteria Sessions*, a series of lunchtime recordings and radio workshops at the Multicultural Arts High School in collaboration with Lavie Raven and Ayana Contreras, which culminated in a live radiocast. How did you come upon the cafeteria as a site or an idea for work, and what effect did that site have on the work?

Jim Duignan: The site had all the effect on the work. It was something I had thought about when always looking for neutral ground. When I started working with youth, it was clear that being out of the classroom was important. Part of that is just remembering what it was like to be at Chicago public high schools when I was in school and thinking about the activation of the hallways and the cafeteria and areas outside the building. That was

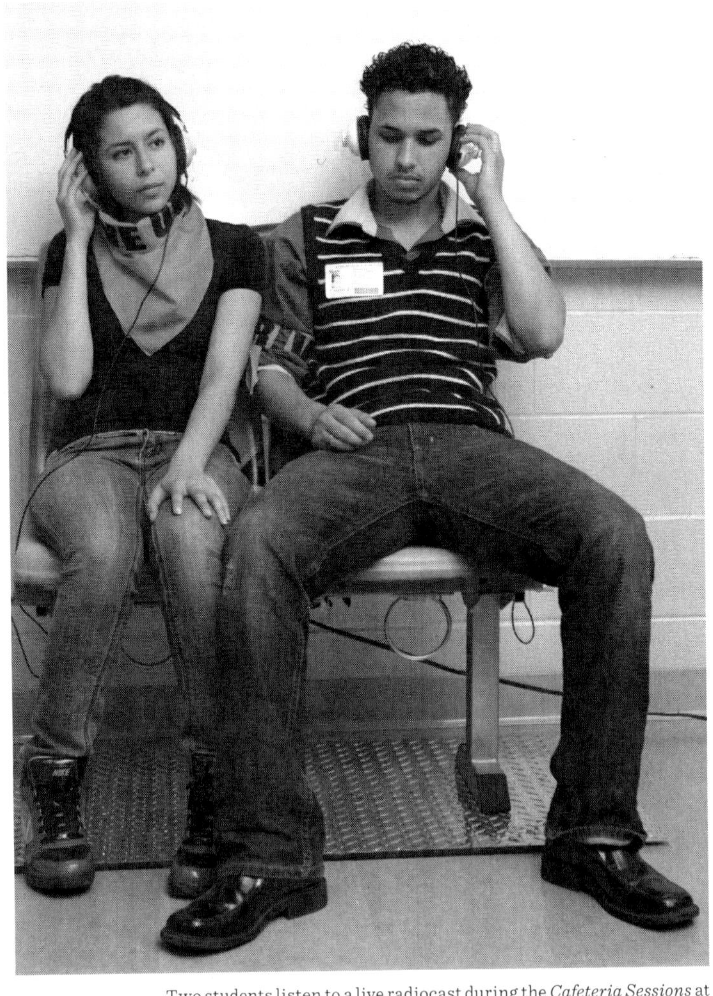

Two students listen to a live radiocast during the *Cafeteria Sessions* at Multicultural Arts High School in Little Village, 2009. Courtesy of Jim Duignan.

where all of the energy existed. It seemed a prime space. In the *Cafeteria Sessions* we were recording very personal stories about the students' lives and it seemed an appropriate space because on a secondary level, there was this activation—of being with their friends in this highly energized space. I don't think that would have worked anywhere else—in that building, anyway.

SS: Phil, you look at classroom space itself as content for art making and pedagogy. How do you think those explorations have impacted the students? What are some of the things you've seen unfold from that choice to focus on space?

Phil Cotton: My whole concept at the beginning was to get students to understand that the space of learning was not just a cube—the building, the classroom, the seat—but every aspect from the time you wake up to when you go to sleep is a part of the learning process.

In the classroom, I tried to have a lot of cues that would inspire students to think about the world and to produce things they could use. Our first project was to create their own thrones, their own chairs. They came up with ideas for the throne, because it seemed that the teacher's chair was always bigger and more important than the student's chair. I wanted to obliterate that. So we created chairs, these symbols of their ownership, and that's how it started with the classroom.

SS: Jorge, describing the 2001 project, *Residue of Having Been,*[1] where you worked with your high school students on gathering residue or remnants of the evidence of life, you wrote, "Ultimately the mess (of the remnants) may reveal more about the creator and its observers than any finely tuned sentence or object." In your video, *Monumento* (2010), the narrator states that the evaluation of an artwork should focus on what remains or what sticks from the experience of making, referring to the experiential residue as "monuments." How do you see the relationship between the mess and the monuments in classroom work?

Jorge Lucero: At a certain point you collect enough experiences together as a group, whether it's with students, or your colleagues, or with the staff in your school. If you choose to attentively live that life with those people who you're around all the time, then you also collect enough "things" associated with those experiences. Actually, the only thing you may be left with after all that "living" is a seemingly disjointed aggregate of ephemera that ineffectively documents such lived experiences (for example photographs, bureaucratic documents, recordings, artworks, emails, and various personal recounting by the individual participants). Still it is this somewhat invisible collection of evidence that serves as the triggers for recalling these experiences—talking about them, evaluating, assessing, and perhaps building upon them.

These are the "monuments" I was referring to in that video. I wasn't talking about monumentality in the conventional sense, although I was talking about how we use all kinds of monuments in order to remember, reflect, and infer. The monuments I speak about in the video are presented as objects that trigger remembrance or inference based on the narratives associated with those objects, which then propels their observers to act, react, assess, or be contemplative. In this way the monument can even be small, prone to subjectivities, inconsequential, perhaps fleeting, and frequently undervalued by those who may not have any relation to those particular pieces of residue.

I arrived at this idea about how monuments can be "used" through conceptual art, which in many ways is an absent way of working or thinking about art with students in schools even though many students are frequently asked to put words to their artmaking. The idea that the object can actually be the point of projection for these narratives to be told and further worked from is fascinating—that the objects, in and of themselves, can be the point of meaning. From these monuments we can come together to talk about ideas that make concrete again our lived experience (such as our neighborhood, our classroom, and our daily life.)

SS: Phil, you make models and prototypes with students, forming a kind of monument around which they come together to talk about ideas. In the example of the neighborhood *Identity Museums*, done with South Shore High School, School of the Arts students in 2008 to 2009, how did you see creating those models as encompassing the students' encounters with their lives?

PC: The *Identity Museums* project was interesting because in the neighborhood around the school, there were no museums, but there were a lot of vacant lots and boarded-up buildings. We wanted to conceptualize and even theorize about what the environment might look like if you could create your own museum in this location. We used the idea of an identity museum to get students to create their own environment with their own influences—family members, portraits of family members, people who were close to them, things that were close to them—and place them in these museums, and then locate these museums around the different sections of the neighborhood. That process of envisioning a museum and purposefully locating it in itself was empowering for them. They felt, "Hey, we can do this." I said, "Yeah, you can do this. You can put the money together. You can go out and rally people together to create a small one. Start up with a storefront. It doesn't have to be a large building. You can start up with a very small storefront and produce a museum."

SS: Jim, you've articulated the importance of open questioning as part of the process in projects like *Gang-Proof Suit*. I wonder if you might talk about questioning itself as part of this practice.

JD: There's this dance with various groups that I work with. We need a lot of time to get to know one another and to trust each other, and to think, what are we doing here, what is the particular outcome of this dialogue? When I work with young people I want to understand how they see this community that they live in as a kind of educated site. How is their family involved in their sense of themselves? What kind of neighborhood do they want to live in?

A lot of that early time together is about finding the conditions to make this process of mutual questioning happen in an authentic way. *Gang-Proof Suit* was a six-month series of conversations and collaborative art project in 2000 with a group of sixth grade students from San Miguel, a school in the Back of the Yards neighborhood, and a team of artists. We asked: what do you love, what are you afraid of, and what do you think about this city, knowing that in some of these neighborhoods, everyone is implicated in everything. It was about building cooperation within a project that could identify the young people as producers, as agents for their own questions, and not worrying about it going into a gallery or a museum or a book. We were able to keep this quiet for two years. There was something important to that sense of us wanting to work together in private. Secrecy was also important in a very pragmatic way: I knew one of the young person's father was a gang leader so it was important to close ranks and assure the conversation would stay in our place only.

SS: Phil, I know the kinds of questions that you generate for yourself. How does that process happen and what's the relationship between your own questions and the students' questions?

PC: It starts out with an open dialogue about the state of their world. Right now we're working on a prosthetic design project at Daniel Hale Williams Preparatory School of Medicine because the students noticed that a lot of people in the neighborhood are missing limbs. We started to ask, what's the least expensive way that we can create prosthetic devices for these individuals that won't cost thousands and thousands of dollars? The students start saying, "Well, we could do this." We're experimenting with cheap materials. We're looking at the state of where prosthetics are now. Just to do something that's affordable is a big thing. So I let them frame that idea and then I come back with my questions. An arm or hand or leg— what is the part of the body that you use the most? What do you think is needed the most? What kind of movement do you want to see happen? What is needed? Who's going to make this part?[2]

JL: I want to highlight what Jim said about keeping their activities a secret when they were working on the *Gang-Proof Suit*. I wrote down this phrase about how the work of teachers is almost always automatically secret. The thing that gets evaluated or the thing that comes to the surface is usually not the true indicator of what's happening inside of the classroom or all of the interactions that are happening in the hallways and in the lunchroom and all these places.

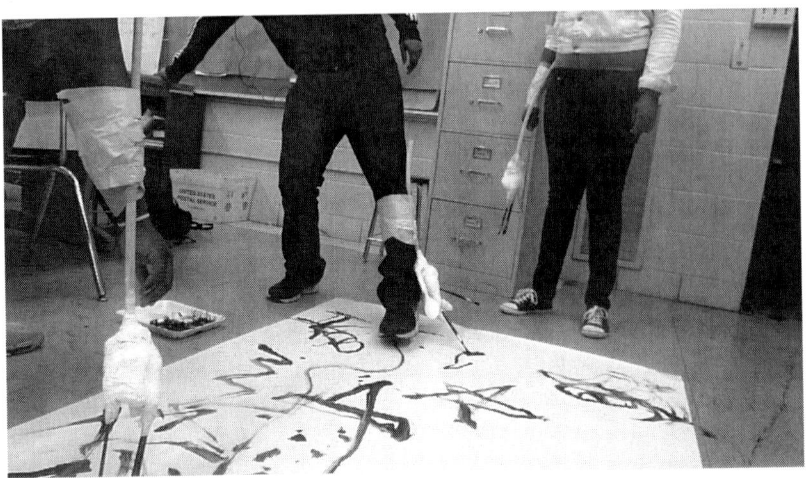

Students take part in a prosthetic design project at Daniel Hale Williams Preparatory School of Medicine, 2013-2014. Courtesy of Scott Sikkema. Photo: Margy Stover.

That made me think about social practice. What has led to the vitality of social practice in Chicago? Part of it has to do with some element of secret. Sometimes the work is not seen very well, but that doesn't matter. People continue to do the work. Sometimes the work takes a very long time, so it's very difficult to show it. But people continue to do it. It's certainly visible to all of the stakeholders but to the outside world so much of it goes unseen. Yet this latent-ness gives it its vitality. There's a corollary between what's happening in the classrooms in terms of how things gather steam in life, and what's been happening in social practice in Chicago.

JD: Yes, the idea of secrecy in social practice is a parallel condition of teaching: only what is visible gets shared or seen outside the process of building. That process of building requires improvisation, risks, connecting to students around the creation of work. I agree completely with Jorge; it is part of what I too think about, especially with the *Gang-Proof Suit*.

SS: Thinking about invisibility and questioning and things that you can't articulate, I am reminded of an article you wrote when you were a high school teacher, Jorge,[3] One of the passages is about showing students the elements of the world without giving away the mystery. Can you talk more about that aspect of maintaining the mystery?

JL: Inarticulability doesn't necessarily equal ignorance. You might not be able to say something, but it doesn't mean you don't know it, and it doesn't mean you don't know about it. How can we support more open-ended processes of learning? How can we learn and grow and develop new questions without always having to feel like, okay, now we're done with this project—let's put it away and move on to the next thing. I'm done with getting to know you. You're no longer my student. Don't say hi to me in the hallway anymore. Of course you're not going to do that because that would be crazy, right? We don't live that way. That's not how life works. As teachers and as artists I feel we need to emphasize that education is about knowing, is about growing, but it's not necessarily about holding onto or defining or capturing or being able to have the right words for it.

JD: We're also really adept at these very poetic, elegant elements that come into work that we don't feel any need to define, but we can use at our disposal. I think about the *Gang-Proof Suit*. We were at 48th and Damen, and Wood is two blocks over east. A kid was saying to me, "You can't cross Wood." I'm like, "I can't cross Wood?" I mean, do you really think that nobody can cross Wood because you don't cross Wood? How much of what you know is about this sense of your space and mobility and just understanding? Some of the projects aren't art, you know? But there are all these things that shape the project, like these conversations that alert you to what the students know.

JL: That's where the time element becomes so important because maybe the kid can't say it to you at first, but maybe after you've spent three weeks or three months with them—

JD: Six years.

JL: —or six years, you're like, "Oh, I know that he knows this," or "I know that she knows this."

JD: Well, that's what I have to assure them of—that I'll be there with those sixth graders until they're done with high school. You think about this idea of pacing, then exposing themselves. That's where these surprises happen—where you can take time. It makes me think of your prosthetic project, Phil. The prosthetic is such a great metaphor for what you rely on, what lingers.

PC: I look at time as different spheres for my kids. They have the sphere in which they're inside the classroom. They have their own sphere in which they're inside their house or on the way to their house. All of those are learning environments. I try to get them to take advantage of that—that it's not just the time that you're here in school where you're going to learn.

SS: I like that notion of spheres. There's something about the interactions between the internal sphere and the external sphere. The internal sphere is school; the external sphere is whatever that might be—the community, the neighbor, the artist. The interaction of those spheres generates something. Chicago does have a particular history of these external-to-internal relationships, whether you take it back to Jane Addams's Hull-House or to the teaching artist movement that's been happening strongly in Chicago over the past twenty, thirty years. There's something about that internal/external that generates a particular kind of social arts practice or socially engaged art here.

I want to ask the three of you, what's your take on this? Social arts practice, socially engaged art—do they naturally fit together in school? Is there a kind of division in school-based work? How do you see the two relating or not relating?

JD: I think we have to find out what social practice means, how it's now this theme around many different constellations of activity. When I think beyond making, I can think about a community as a medium, and about conversation as part of that content. Those are ideas that come from a community arts movement; in Chicago, an early mural movement. People like Jane Addams and Saul Alinsky—those are people in a social frame who were influential in terms of how to understand art. Social engagement was something that came from that kind of community framework.

In the 1970s or 1980s—and there wasn't really a "social practice" term then—I saw people working through it in high schools. It's been incubating for a long time. There's another relationship between the contemporary art world, even in Chicago, and the way in which art teachers are working in schools, right? I think in high schools, we were beginning to take inspiration from places like Hull-House, imagining the social settlement as an art school. There was a utilitarian history that we were understanding and putting into practice in the schools. There were other ways we thought about making work in the schools that I've seen happening for a long time—far longer than in the art world. As a model for a social center, a school, an art center, or for a park, Jane Addams had a framework that was about bringing people in who had things and introducing them to people who needed things. It is the most simple, elegant philosophy about using one's life. It's ground zero for my work.

PC: I think social practice and social engagement in art can overlap and exist in the same environment. I'm not sure about the definition—what is socially driven. I would not want to have an art that had just one agenda.

I look at this art process as gyroscopic: things are evolving around inside each other and outside of each other. This whole social idea of who we are, what we are, and what we're supposed to be—what is that really about? Who's saying we have to be x, y, z? Are we defining ourselves or are we being defined? I like the idea of the art process as being expansive, but in the same sense I'm concerned about society and the world we live in. You have to have that sort of sandpaper thing happening and then you have to have this smooth thing happening. It's not all going to roll down the road comfortably all the time but you learn a lot from it.

JL: If you want to be a socially engaged artist in Chicago, there might not be a better gig than to be in a school doing it, because, for one, it opens up resources for you and it's a ready community. Two, it also holds your feet to the fire. It tests your politics. It tests the strength of your commitment.

This conversation occurred on February 21, 2014 in Chicago.

1 This project involved students from the Northside College Preparatory High School and was subsequently exhibited at the University of Illinois at Chicago's Gallery 400.

2 The students were inspired by the need for prosthetics, and they actually produced prosthetics to be used by people in the neighborhood.

3 Jorge Lucero, "Running in Place is Dumb/Great," *Teaching Artist Journal*, 4, no. 2, (2006): 92–99.

The Free University Movement

Rebecca Zorach

The "free university" movement in Chicago began in 1965 with a Students for a Democratic Society school called simply The School, and by the early 1970s, free universities and other pedagogical experiments—whether in and around campuses, sponsored by activist groups, or totally independent—were flourishing. Some focused on social research and community organizing; others emphasized feminist or queer consciousness-raising. Offerings of the University of Chicago's Experimental College provide a pungent taste of the Age of Aquarius: in spring 1970, they included Ethnic Dance, Alien Civilization, Music Instrument Building and Repair, Medieval Combat Training, Crafts Co-op Workshops, Bhagavad Gita, The Black Arts, Calligraphy, Folk Guitar, The Life and Teachings of Avatar Meter Baba, and Environmental Design. Instruction was often provided gratis, but that was not the primary meaning of "free": free universities were intended as education for freedom, liberating students and teachers from authoritarian university structures and preparing them to challenge the status quo. Students at the University of Chicago were also involved in a Free University created by the Center for Radical Research (CRR), a group that included both faculty and students, to train activists in the summer of 1967. Materials from both the Experimental College and the CRR's Free University, housed in the University Archives, are presented on the pages that follow.

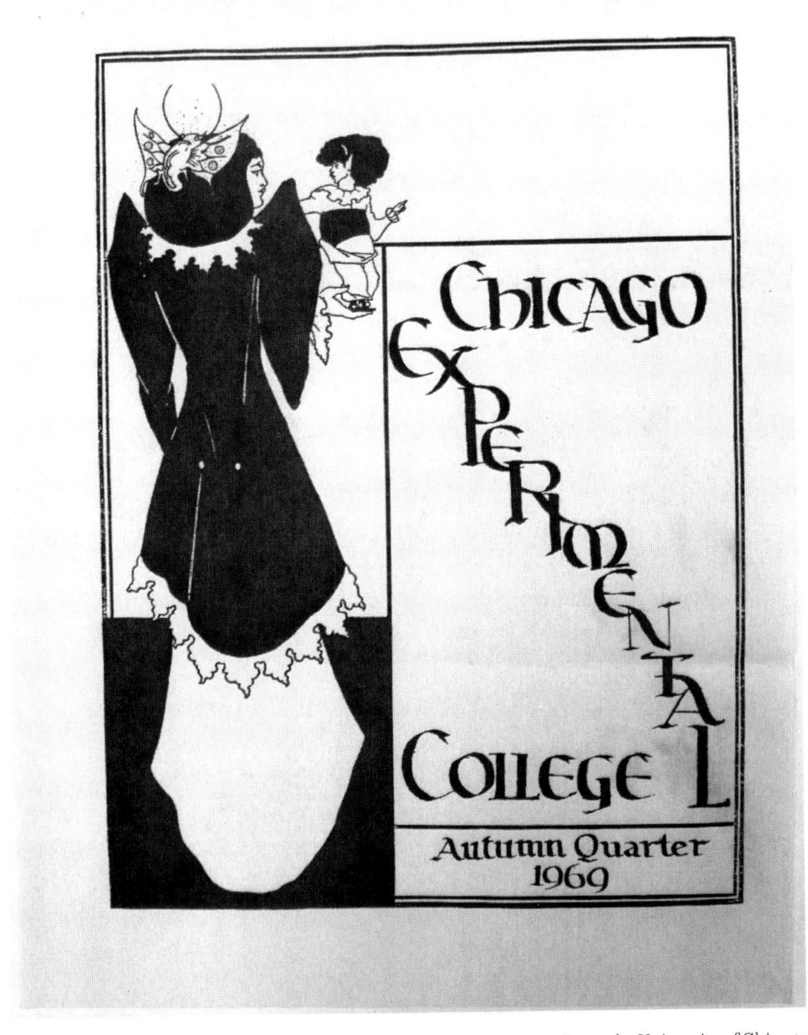

Materials published by the Chicago Experimental College in 1969. From the University of Chicago Office of Student Activities Records [Box 15, Folder 16]. Courtesy of the Special Collections Research Center, University of Chicago Library.

THE CHICAGO EXPERIMENTAL COLLEGE

Because a series of academic classes alone does not represent a satisfying and creative educational experience to many students, and because the University is apparently construed more as an institution than as a community, the Chicago Experimental College strives to create a more balanced campus life through the variety of the programs that it offers. It does not aim to compete with the established academic programs, but instead seeks to enhance them by applying unusual approaches to conventional topics, and by organizing workshops and seminars in fields that are either unavailable or considered inappropiate for inclusion in the standard degree programs. CHEC considers itself a service to the Hyde Park community, a means of setting up and publicizing programs which generate serious interest, by securing use of university facilities, and by helping to defray the costs of course materials and supplies. <u>All programs are tuition-free</u> and open to the entire university community--students, faculty, staff, and residents--subject only to the limitations in size requested by course leaders for the benefit of the individual members. Anyone may sponsor a course, if he will accept responsibility for leading the discussions and programs or can secure a qualified instructor in the field of his interest. The Experimental College welcomes all suggestions and ideas for projects and innovations.

Materials published by the Chicago Experimental College in 1969. From the University of Chicago Office of Student Activities Records [Box 15, Folder 16]. Courtesy of the Special Collections Research Center, University of Chicago Library.

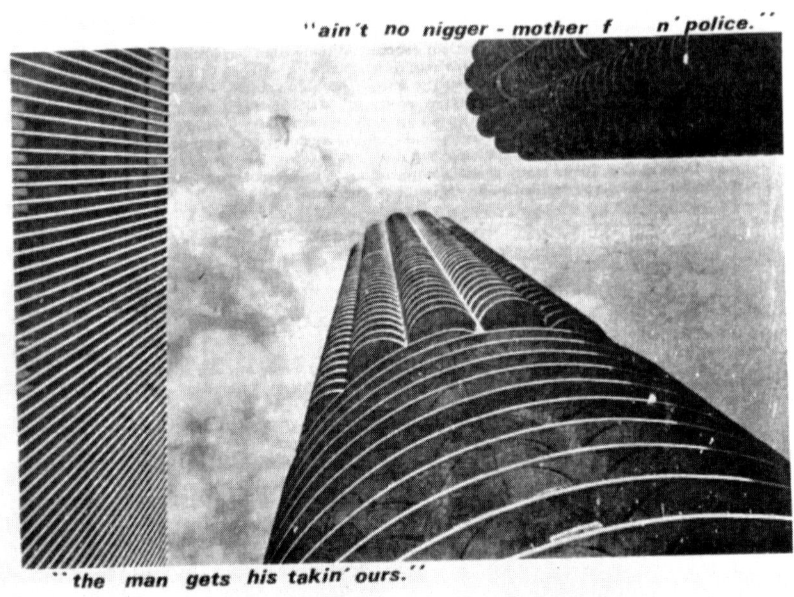

A FREE UNIVERSITY

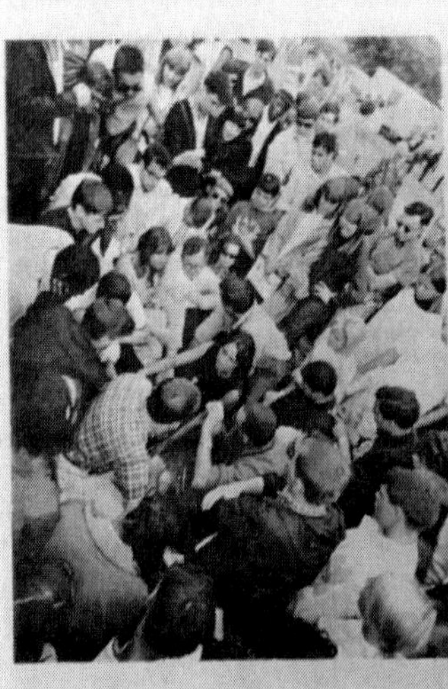

Students returning to the campus from movement activities have been concerned with the lack of relevant
courses dealing with pressing social issues. Free
universities have been the most concrete expression
of this discontent. The free university offers an alternative to a system where learning is confined to
traditional channels that do not satisfy our curiosity
or our passion for involvement. We know that the
university devalues passion except in the pursuit of
careers, insisting that values have no place in the
thinking life. It splits thinking from action and treats
the educational experience solely as an apprentice-
ship for dutiful mediocrity. It is not surprising that
the university shapes its students to fit certain molds
in light of the position of the university in our society.
Thinking which is at odds with the dominant social
values is discouraged. As an established institution
the university is itself deeply immersed in perpetua-
ting the status quo.

Materials published by the Center for Radical Research in 1967 [Box 15, Folder 6]. Courtesy of the
Special Collections Research Center, University of Chicago Library.

POLICE BRUTALITY, URBAN RENEWAL,
INHUMAN AND DEBASING RELATIONS WITH
WELFARE AGENCIES AND "CHARITY"
HOSPITALS, HIGH RENTS AND POOR
HOUSING, JOB DEPENDENCY ON DAY LABOR
AGENCIES----------problems such as these
faced daily by the poor are the cause for such
statements.

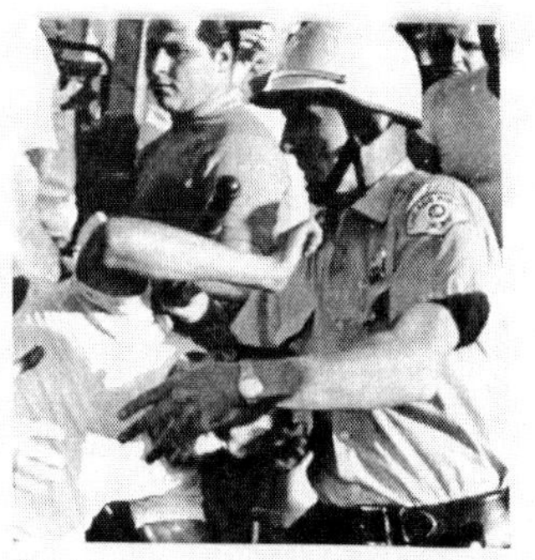

For years city and private agencies and community organizations have attempted to deal with people's specific problems and in some cases with broader issues. But with few startling, limited successes, even the most powerful groups have COME UP A-GAINST IT. Early dramatic civil rights activities such as sit-ins, freedom rides, and voter registration drives led to token national legislation such as the Civil Rights Act of 1964 and the Voting Rights Act of 1965. The passage of these acts has yet to change the conditions of the masses of poor---Negro, Latin or white. Lack of power against the political, economic and social system and lack of specific alternatives to that system have isolated our few victories. In terms of broad change the movement techniques for success have been rendered ineffective. It is painfully clear we must find new techniques, resources and ideas for moving against poverty racism and political powerlessness.

THE CHALLENGE

To meet the challenge offered by the political machine in Chicago and the economic sources which back that machine, a union of community organizers in Chicago has formed the School of Community Organization. The School hopes to give major impetus to a major attack on such problems as police brutality, high rents and slum housing by directly attempting to alter the existing power relationships between the Chicago Police Department and Chicago youth, and the landlord and tenant, the poor and the Democratic machine.

Political and economic power for the poor must become explicit, working objectives. Staff and financial resources must be directed towards creating and strengthening organizations of Negro, Spanish and white poor. Independent ghetto organizations must be built on a ward basis which compete with the machine for power. To the moral dimension of the movement, we must build a political and economic dimension. Negroes must be organized to fight and change the financial institutions that prevent them from owning their own homes and businesses. The poor must take political power in the wards they dominate numerically. A staff of 300 or more organizers must be recruited and trained and put to work helping Chicago's powerless to build powerful, self-governing organizations.

Materials published by the Center for Radical Research in 1967 [Box 15, Folder 6]. Courtesy of the Special Collections Research Center, University of Chicago Library.

The Creative Audio Archive at Experimental Sound Studio (detail).

COLLECTING STORIES

Collecting Stories

Some stories shape our imaginaries. They linger and continue to matter from year to year, from generation to generation. Others that were once lost resurface to provide new inspiration. But some only ever circulate within narrow confines; others slip from consciousness altogether. The texts gathered in this section directly address history through the concept of the archive. They represent different strategies for sifting, collecting, and broadcasting the stories that comprise the history of socially engaged practice in Chicago. They call into question both the means and ends of preservation. Are accessibility and use more important than preservation? Who gets to decide what is worth saving? How might the fruits of such efforts be most effectively made accessible, in what forms, and for whom? What about questions of power and access? What are the most effective uses—and perhaps the most creative misuses—of these collections? And what platforms are best suited for the entwined work of documentation and dissemination?

This focus on different approaches to the archive opens up a consideration of the contested role of institutions, such as museums and libraries, as keepers of cultural heritage. Librarian David Senior considers the presence of Temporary Services booklets and the New York–based project Political Archive Documentation/Dissemination (PAD/D) in the library of the Museum of Modern Art, as well as the traces of similarly progressive histories from Chicago's past within the collection of the Newberry Library. He reminds us that even institutional attitudes can change and greater inclusiveness is possible over time. Marc Fischer's conversation with Allison Schein and Tempestt Hazel arrives at questions concerning archiving from the perspective of independent projects that occasionally but warily over-lap with institutional efforts. While appreciating the roles that big institutions can play, embracing the potential of collaboration with independent archiving projects that often address histories that have been marginalized, they note potential conflicts such as preservation versus access.

Both the conversation between Philip von Zweck and Duncan MacKenzie and the selection of excerpts from "5 Questions on Socially Engaged Art in Chicago" call out the growing importance of dispersed, web-based projects as means of collecting material, adding to the plurality, and reaching wide audiences. It is important to note the latter text is housed within the website of another key archive, Never The Same—a project organized by Daniel Tucker and Rebecca Zorach—not only to gather tangible ephemera related to socially engaged practice, but also to collect and share stories that bring those mute materials to life.

Such projects take varied approaches to the pros and cons of collaboration between independent archiving projects and larger institutions. Those institutions can offer expertise, resources, and long-term stability, yet they may not share the same ethical, political, or aesthetic commitments of DIY initiatives. Collaboration between two such enterprises will be shaped by negotiation with some inherent tensions. Solutions range from guerrilla infiltration, to sustained partnerships, to a shared commitment to work independently. The kind of work and thinking embodied in such projects has the potential to shape a useful debate about two key issues: what is preserved—by whom and for what reasons—and what is the optimum balance between preservation and access.

—SS

File Under: Radical History

David Senior

Most prominent movements in arts and culture of the twentieth century were essentially motivated by a rejection of the existing organization of cultural institutions. This story runs consistently up to today. In the visual arts, this rejection often reflects attempts to navigate around the traditional relationships between artists and art galleries and museums by developing alternative sites of exhibition, publication, screening, and performance. Yet a paradoxical issue arises when researchers look for the primary documents of radical modernity: in order to consult historical avant-garde materials, we often must rely on large institutions' libraries and archives.

Given the original social and political intentions of the historical and contemporary spaces and collectives, there is an obvious tension between the legacy of such practices and the condition of being housed within the very entities that they were critiquing. Yet there is a pragmatic reality behind this scenario. As groups dissolve and traces of these histories scatter amongst individuals and collectors, libraries and archives represent potentially stable repositories. They also remind us that institutions are growing organisms that have the potential to change over time, supporting practices that may have been excluded in the past. Two different collections, the Newberry Library in Chicago and the Museum of Modern Art Library in New York, are presented here as case studies in which we can follow the thread of materials relating to politically engaged groups and individuals in the arts and letters that have traveled from personal archives to institutional settings.

Materiality and Personality within Institutional Archives

While recently spending a large amount of time researching within the ephemera files in the library of the Museum of Modern Art (MoMA), where I currently work, I noticed that some of the newspaper and magazine clippings in these files had labels attached from press clipping services. From what I can gather, the library subscribed to these services for a period of time in the 1950s and 1960s to gather materials in the international popular press on subjects relevant to the museum's collection and its curators, as was standard practice for businesses as well as libraries and archives attempting to document specific subject areas and individuals. They evoke a past era replete with the buzz of news desks around the world, a time when media accumulated mass, and huge staffs populated buildings to produce daily newspapers. The labor of organizing the vast amounts of serial print media produced at this time prefigures automated, and subsequently, digital modes of aggregating information: at the clipping bureaus, an underpaid work force culled the news of the day, reading solely for the sake of harvesting data. As I have found in the MoMA Library's files, these clipping bureaus were also used to cast a global net on artists and exhibitions around the world. This method established an assembly-line model for archiving print periodicals, creating blunt efficiency within a business of organizing and dispersing texts.

When we think of processes of archiving print culture, quite the opposite kind of labor is often responsible for the founding of archive collections. Through very direct and personal involvement with materials, the shape and tone of archive collections are formed by the work of passionate individuals with a particular vocation: librarians and archivists, and also independent collectors, activists, and scholars. The ephemera may be annotated or otherwise marked-up; these traces reflect the hands the materials passed through on the way into an archive. An archive generally denotes a place, a home, a repository in which things live. Archiving is a generous gesture, a gesture towards how we think about thought and an idea towards preservation. A safe haven. A space apart. The specific character of any archive—its proposition—is bound by the context, the who and what to be archived as well as the sensibilities of the individuals who prepare and guide materials into safe places for posterity.

Independent archivists or collectives often create and structure collections of materials outside of any institutional setting, but over time, these collections may get absorbed into institutions. Maintaining an awareness of the intentions of the original archivists is essential to a process of animating the collections that preserve and rearticulate radical ideas, movements, and individual works. In the library collection at MoMA, for instance, it is quite common to find print materials that were first preserved and maintained by devoted scholars, artists, or art workers active in various scenes. The history of these collections can relate social and political conditions that were not inscribed in the official historical record, or certain geographic, race, gender, or class identities that were underrepresented or completely disenfranchised in their contemporary setting.

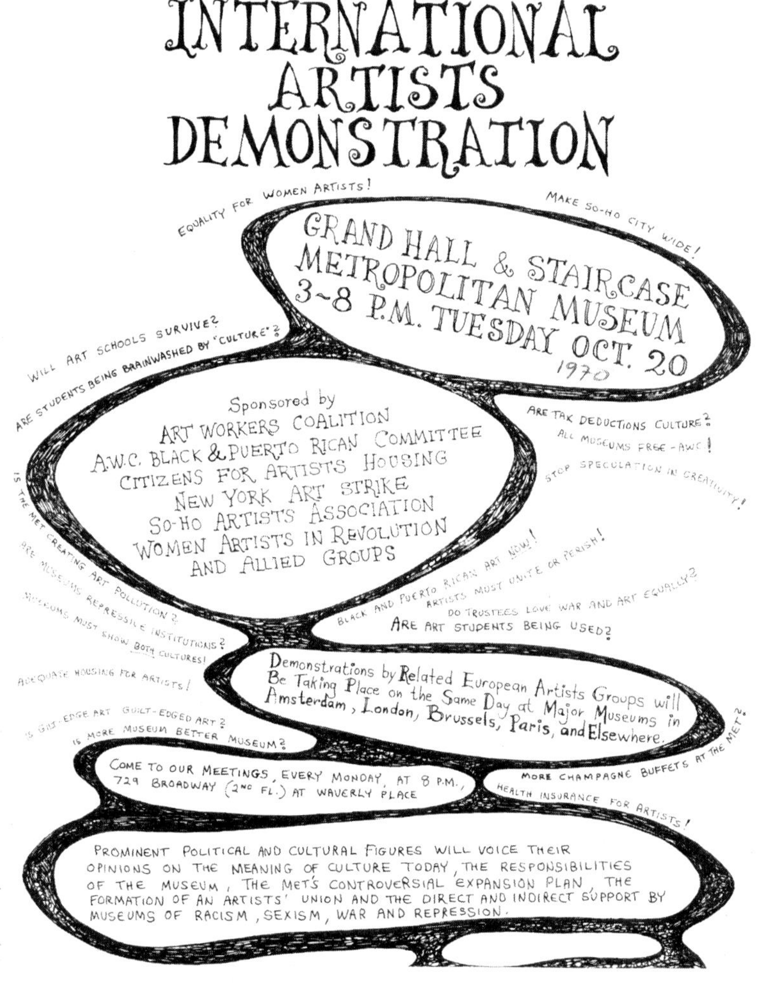

Flyer from the Art Workers Coalition file from the PAD/D Archive at the Museum of Modern Art Library. Courtesy of the Museum of Modern Art, New York.

PAD/D and MoMA, New York

The Political Art Documentation and Distribution collection (PAD/D) of materials from the 1980s and early 1990s, now held by the MoMA Library, offers a prime example of this type of archive. An activist arts organization, PAD/D was initiated by the curator, writer, and activist Lucy Lippard, who called a meeting in 1980 at the artists' book distributor/publisher Printed Matter in New York in order to establish "a progressive artists' resource and networking organization" and to address the need for an archive of "socially responsive art."[1] The director of MoMA's library, Clive Phillpot, was an early PAD/D member, helping to name the organization as well as advise on the archive. Throughout PAD/D's existence, Barbara Moore and Mimi Smith served as the main organizers of the Archive Committee. The organization issued an open call for the archive and received a rich range of materials: announcements, press releases, photographs and slides, publications and posters, continuing to evolve in a deeply collaborative, community-based fashion. Members of the group held archive meetings to sort incoming materials and cross-reference them for future researchers.[2] When PAD/D disbanded in 1990, the archive moved into an institutional home, with Phillpot brokering its donation to the MoMA Library. Smith and Moore continued for several years more, working onsite to help process the materials. The trio also organized a small library exhibition and publication in 1993 to commemorate this labor and the inclusion of the archive in the library.

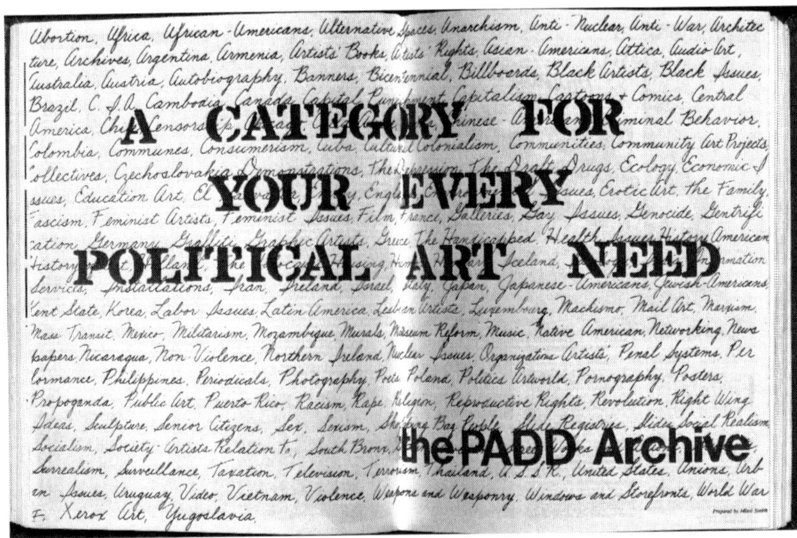

Advertisement listing all the PAD/D Archive's subject headings, prepared by Mimi Smith, published in *Upfront: A Publication of PADD* 9 (Fall 1984), 22-23. Courtesy of the Museum of Modern Art, New York.

The placement of the archive in the Museum of Modern Art may have raised some eyebrows, since MoMA had been a target for decades within the art and activism communities in New York. To his credit, Clive Phillpot was able to represent the library as a hospitable space for the archive, providing needed resources. At the same time, the PAD/D collection provided a complex and rich new resource for the library, adding materials that would have never entered the doors of the institution in any other way. In many ways, the full breadth and energy of the archive has yet to be fully revisited in a public setting. Curators and researchers consistently consult the holdings, but a great exhibition is waiting to happen in terms of the graphic history of the politically dissenting artists and artists' groups contained in the PAD/D archive.

Modern Manuscripts and the Newberry Library, Chicago

My first experience with any type of archive collection was at the Newberry Library in Chicago, where I was hired right after college as an assistant in the Special Collections Department. The library itself is a remarkable place, filled with wide-ranging treasures and the Modern Manuscripts Collection provided a unique introduction to particular, resonant Chicago histories. Most memorable were the manuscripts and papers of various literary figures. Many of these collections were marked by significant undercurrents of class struggle and by affinities for social justice and political organizing. The archive's holdings made vivid the dynamic interweaving of the lives of artists and writers and the political causes aligned with the radical left in Chicago during first half of the twentieth century.[3] It also established clear connections during this period between radical leftist politics and activism surrounding labor, free speech, and social justice concerns and the figures of the Chicago Literary Renaissance—a notable cadre of writers, critics, and journalists who developed a significant scene for new literary genres—as well as the small and vibrant cultural institutions that supported their activities.

Although initiated within the Newberry, this aspect of the Midwest Manuscript Collection resonate with PAD/D in that these materials were gathered and preserved because individuals who recognized that these documents could tell a particular and necessary story about the history of a place, a community, a radical potentiality. Stanley Pargellis, who started at the Newberry in 1942, originated the idea for a Midwest-focused collection by gathering the papers and correspondence of individuals and organizations active within Chicago's arts and letters scene. The broad agenda for the collection focuses on Chicago and the Midwest from the early nineteenth century and now includes more than six hundred collections of materials ranging from the arts, business, Civil War, clubs and organizations, family papers, journalism, literature, music, politics, railroads, religion, social action, theater, and women. The collecting activities were shaped by Pargellis's connections to such individuals as Floyd Dell, an editor of the *Friday Literary Review* and of the radical magazine *The Masses*, with whom he corresponded closely, and his vision to provide a home for materials that might otherwise be lost.

In the past decade or so, the Newberry staff has been especially active in building, developing, and sharing the collection. This is a decisive development for the stewardship of these materials. Many researchers utilized the manuscript collections during my time at the Newberry, but it seemed, nonetheless, that they were somewhat hidden. Under the guidance of Martha Briggs, who has overseen the Modern Manuscripts Collection since 2005, the library has increasingly worked to make these materials more accessible. With clear finding aids available online, these rare materials are now accessible to a broader public.[4] This increased access is a vital development in cultivating new researchers and recognizing the dedicated labor of those who preserved and maintained the histories to be discovered found in these papers. The institutional and independent labors of archivists have now been woven together as a dynamic historical accounting of figures and organizations that helped shape the cultural and political life of Chicago. Yet an institutional challenge remains to create a proper setting for the archive to continue to live and grow as a unique and radical resource. Growth in this sense most directly occurs when the collection is animated by diverse researchers, including socially engaged contemporary artists and writers who draw inspiration from these historical materials.[5]

Artists' Publications at MoMA: Chicago in New York

One of the main agendas for MoMA's library is to continue to build a repository of artists' publications. I often describe this format as especially significant as a cheap and effective format for dispersing contemporary art. The book can work as another kind of public space in which the author can shape a relation with an audience on their own terms. For conceptual artists or artists who work with performance or other site-specific and time-based media, the book itself can become a little archive for art actions and ideas. So in many ways artists' books collections are archives of archives. With artists and collective groups who use the format over time, the production of these published works often traces a network of activities, places, and collaborators.

The more than one hundred booklets produced since 1998 by the artists' group Temporary Services, which originated in Chicago, exemplify this idea of a publishing practice that develops as an operative archive for diverse range of past exhibitions, events, and collaborations.[6] When these materials were first filtering into MoMA's library from Printed Matter, I consistently noticed the content, which often engaged with historical, political, and folk histories of Chicago that I had first encountered at the Newberry. The booklets' spirit caught my attention as well since many projects involved collaboration with other groups and artists with shared affinities, often with an implied ethic of free exchange, convivial discussion, and blurred identity between art and activism. There were also booklets that resembled how-to manuals, small exhibition catalogues, and personal zines. In terms of art categories, the practice was hard to pin down, especially in a context where the vocabulary and academic discussion of art and social practice had not quite occurred yet.

One booklet pulled together several key strands for me in regard to my own work as a bibliographer. It documented Temporary Services' *Library Project,* in which group members intervened in the stacks of the Harold Washington Library Center. They assembled books from a variety of artists and other types of self-publishers and placed them within the shelves of the lending library's holdings. This gesture was a kind of guerrilla attempt to insert materials that usually circulated outside of mainstream channels into the largest, most accessible lending library in Chicago. The project was successful in that, upon discovery, one of the librarians agreed to keep the materials and cataloged many of them as a set, giving attribution to the Temporary Services project within the library's catalog record. This kind of library intervention conflates several of the ideas that I have sought to suggest here. In this case, an artists' group directly inserts a particular archive of collected materials onto the shelves of the existing collection. They created a kind of performance that mirrors a pattern of radical influence of individual artists and artists' groups on the institutional archives and libraries of modern and contemporary art.

When Lucy Lippard was asked to write about the importance of artists' publications in the mid-1970s, she responded that the decisive aspect of these little books was in their ability to disseminate information, "propaganda" in her terms.[7] Such production can resemble a kind of pamphleteering that allows for the cheap and easy distribution of works and ideas. If the work can be this little booklet that you can take home or share with friends, it offers a positive complication of the conventional methods of staging an artwork. The Temporary Services booklets fall within this lineage of art production through pamphleteering, through the consistent dispersal of their propaganda. Like the PAD/D archive, the artists and art workers who authored the Temporary Services collection of booklets have charted various places, individuals, organizations, and ways of working between the large and daunting categories of art, activism, radical politics, and urban history and development, among other things. The booklet format suggests a continued conversation, one that can be revisited through the publication. Temporary Services offers PDFs of these booklets on its website as an additional means to perpetuate these conversations and to keep these texts and ideas moving through the world. So while, on the one hand, library collections are part of the act of preserving this published archive of works, on the other, efforts such as Temporary Services' publishing work allow library collections like the MoMA Library to continue to be relevant hubs for the consideration of contemporary art and its many possible forms.

The conversation around artists' publishing brings up the larger question of independent archives and the labor needed to document activities that fall outside the collecting scope of official institutions of record. Publications such as Temporary Services' booklets and other on-the-ground archival gestures, help keep DIY work a part of our cultural memory, which is so significant in our time in which media formats have significantly changed. Thus, it seems even more necessary today for these alternative efforts to continue, especially since there is no assurance in regard to the "archival-ness" of digital content. As it now stands, there are no definitive models for adequately archiving digital materials. This ambiguity creates a very vulnerable condition for libraries and archives. So while search engines and other digital content tools have transformed how we can find information, the longevity of these new tools remains an open question, and in any case the standard search model is one that merely continues the legacy of the newspaper clipping services as a comprehensive, automated, impersonal method.

Past examples in radical archives, such as the ones described above, suggest that we will continue to be dependent on inspired acts of collecting by individuals and groups outside of conventional settings. The collectors—those with the habit or disease of assembling and preserving particular genres and formats of our print culture and now our digital culture—will continue to assist us in forming more comprehensive views of our cultural history. As information becomes more and more centralized within specific media languages, it is not hard to imagine a growing importance of decentralized strategies for preserving and dispersing our texts and images—and it seems all the more crucial to develop new creative responses to both the possibilities and the challenges of working with, and within, institutional collections.

1 Lucy R. Lippard, Barbara Moore, and Mimi Smith, *Political art documentation and distribution: the PAD/D Archives* (New York: The Museum of Modern Art Library, 1993), 4.

2 They organized materials in alphabetical order by artist or organization name and also developed a set of subject headings that cross-referenced the materials for easier access for researchers. One issue of *Upfront* contained a full-page spread that listed all these categories being used to organize the archive's holdings. A perusal of these categories gives a view into the scope of materials being gathered and organized: Anti-Nuclear, Graffiti, Gentrification, Museum Reform, Nicaragua, Non-Violence, Pornography, Reproductive Rights, Surveillance, Unions, Xerox Art.

3 The correspondence and activities of key progressive figures and groups including Nelson Algren, Sherwood Anderson, Slim Brundage, Malcolm Cowley, Clarence Darrow, Floyd Dell, the Dil Pickle Club, IWW, Charles H. Kerr Company, and Mary Field Parton can be documented through the archives.

4 Several substantial web-based exhibitions of archive materials are now available, along with a list of all the different sets of archives within the Midwest Manuscript Collection as well as the finding aids for each of the more than six hundred discrete collections.

5 For instance, one can see a recent online exhibition on the town of Pullman, created by a graduate seminar at the museum, using materials from the Pullman Company archive, or notice the collection of papers by Elliot Gorn on his research on Mother Jones. Gorn was a regular researcher when I worked at the Newberry as he was working on a biography of Mother Jones, and the library has since acquired his papers from this research.

6 Initially, I was not aware that the different booklets were part of a series. They generally all had similar dimensions, but with some material differences: some had more glossy paper while others were more minimal, zine format. Some booklets are branded with overt references to Temporary Services and the details of the exhibitions and events they were produced for, while others were less clear in their attribution and origin.

7 "One of the reasons artists' books are important to me is their value as a means of spreading information—content, not just esthetics. In particular they open up a way for women artists to get their work out without depending on the undependable museum and gallery system…I'm talking about communication but I guess I'm also talking about propaganda. Artists' books spread the word—whatever that word may be." From the *Art-rite* special issue on artists' books, *Art-Rite, no. 2*, (Summer, 1973): 10.

Archiving Chicago's Experimental Creativity

Marc Fischer, Tempestt Hazel, and Allison Schein in conversation

Marc Fischer: There is a continual struggle in collecting, preserving, archiving, and creating access to histories of art and other forms of creativity that are socially engaged, political, experimental, ephemeral, non-commercial, or represent the types of work that museums and other public archives might not know what to do with—assuming they are even interested in the first place. Many of the projects produced out of these practices are complicated and don't result in the kind of neat, single-object masterpieces that art museums tend to collect. These general concerns also shape the history of socially engaged and collective art in Chicago. Perhaps because the city has a particularly rich history of such work, Chicago also has more than a handful of people who are strategizing how to save these histories, activate them through exhibitions and events, and keep them accessible for future generations of artists, historians, curators, and activists, as well as the general public. Without people to help track down this material and collect accurate meta-data while everyone is still alive or close enough to the history to remember it, many histories that are ripe for discovery or ré-discovery are seriously at risk of disappearing from memory and record.

Allison, as archivist at Creative Audio Archive (CAA) at Experimental Sound Studio, and Tempestt, as founder of Sixty Inches From Center, you both are working to preserve and create access to important materials from some of Chicago's lesser-known, less-recognized creative practitioners through independent initiatives as well as by collaborating with a long-standing institution like the Harold Washington Library Center to make its archive more inclusive. You are also working on projects and missions that intersect with my own history, so I thought it could be great for all of us to come together to talk about socially engaged art and experimental culture in Chicago archives and libraries.

I approach these concerns as a member of the group Temporary Services[1], and as the administrator of Public Collectors. I created the latter in 2007 as an initiative concerned with collecting and archiving as creative endeavors, and with preserving histories and subjects that exist on the margins. Public Collectors recognizes that many smaller organizations and individuals maintain cultural holdings that are as significant as anything that larger institutions deal with, and that private individuals often attain a level of connoisseurship around the stuff they own that rivals the knowledge levels of museum curators and cultural historians. Public Collectors calls attention to those collections and helps make private holdings more accessible.

I want to start by describing a project in which Temporary Services secretly intervened within a major institutional collection. In 2001, we organized *The Library Project*: we worked with artists, authors, and publishers to add one hundred small press and self-published books to Harold Washington Library's collection without the library's permission.[2] We altered each of these books to make it look like they were already owned by the library. They had rubber stamps that said Chicago Public Library on the edges of the pages and due-date cards, and we gave them the same kind of protective treatment that the library uses.

The idea of placing things throughout the library was to expand the audience for experimental art. Artists' books almost never get to coexist alongside popular literature. They have their own kind of specialized stores, places like Quimby's Books in Chicago or Printed Matter in New York. So the project gave us latitude to put the books wherever we wanted within the building with the artists' understanding that if the library found these books they might catalog them differently or choose not to keep them.

Once the librarians discovered the project, they valued it. They created a WorldCat record and the books that they have found are stored in Special Collections as part of the Chicago Artists' Archive.[3] When we realized that they have that collection, we started giving them Temporary Services publications. We also try to promote the work they're doing with the Chicago Artists' Archive. It's really a remarkable and important thing that anyone who is even remotely established as a Chicago artist has a place that will preserve a record of their practice.

So Allison, could you describe what Creative Audio Archive does at the Experimental Sound Studio?

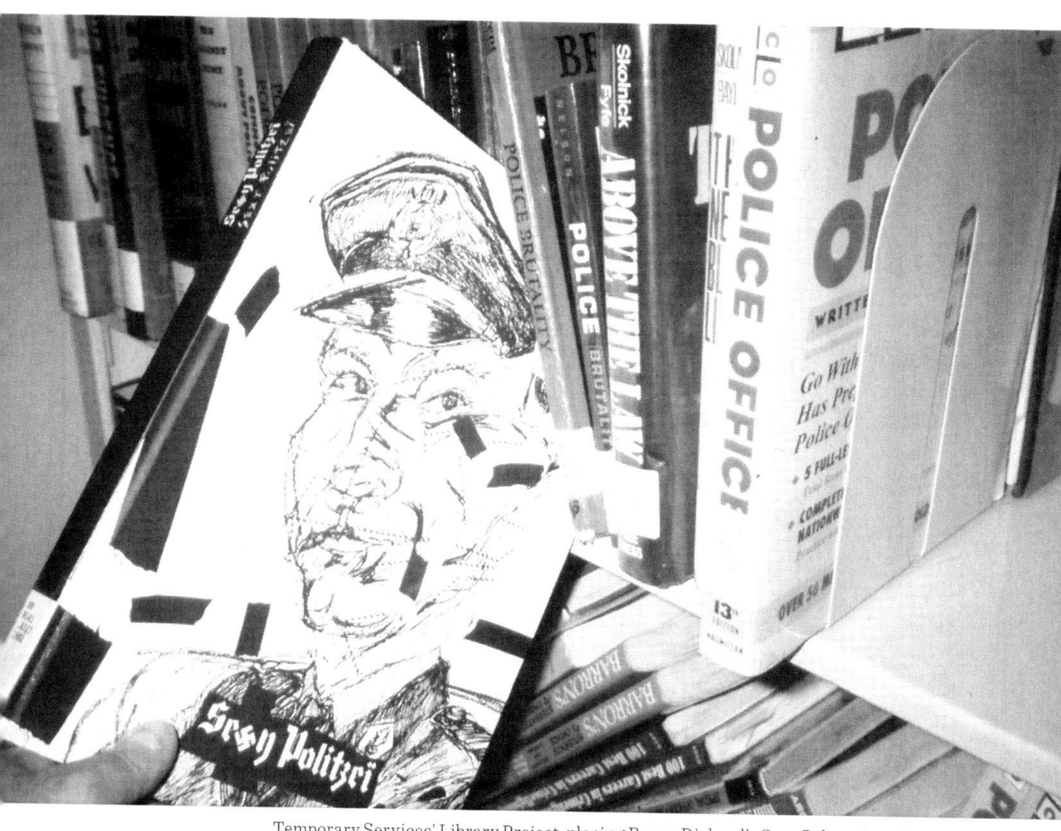

Temporary Services' Library Project, placing Bruno Richard's *Sexy Politzei* into the Harold Washington Library Center. Courtesy of Temporary Services.

Allison Schein: Sure. The Creative Audio Archive is an initiative born out of Experimental Sound Studio (ESS) because they saw a need to preserve improvisational and experimental music in Chicago. They felt that there was no home for a lot of important documentation to make it accessible and preserve it for the community. Right now we have five collections. We have what I call the organizational collection, which is the Experimental Sound Studio Collection that covers all of ESS's public programming since its inception in 1986 at any location. Then we have the Sun Ra/El Saturn collection, mostly on quarter-inch reel and cassettes, that ranges from Sun Ra's lectures to his rehearsals to his answering-machine tapes to popular Western music reinterpreted as tangos. And if you've never heard the tango version of Creedence Clearwater Revival, then you're missing out.

We also have a collection of spoken-word performances at Links Hall curated by Michael Zerang, and the Malachi Ritscher Collection, four thousand pieces of various media—everything from Hi-8 to 2-inch to DAT to cassette to CD. There's also a collection of material from the Art Noise Necessary Arts Collection. They were a sound collective that documented the experimental and electro-acoustic scene in Milwaukee from about 1979 to 2012.

MF: The Ritscher collection has been really important to me. Over the past year, Public Collectors has been collaborating with Creative Audio Archive to tell the story of the late Chicago documentarian and activist Malachi Ritscher, whose concert recordings and selected personal effects are being cared for by CAA.[4] It is a reflection on Ritscher's extensive work documenting Chicago's improvised music scene and also a study of the complex issues surrounding his death: in 2006, Ritscher immolated himself publicly, in protest of the Iraq War. The mass media did little to acknowledge his death and the politics around his action, which were made explicit in a statement on a cultural calendar website that Ritscher maintained. That site, savagesound.com, is yet another archive of a particular period in Chicago cultural history.[5]

Part of why I wanted to work with the Malachi Ritscher Collection is that in addition to finding his work and his story so moving, the collection provides an extraordinary way of looking at Chicago: its musicians, its venues for music, performance, and other kinds of art—many of which are now gone. I wanted to amplify the layers of history there. His example is a valuable one to study also in regard to the sheer magnitude of what one exceptionally dedicated person could document within fairly modest means. The recordings I've heard so far sound fantastic, and there is such a wealth of amazing listening that is waiting for people to absorb.

Tempestt, could you talk about the formation of Sixty Inches From Center and how your work began to include a partnership with the Chicago Artists' Archive?

Tempestt Hazel: I was coming out of school with an art history degree trying to figure out what to do that wasn't your standard trajectory of teaching or continuing with school. My original partner, Nicolette Caldwell, and I found ourselves in artists' studios, going to shows, going to lectures. I would often record things or take photos. So I eventually had this mass of material on my hard drive and at a certain point I thought: what do I do with all of this and why should I keep it to myself? We made Sixty Inches From Center as a platform, an outlet for this documentation. It started as a kind of online magazine, but archiving came into play quickly and we started collecting material more intentionally and feeding it into the Chicago Artists' Archive.

MF: That's such a contribution.

TH: Well, I look at it like this: We all should be trying to contribute. The librarians actively go to different places and collect ephemera, but I think that's really the extent of what they do, which is where Sixty saw a need that could be filled. We realized we could actively collect material for the archives outside of the ephemera that the librarians might just pick up at a coffee shop.

MF: Sixty Inches From Center recently partnered with Chicago public radio WBEZ in a drive throughout the city to gather documentation and material for that collection. Could you talk about that project?

TH: Soon after Sixty first started, we met Breeze Richardson, who was in charge of community partnerships and collaborations for the station at the time. We started brainstorming and that evolved into events. We've done a series of sessions that take the form of open office hours. We set up in neighborhoods around the city; artists come to us; and we do an audio interview with each person and get some brief information about their career. They can also bring ephemera and we will go through it with them, and if they leave material with us, we will deliver scans to the Chicago Artists' Archive. We held events at community bureaus of WBEZ in Humboldt Park, Little Village, Englewood, and Rogers Park. Later we partnered with other institutions, but WBEZ was the first.

MF: That list of neighborhoods suggests that you were trying to reach out to people who might normally be underserved by the city or perhaps by—

TH: Art history. Sixty was also a response to having gone through an art history program and being frustrated by the things that I just never learned about. According to my curriculum, these people weren't making work or wouldn't have been important. As an art historian, you can just slip into this whole art history thing as it exists, but we really wanted to carve out own section and be able to really have an impact.

MF: Recognizing what's missing and who is missing from history and doing the work to get that material included—particularly while many of these people are still alive—is politically important. You've recognized that there's a place that will care for people's histories and you can go and collect material to be preserved. You are intervening and making sure that art history from the far North Side or South Side or West Side gets included in the story of Chicago art at an official city resource that historians of the future will use.

And what's particularly exciting at the library is that everyone's material is treated equally. When you see what is at Harold Washington Library, there's a long list of names. It's similar on Creative Audio Archive's website. You can search for a name or concert venue or year. There's something nice about the fact that all of these people coexist in alphabetical order; one person doesn't get a bigger font than someone else. There is no hierarchy.

Chicago has other DIY Archives, like Never The Same, Read/Write Library, and the Leather Archives & Museum, that don't have institutional affiliations. In the case of the Leather Archives, things related to peoples' sexual lives generally don't find an easy public home in the archives of larger institutions and museums. Even when museums have those things, you'll probably never get to see them.

As a counterpoint there are also a few important and relatively accessible archives in Chicago that intersect with larger institutions. The School of the Art Institute houses a few: the Video Data Bank, the Roger Brown Study Collection, and the Joan Flasch Artists Book Collections, that also manages the archives of N.A.M.E. and Randolph Street Gallery. An alternative art history is told through Randolph Street's archives; they presented every experimental, cutting-edge-at-the-time kind of artist from the 1970s until the space closed in the late 1990s. The Flasch Collection is particularly important to Temporary Services, because it's the one place that has all of the more than one hundred publications we've made, plus ephemera.

With some of those kinds of collections there might be just one person at that place who becomes the locus for why a relationship flourishes between a contributor and this larger institution. I met Doro Boehme from the Joan Flasch Collection while I had a job at the Art Institute in Visitor Services and came to the library on my lunch break. I got to know her and just started giving her things in about 1997. Then Temporary Services formed the next year and she met other members of the group. It was because of that friendship that we started giving them things and working with them. I'm not sure if that would've happened if we never met. We certainly don't have a relationship like that with the Ryerson Library at the museum, which is on a different scale and feels more exclusive.

TH: The Ryerson is actually pretty open. They have some collections that parallel the Chicago Artists' Archive. About a year ago I introduced the librarian of the Harold Washington to the librarian at the Ryerson, and they are now exchanging duplicates of things. We're also trying to figure out some kind of loop to where all of the materials that are donated to Harold Washington can also be sent there.

AS: The notion of gatekeeper is evolving. Coming from the outside, like we do, we can sometimes impact larger institutions. You did that when you brought the librarians together from those two institutions. But there's always the old guard, or at least the perception of it: librarians with stern looks on their faces, their glasses and their cardigans, who don't necessarily want things to change. So it's up to us to challenge that. It's hard, but it can be very rewarding, as you know.

MF: To continue in that direction, what tensions—perceived or actual—might come into play for artists and more DIY or community-based initiatives when they collaborate with bigger institutions? What are the costs or potential areas of danger? What are the benefits? Intellectual property is one issue, and certainly there are artists whose practices play a lot more fast and loose with copyright than institutions can always accommodate.

AS: Well, artists or DIY initiatives typically have specific ideals around how their collections or archives will function. If relinquishing materials to larger institutions, what's to say that future archivists will actually honor the donor agreement? Or the donor agreement might not have teeth that would restrict the institution too much, saying "You need to do this." I mean, it's up to the institution. Or materials just get locked away. The worry is that artists will give collections and then they disappear into institutional archives—maybe processed or not—and never see the light of day. So all of that raises questions about whether the repository you donate to understands what that collection means, if they understand the issues, or if you can educate them. Is a large institution going to best represent you?

Lack of clarity about processes and access can also create hassles for researchers. We'd all benefit if the archivist community or the gatekeepers came together and had open, honest conversations about access policies and how to make them more consistent and transparent.

MF: Part of Temporary Services' decision not to ask permission to put books in the Harold Washington Library was that we thought that they would probably say yes to some things and no to others. We wanted to give people the possibility of having experiences with a range of fragile, hand-made, or one-of-a-kind books that people submitted to us, and we knew that if we asked permission it was just not going to happen.

AS: Maybe small or under-resourced repositories do not really know what researchers need or do not have the time or staff to devote to the collections. With larger institutions, other issues create tension, because locally or regionally it might make sense for a collection to go in a certain direction, but maybe the collection keeps a traditionally art historical or less contemporary focus. That doesn't create a good community

TH: No, not at all. For me, that is part of a larger issue—funding for this type of work. Materials and archives are coming out of people's attics and basements every day, and we have nowhere to put them. Some small institutions just don't have the manpower to accept or manage new materials. So who's going to take that on? And how are they supposed to give me as a researcher access to it when they can't really keep track of what I'm fumbling around with?

MF: As a counterexample from New York, there's the Interference Archives where one of the founders, Josh MacPhee—who was from Chicago— recently told me that some of their stuff gets used to the point where it's falling apart. So, ultimately, is it more important that it be preserved and no one ever gets to see it, touch it, and draw inspiration from it, or to allow that so some-one can make new work because they had that tactile experience? You can think about care in different ways. Protecting the objects is one kind of care, but some collections are so well cared for that no one will ever get to see them.

A detail of the Creative Audio Archive at Experimental Sound Studio. Courtesy of the Creative Audio Archive at Experimental Sound Studio. Photo: Jason P. Holmes.

AS: You're never going to have unlimited resources, so you need to focus on priorities. For some collections, what's most important is that it's tangible and used, not that it's preserved to an externally imposed perfect standard of preservation.

TH: I agree. For me, when I think about archives and collections, it's all equal—preservation, education. Both are on the same level of importance.

AS: Right, exactly. It's about the goal of the collection and also the nature of the media that it contains.

TH: Yeah, which is why Sixty's partnership with Harold Washington is so important. They have the staff—even though they're overworked—and the space to house all of this. We don't actually have to house anything. It really helps us to be able to give the archives over to people who know that process and that's what they do, so as to not call ourselves archivists because we're not. We're—

AS: Facilitators.

This conversation occurred on January 24, 2014 in Chicago.

1 Temporary Services formed in Chicago in 1998; the other member is Brett Bloom, who lives in Copenhagen. We produce exhibitions, events, projects, and publications and often work in collaboration with others. We're also interested in creating platforms and infrastructures that give visibility to people whose creativity isn't recognized in mainstream art worlds.

2 Though the project had many international participants, some of the (then) Chicago-based participants in Temporary Services' *Library Project* were: Janell Baxter, E.C. Brown, Salem Collo-Julin, Jim Duignan, Emily Forman, Paul Gebbia, Helidon Gjergji, Kenneth Hirsch, James Hugunin, Rob Kelly and Zena Sakowski, Nance Klehm, Kathleen Kranack, Stephan Lapthisophon, Cindy Loehr, Rebecca Moran and Rosie Sanders, Leah Oates, Stephanie Ognar, Trevor Paglen, A. Laurie Palmer, Robert Peters, Michael Piazza, Jennifer Ramsey, Karen Reimer, Van Harrison, Dana Sperry, Deborah Stratman, Pedro Velez, and Oli Watt.

3 See: http://chicagoartistarchives.blogspot.com/.

4 The project titled "Malachi Ritscher" was presented in the 2014 Whitney Biennial at the Whitney Museum of American Art, and shown later in 2014 in the Audible Gallery at Experimental Sound Studio.

5 Marc Fischer's essay on Malachi Ritscher can be read here: www.publiccollectors.org/Malachi_Ritscher_Whitney.pdf.

Talking in Public

Duncan MacKenzie and Philip von Zweck in conversation

Duncan MacKenzie: The question of institutionality plagues both our practices. I'd say your projects, Philip, since the mid-1990s—*VONZWECK*, the *Much More* lecture series, the *Much Much More* lecture series, *Something Else, Blind Spot,* and *Temporary Allegiance*—have used the form of "new institution" as set-dressing and framework to create unexpected social connections and personal experiences, whereas Bad at Sports (B@S) for me is a kind of pseudo-institution.

So why construct new institutions? Shouldn't we be supporting the great institutions we have? What demands do these other institutions make and what do they enable?

Philip von Zweck: It doesn't have be an either/or, right? It's not as if you can only like the Museum of Contemporary Art Chicago (MCA) or B@S; you can do both. You can understand that their constituencies aren't necessarily the same. The MCA and the Art Institute of Chicago (AIC) don't simply exist to support artists in Chicago. They serve a broader public and that opens up room for other kinds of institutions. In our own projects over the past fifteen years, we've worked as community documentarians, oral historians, and platformists and facilitated other arts of Chicago's contemporary art world. But for you to do B@S or for me to do the *Much More* lecture series and the *Much Much More* lecture series, isn't to say that we don't also want to see the "Artist Connect" talk at the AIC or that I'm not interested in going to a lecture at the MCA. It's to add to the plurality; it's to better represent or to provide more opportunities for dialogue, for conversation, that we think is important, and to support different parts of the community other than, perhaps, the part that the MCA, AIC, or any other institution exists to support.

DM: My impulse in starting B@S with Richard Holland was specifically to address an art world that was being radically underrepresented and unsupported. We had the notion we could make a radio show that no radio station would do, because it's too narrow, it's about contemporary art, and is laced with vulgar jokes. Our plan was to do a show like the Howard Stern cast would do if they worked for the BBC news and only talked about the nuances of contemporary art. Now we run a platform dedicated to talking about art the way that artists talk about art with other artists. So we treat art roughly. We use it as jokes, punch lines; we make light of other artists, and we taunt the avant-garde cultural producers, all the while maintaining our fierce commitment to art. The show doesn't exist to challenge other art information sources—but its catalyst was Chicago's failure to support its most interesting artists and our hope was that we could help change the community we live in. We identify that community as the contemporary art world; I think most artists experience their art world as a community.

PvZ: B@S plays pretty nicely with institutions. You have curators on. You often have artists who are coming through town because of an institution. So clearly you're not viewed as undermining any of those institutions, but at the same time you have your own space, your own authority. They're not editing or getting a final say. Do you feel that conditions at those institutions are improving in terms of how they respond to the local art community and do you think that B@S has an impact on that?

DM: In 2005–2007 we talked a lot about the underrepresentation of Chicago artists in local museums, but we weren't the only ones; a lot of other Chicago arts personalities were also asking where is all the Chicago stuff? And to their credit, the MCA and the AIC, over the last seven or eight years, have done a bang-up job of making sure that they are representing Chicago and not in a kind of ghettoized *12x12* show or a patronizing kind of way, but as equal to anything being made anywhere in the world.

PvZ: We've talked about wanting to add to the spectrum, but maybe in a more granular way, what does it do and how does it work?

DM: What's important to me is not allowing the capital "I" institutional spaces to lock down how we speak to each other, shove us into the opaque-ist dialect of "International Art English," or allow our competition for their attention to accidentally "Lord of the Flies" our art communities. I think that everything we can do to counter the feeling that we, as artists, are in competition is vital. I want to feel invested in how my art world is working and what people are doing and making. I want to live and work in the land of *Super Friends* not *Game of Thrones*. B@S has tried to operate with openness, to be welcoming, and to support all of the contemporary art voices. For me, creating the context for conversation is the key to all of that—understanding and being open to the ideas of all the other people who are invested in sharing a community.

PvZ: Then to what extent do B@S or other non-institutions operate as gatekeepers? My projects have worked in different ways. *Something Else* was a radio program that was 100 percent submission based, but with the caveat that the work couldn't have another outlet. So if it was punk, it went to the punk show; if it was hip-hop, it went to the hip-hop show. And if it had nowhere else to go, then I would play it. I didn't have to know the people who made it; I didn't have to have a resume. Likewise with *Temporary Allegiance,* people just sign up and drop off a flag and it flies. *VONZWECK* was slightly different in that I needed to know people, because I was inviting them into my space and giving them keys to my apartment to have a show.

DM: We do occasionally get accused of gatekeeping, but for us the requirements are simple. One of us who works at B@S has to be interested enough that they're going to donate their time to research, talk, edit, post, and continue to support the work of the person to be interviewed. If one of us is into it, we are into it. It has to be that way, as B@S works without an economic spine: we make just enough money to cover our rent and after that everyone works for free. We choose the no-model business model specifically because we don't want to be gatekeepers, and we don't want our relationship to culture to be about hustling ads.

But with the *Much More* lecture series you were creating a context to have a conversation with fourteen or fifteen people at most. Someone came in and delivered a lecture and then there was a genuine opportunity to have a real conversation. It's similar in spirit to a salon-style conversation, where you have a very small, insular group in which everyone knows everyone else by name, and you have a meaningful conversation that has ramifications, that can change the participants.

PvZ: When that started, I thought, who are the people I know who aren't getting invited to give a big public talk somewhere in Chicago, who still have things to say, things I want to know about their work?

DM: But how did that transition as you moved to the *Much Much More* lecture series and involved the Chicago Public Library? You were nesting the lecture series inside of another institution and a major one.

PvZ: The *Much More* lecture series really was just on hiatus for a few years; I restarted it as *Much Much More* after the expansion of the Humboldt Park Branch of the Chicago Public Library. I brought a projector because they didn't have one. They said, "You can make flyers and hang them up," but they don't promote it in any way and they don't attend and there's no underwriting. I just use a room that's provided as public service to the people of Chicago, and since the space is much larger than my living room, I can now accommodate many more people. The *Much More* lectures at my apartment were always filled. I always had to cut off enrollment because I would run out of seats. Now with *Much Much More*, even though I'm getting about as many people per lecture as I got in my living room, people don't have to RSVP. Anyone can come; anyone can show up. It opens up an unpredictable and different dynamic.

DM: When B@S nests inside of an institution, we use a kind of artist model. We go down to Miami to do a project with Cannonball, and we play residents. We do a big project, and then we go away. Or we go do something with the Contemporary Arts Museum in St. Louis and it lets us interact with a different community. It is an obvious relationship, but that creates new conversations and keeps us walking the line between artists and journalists.

But in this context we're talking about you using an existing part of social infrastructure, the library—a location outside of the usual art world context. Then you nest a potentially subversive program inside of it, creating a kind of cuckoo's-egg structure in which existing public infrastructure accidentally provides for an unanticipated cultural outcome.

PvZ: Pretty much all of my projects might fall into this category. I wouldn't have used the term social practice, because I hadn't heard that term and it wasn't even around in 1995, but now I think they fall into a form of social practice. The politics are implicit instead of explicit and so maybe don't get thought of that way, but they're all about taking advantage of something

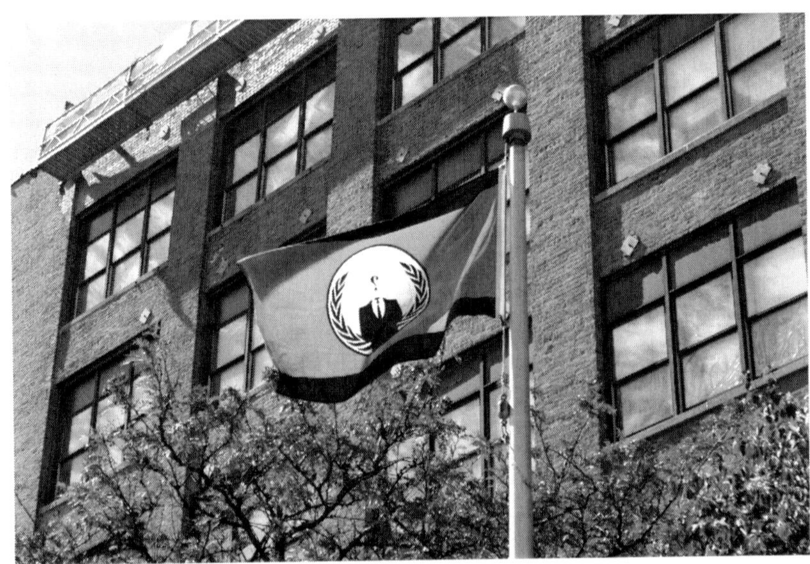

Amy Corle, "We are Anonymous. We are Legion. We do not forgive. We do not forget. Expect us." July 15-22, 2011. Part of *Temporary Allegiance*, Gallery 400, University of Illinois at Chicago. Courtesy of Gallery 400.

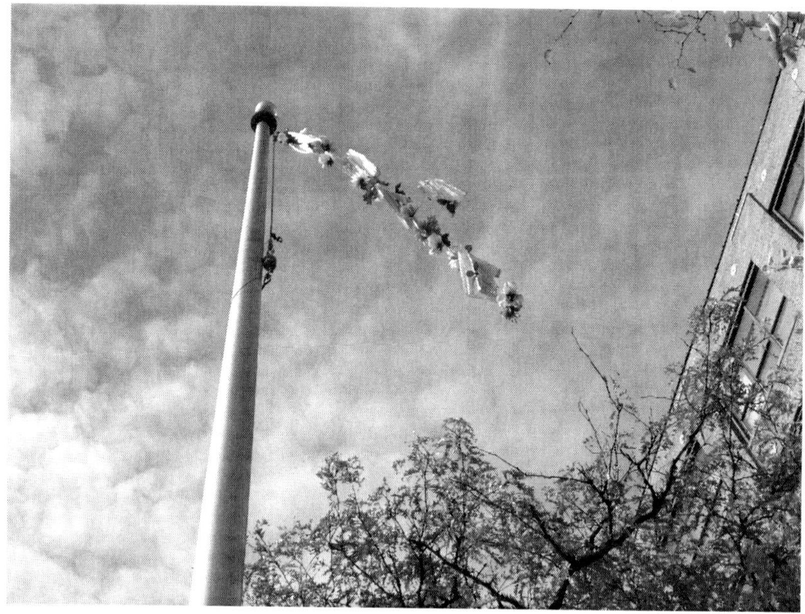

Di Delgado Pineda, *Ofelia No te Rajes*, November 8 – 15, 2013. Part of *Temporary Allegiance*, Gallery 400, University of Illinois at Chicago. Courtesy of Gallery 400.

that already exists. It is embedded in the ethos of each project. For instance, *Something Else* was only possible because Loyola has a radio station that was so uncool that no one wanted to do shows on it, because it was kinda' all Top 40. And, thus, I could get four hours a week to do something that no one else was doing. It was a way to re-direct and re-value something that belongs to the public, in this case the airwaves.

DM: What about the *Temporary Allegiance* project? It seems like that is a moment of explicit politics.

PvZ: I do think that is the most explicitly political of my projects, but I also think there's something political about turning a radio show on licensed radio into an open forum for people to send work in, whatever they want to send in. Although I never couched it as political, I think it is: the airways are licensed but still owned by the people. I think *Temporary Allegiance* is seen as political, in part because of its name and in part because it sits on state land.

DM: And it's about flags.

PvZ: Yes, it came as a direct response to the jingoist patriotism of wearing American flags after 9/11 and the invasions of Iraq and Afghanistan. There was a period in which Obama, as a presidential candidate, was raked over the coals for not wearing a flag pin. It got to a point where it seemed that in America you were no longer allowed to *not* have a flag on or to not fly a flag, and that seemed to be completely contradictory to democratic notions.

DM: How "free" is that?

PvZ: Exactly. That was exactly where *Temporary Allegiance* came from, instead of making a picture of something, instead of making agitational propaganda, a picture of a flag that says, "Why don't you get to choose?" Well, let's just try and make an actual thing that offers a choice.

DM: I feel like that is the politic that has for the last fifteen years, and maybe always, held our Chicago art world together. If we feel like something we need doesn't exist, we make it and work to help it find its public. We grow institutions like mushrooms because maybe the more ways we have to bind ourselves together, the more we can build that better, newer world—and the more freedom we have to articulate ourselves, the more we see our place in that world.

This conversation occurred in April 2014 in Chicago.

5 Questions About Socially Engaged Art in Chicago

Project by Creative Time and AREA Chicago

Question 3: *Describe a local cultural event that productively expanded the social networks that your practice operates in. That is to say, the event produced a new sense of community that had political potential.*

travis: A recent political event or cultural event that impacted my work and my self was the death of Dr. Amadou Cisse here on campus [University of Chicago, November 19, 2007].[1] A lot of people had political responses, especially since he was black and was murdered in the black community. There was a lot of bloodletting on both sides of Stony Island. Being out there every day, listening to what was happening, listening to the input had an impact upon me. Also, noticing how the students who are activists on campus began to look at their work in the community and actually step up that work was really interesting to me. My relationship to the police force is something that I'm going to be doing in a piece later, but it was a very personal experience when the roundup was being handled; I was on the street before people were arrested. Most people don't know the number of people, black men, who are on the street and rounded up summarily, simply because [their] skin is black. And yes, it did happen right here on Stony Island to me. But on the other side of that is that after the arrests were made, I suddenly found that campus police were smiling at me when they had never smiled before.

Sara Black: A few events that have brought a number of practitioners together in a critical way that I would include are *Pathogeographies: or, Other People's Baggage*[2] project, the *Pedagogical Factory*[3] and the latest conference at Mess Hall (What We Know of Our Past, What We Demand of Our Future, January 2008[4]). Those were pretty important experiences. And of course, numerous events here at the Experimental Station[5]. I would like to add that for me, a lot of the visibly political activities organized around these events and spaces were less exemplary of the thing that is Chicago than the conversations, discussions, gatherings, dinners that have happened peripherally to the artwork or political activities. It's in this peripheral activity that I see evidence of a culture being produced: a culture that is enacting what I think of as a true democracy with responsibility, empathy, and creativity at the heart of it, where the values suggest that everyone finds the greatest freedom when everyone acts to maximize the freedom of others, where we are only as free as our most disenfranchised person. That's something that I have found in this community here that is really exciting and stellar and particular to this group of people in Chicago.

Rebecca Zorach: When we corresponded by e-mail as a group about this question, we cited a lot of the things that have already been mentioned, so I won't go over them. One of the things that emerged for me is the fact that there wasn't necessarily a sense of a community being formed in that moment, but rather a set of partial moments where a connection was made or a network at an individual level was advanced. This is an ongoing creation of community that can't be situated in one particular moment, but rather is something that happens over time, over a number of different encounters and different relationships. The other thing I would add is that coming from the point of view of Feel Tank[6], I think sometimes community is forged through a negative identification or bad feelings as much as through a positive experience; for instance, through resistance or protest or the negative feeling of existing within a bad institution that you want to change. It's not always just a matter of going to a great art event where people feel community, but actually experiencing something bad that you want to change.

Jon Pounds: Within the politics of the local, one of the things that I hear in Chicago is that we've continued to see this real dissolution of the distance between artists and the audience, between the artists and the public. All of us are describing various ways in which the work is generated out of open-ended explorations; in some cases, the audience becomes a part of the performance, and that's a welcome piece of it. That's a really positive thing. One of the things that I would say we probably believe collectively is that everybody is more creative than they're asked to be in the course of their ordinary lives. And that we, as artists, to use that honorific term, have some responsibility, not only to make our work and our life meaningful for ourselves and to make a living, but also to help other people to create the context in which they can experience their own creativity. To understand and impart why they are part of a larger creative community and not a larger divided community.

Deborah Stratman: The "ASK ME" event that Laurie Jo Reynolds organized at the Cultural Center (and later, the Museum of Science and Industry, though I didn't attend that one) a few years back was an incredible act of socio-cultural expansion.[7] I spent a couple of hours there, as did many of the other strangers/visitors I met there while drifting about and stopping in at various information stations where a wild array of "specialists" held forth on their chosen specialty. It was an incredible constellation of generosity, democracy, agency, and human expertise.

Anne Elizabeth Moore: Local as in Chicago, or local as in "I was there myself?" I do a fair amount of work now nationally and internationally, which has been really great but has taken me out of Chicago for much of the last year. In Chicago, at *Punk Planet*[8], the long-standing independent cultural politics magazine I ran for three years, every event we did, from putting out an issue to throwing a literal event in an event venue, expanded both our social networks, our collaborative opportunities, and the political understanding of the issues we addressed with the mag. But for the most part, I don't know that events necessarily have the kind of potential to spark political change. I think they can spur engagement, but change comes out of sustained communication, out of relationships between individuals. And that requires a lot more work than a single event.

Theaster Gates: The event is more like a geographical phenomena: the Experimental Station[9]. Dan Peterman and Connie Spreen at 6100 South Blackstone have provided a place from which many kinds of cultural feats could launch. My practice has grown so much out of the friendships developed at this place, so it's quite difficult to understand exactly what happened. What seems clear is that there were reasons to come to this space. The space was open to hosting interesting ideas, Dan Peterman has an amazing cultural reach and has been an important critic to my art practice, and finally, many of the people interested in political engagement know that they have a space for shared values at the Experimental Station. This means that even though I am not sure of a particular curator's name, if [he or she is] coming through the station, I want to be there. I trust that the curatorial edit is one that will engage me and the people coming represent a set of values that I believe in culturally, creatively, or otherwise. If there were to be an event to speak of, it would be a conversation that reflected on an exhibition at the Renaissance Society, *Black Is, Black Ain't*[10]. The event brought together scholars from the Art Schools with South Siders who had interest in collecting and knowing about Black Art along with a whole cadre of other listeners. The event was heated and loaded with race, class, and institutional tension, but it was sixty of the most passionate people who rarely get to be in the same room. Making space for the margins to meet is something that the Experimental Station is becoming masterful at.

Aay Preston-Myint: Last year, the Chances [Dances][11] organizers decided to use surplus funds and donations in order to create a float for the Pride parade [Annual Chicago Gay and Lesbian Pride Parade]. Rather than stage an intervention or feeder march, we decided to participate in the parade in order to gain more direct access to parade-goers as well as to repoliticize an identity-based event that has, over time, become co-opted by commercial sponsorship and promotes and exploits material and consumerist tendencies in the (gay) mainstream.

With the help of many of our Chances DJs, performers, and attendees, we constructed a witchcraft-inspired float asking spectators to "Summon a New Queer Reality," continuing the tradition of the "witches" that came before us—twenty-seven queers and allies selected for their contributions to culture, activism and justice. [...] The event made connections with paradegoers who were surprised to see some of their unsung heroes represented at the parade, or maybe did not expect to see political and educational information relevant to their identity. We also fostered connections with other organizations that heard of the project. [...]

Mike Bancroft: The dedication ceremony of the *Respect Signs*[12] memorial mural at the corner of North and Kimball brought together almost 100 people early on a Saturday morning in May [2008]. Attendees were an unlikely mix, from politicians and church leaders to families and local press. A reckless driver killed Alicia Coria and her sons Ivan and Diego Castro. Diego was in Nellie Windsor's third grade ESL classroom at Stowe Elementary, where I had been doing residencies through the Building Community through the Arts Initiative[13] with IPRAC [Institute of Puerto Rican Arts and Culture[14]]. Responding to the tragedy, we began to discuss how we could honor the memory of this tragic loss, while making the corner safer through a public intervention. Nellie, myself, and artist Anthony Rea helped the youth compose idioms and create life-size black plastic silhouettes of themselves. [The slogan] "Respect Signs" was selected and woven into the fencing with metallic Mylar streamers in Spanish/English, with the kids silhouettes zip-tied to the fence walking towards the corner. From this project, we have connected directly with the Alderman, the Congressman, and the Lieutenant Governor directly. These offices became advocates for the project after witnessing the incredibly diverse group of people mobilizing for healing which was celebrated at this dedication.

Amanda Gutierrez: I think that working and living in Pilsen has allowed me to expand my networks, beyond just art or just social activism. For me, having contact with the work of art spaces such as Polvo[15], the Flower Shop, and the Plaines Project[16] has been really rich—not only because I've shown my work there, but also because they've allowed me an important experience of social practices within art networks. When I was developing *En Memoria*[17], several core questions were formed based on my experience here: What or who represents the "community?" Is that community divided based on cultural and class divisions? Is it really possible to stress cultural and class differences in order to overcome them, and create some kind of interrelation? Is that a utopian ideal?

On the other hand, I see that two of the places I mentioned are already closed, after exhaustive efforts to work within and for the "community," leaving more questions about the relationships between the people who collaborate in these projects and the participants left behind (most of them teens, kids and community artists). I believe that there was a legitimate reason behind their existence: expanding cultural alternatives as a political tactic. But I'm not sure how aware, conscious, or critical the users or participants were during the process, and I wonder about the practical and ideological results of this as a political tactic.

Mark Messing: Redmoon Theater[18] used to perform in Logan Square on All Hallows Eve and eventually drew large crowds. The performance was designed to include as many people as possible in a ritual that was simple and not too specific (i.e. not indoctrinating) but always beautiful, invigorating, and very social. It was the biggest regular event I've seen that wasn't sports-related or beer-related. So it was miraculous in that it brought large crowds of sober people to a public space induced to warm, human, thoughtful interaction. The theatrics, shrines, and sculptural objects were abstract enough so that people could make their own meaning out of the night. It was a little like a protest without a cause. I mean this in the best of ways: one of my favorite by-products of protests and marches is the way they are ad-hoc conventions where you get to meet the organizations serving the movement and you meet other people looking for a hook-up with the cause. So while the event was not politically themed, it created an occasion for people to meet.

As an institution, Redmoon Theater has benefited the community at large in the same way. When the call came to take to the streets en-masse to show American resistance to the invasion of Iraq, many of us formed an ad-hoc theater group easily, through the network of artists existing from formal arts institutions and especially Redmoon Theater. So while Redmoon the Institution did not participate in any street protests, the artists on the fringes of the institution self-organized overnight to bring a focused theatrical element to the protests. This focus not only allowed us to interject a visual statement into the mainstream media, [but we were also] interviewed by media [which allowed us to] throw our own sound bites into the debate. At the least, we were able to contribute to the message that "Not all Americans believe in world domination by force." At the most, we found a way to connect with the long-term organizations building political institutions that do the things cultural institutions don't do.

This excerpt is taken from the project *5 Questions About Socially Engaged Art in Chicago*, which began in 2008 as a project with Creative Time's Town Hall Talks and was later expanded by AREA Chicago, organized by Daniel Tucker and Nato Thompson with editing support from Abigail Satinsky and Mairead Case. Today the archive of this thirty-eight-person interview project is housed at never-the-same.org.

1 Laurie Davis and Steve Koppes, "In Memoriam: Members of many communities remember Dr. Amadou Cisse," *The University of Chicago Chronicle*, December 6, 2007, ttp://chronicle.uchicago.edu/071206/cisse.main.shtml.

2 See pathogeographies.net/. Exhibition took place at University of Illinois Gallery 400, June/July 2007.

3 "Pedagogical Factory: Exploring Strategies for an Educated City," Hyde Park Art Center, accessed January 21, 2015, www.hydeparkart.org/exhibitions/the-pedagogy-project. Exhibition took place at Hyde Park Art Center, July-September 2007.

4 "What we know of our past what we demand of our future," Let's Remake, accessed January 21, 2015, letsremake.info/mnd.html.

5 See www.experimentalstation.org/.

6 See www.feeltankchicago.net/

7 "Experiments... Science and Art," Museum of Science and Industry, www.msichicago.org/scrapbook/scrapbook_events/experiments/.

8 See www.punkplanet.com/.

9 See www.experimentalstation.org/.

10 "Black is, Black Ain't," The Renaissance Society, accessed January 21, 2015, archive.renaissancesociety.org/site/Exhibitions/Intro.Black-Is-Black-Ain-t.595.html?search=1.

11 See www.chancesdances.org/.

12 Gordon Walek, "Mural Memorializes Mother and Two Sons," *Local Initiatives Support Corporation Chicago*, May 14, 2008, www.lisc-chicago.org/news/2521.

13 See www.instituteccd.org/resources/4864.

14 See www.iprac.org/.

15 See www.polvo.org/.

16 See plainesproject.wordpress.com/.

17 See amandagutierrez.net/esp/portfolio/en-memoria/.

18 See www.redmoon.org/.

Enemy Kitchen (Food Truck) at sites around Chicago, 2012. Courtesy of the artist and Smart Museum of Art. Photo: Stephanie Smith.

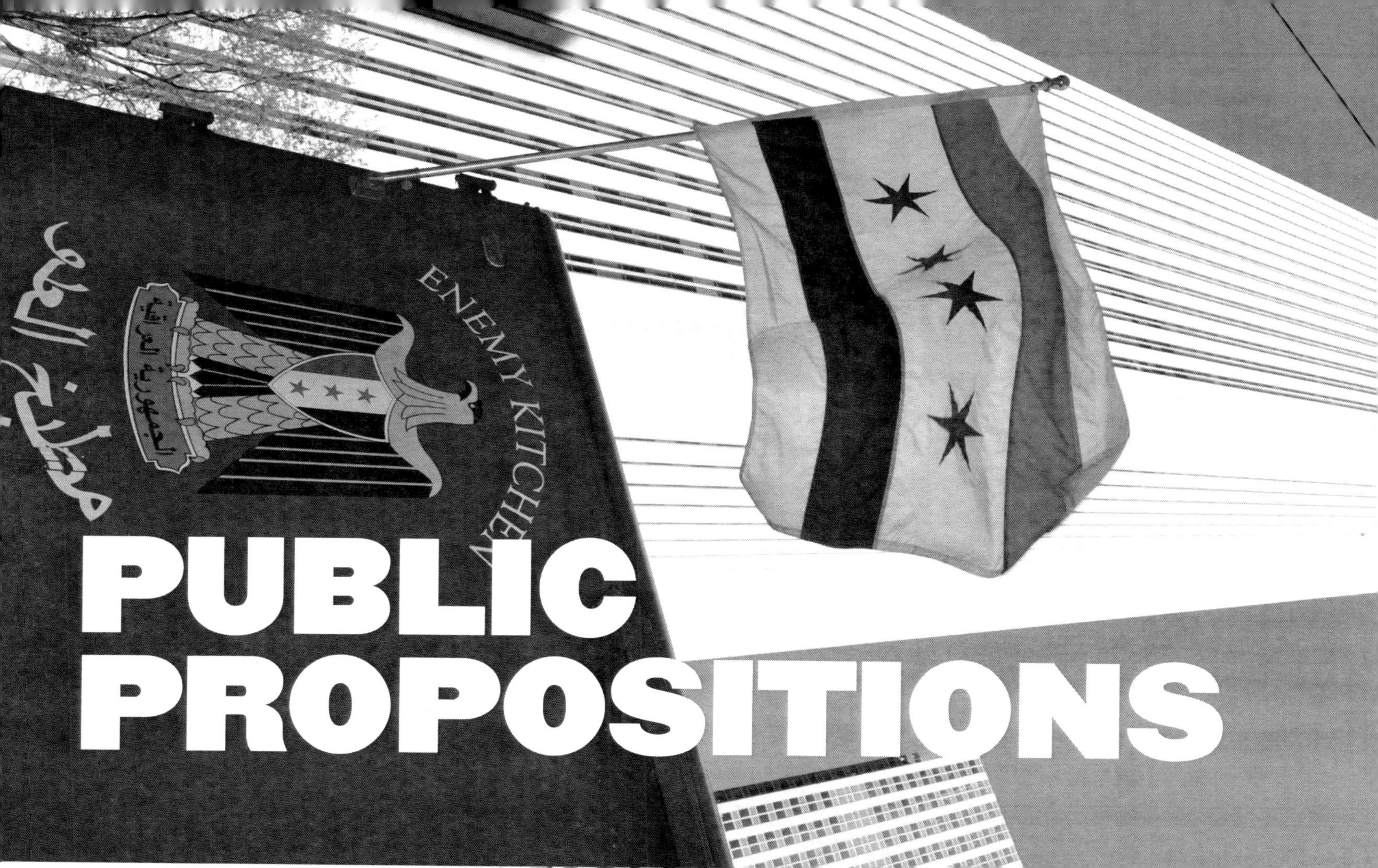
PUBLIC PROPOSITIONS
ENEMY KITCHEN
مطبخ العدو
الجمهورية العراقية

Public Propositions

Recent decades have been a formative period for socially engaged art in Chicago and coincide with a larger trend across the United States: cultural workers and institutions have been experimenting with new ways of reaching publics and addressing social issues. The texts in this section focus on key events and proposals in which socially engaged practitioners moved out into the city of Chicago in order to experiment with different forms of interrelation among artists, institutions, and publics. Their projects challenged audiences to shift their usual definitions as well as modes of engagement with art, institutions, public space, and communities.

As with much recent history of change, the discussions begin in the tumultuous 1960s. Rebecca Zorach discusses how in 1968, Art & Soul, a visionary but short-lived venue, sought to create a cultural hub on the South Side of Chicago. This remarkable venture was a collaboration between the then-new Museum of Contemporary Art, spearheaded by its director Jan van der Marck and board members, and the Conservative Vice Lords. Decades later, the 1990s also proved a pivotal period, when social issues of homelessness, AIDS, identity politics, and more raged. Iñigo Manglano-Ovalle contributes both as a theorist-artist with his 1992 treatise *Does the Public Work?* and as artist-curator as he and Peter Taub reflect on their efforts to effect the idea of site as a locus of possibility at the alternative space Randolph Street Gallery and the program they undertook in 1991, *Counter-Proposals*. Curator and museum director Lisa Corrin recalls her experience of Chicago as social landscape through a bus tour that was part of *Culture in Action*, curated by Mary Jane Jacob. This exhibition across

Chicago and demonstration of public art took place in 1991-1993; its process was as significant as its outcomes.

The impetus toward engagement continued its momentum in the early twenty-first century. A. Laurie Palmer, who had participated in *Culture in Action* as part of the artist collective Haha, writes of her unabashedly political program *3 Acres on the Lake* in the early 2000s that questioned the use of public space and lakefront assets for civic over private interests.

Very recent projects are compelling examples of the energy and activism ongoing in Chicago; they continue to propose new kinds of publics. Michael Rakowitz's *Enemy Kitchen (Food Truck)* was part of the exhibition *Feast: Radical Hospitality in Contemporary Art*, which I curated for the Smart Museum of Art in 2012, an evolution of the artist's original incarnation of this project for More Art in New York. In his discussion, Rakowitz speaks candidly with his collaborators, both Iraqi refugees and American veterans who served in the Iraq War. He confronts the issue of intentional antagonism as much as the notion of human hospitality. This dark but real side of behavior is addressed most directly by Carrie Lambert-Beatty in her discussion of Tania Bruguera's 2009 performance *Generic Capitalism*, part of the experimental art and theory program Our Literal Speed based at University of Chicago, where Bruguera was on the faculty. The performance took place in the more public venue of the Merchandise Mart as it was also part of the programming for the art fair, Art Chicago, that year. This action demonstrates the artist's political agenda in revealing and provoking behaviors. Coming from artists with roots in cultures controversial for many in the United States—Iraq and Cuba, in these instances—such projects generate powerful ripple effects well beyond Chicago and are testaments to this city's ongoing participation in and influence on the wider discourse and practice of socially engaged art practice.

—SS

Art & Soul: An Experimental Friendship between the Street and a Museum

Rebecca Zorach

In the summer of 1968, as the Democratic National Committee prepared to roll into Chicago, the city's Museum of Contemporary Art was entering into an unusual partnership—an "experimental friendship"—with an organization called CVL, Inc. What's remarkable about this organization was that it was the new incarnation of a notorious street gang known as the Vice Lords. The letters stood for "Conservative Vice Lords." Called "Westside terrorists" by the *Chicago Tribune,* the Vice Lords—by their own description—had "ruled the streets" on the West Side.[1] "Cars were stocked with shotguns," they wrote of their past exploits. "Young men were mauled in street battles, and many were arrested and sent to jail."[2] How did such a friendship come to exist? The Vice Lords, like other street gangs in the city, had become interested in working on neighborhood problems in a constructive way; they had "gone conservative" and reinvented themselves as the Conservative Vice Lords, opening several businesses and sponsoring youth programs. Meanwhile, the Museum of Contemporary Art (MCA) was brand new, and its director, Jan van der Marck, was interested in how museums could make more of an impact in their communities—their entire communities. And so, ever so tentatively, this friendship formed and produced an experimental art center called Art & Soul, at 3742 West Sixteenth Street in the neighborhood of North Lawndale on Chicago's West Side.

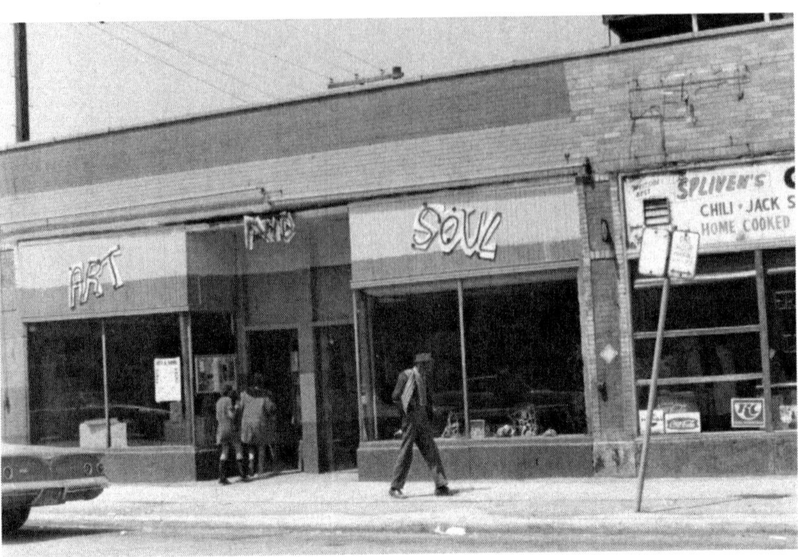

Art & Soul exterior with *Rainbow* mural by Sachio Yamashita, 1969 (mural now destroyed). Mural artwork © Eileen Petersen Yamashita, all rights reserved, used with permission. Photo © Ann Zelle.

What place can such a project have in the stories we tell of modern art of the 1960s? If the standard wisdom about that period is concerned, the answer is "not much." To try a somewhat brutal exercise, let us take the table of contents of *Art since 1900* as our guide to what's considered important in the twentieth century by art history now—and try to imagine a place here for a story like this one. Looking at the chronological table of contents, we would think that African American artists were absent in the fifty years between 1943 and 1993, and that the one thing that happened in art in the entire twentieth century in Chicago is that László Moholy-Nagy died there.

A closer look reveals, as many reviewers have noted, that Hal Foster, Rosalind Krauss, Yve-Alain Bois, and Benjamin H. D. Buchloh could not or would not write about the Mexican mural movement or the Harlem Renaissance, so the publisher was forced to outsource those two entries.[3] The Black Arts Movement, perhaps the only postwar American art movement distinctly affiliated with anything resembling or calling itself a *political* vanguard, is entirely absent—undoubtedly because it is perceived (if perceived at all) as a premodernist rather than postmodernist formation. If some artists in Chicago (or elsewhere) were working in a different visual or political idiom than the New York avant-garde, it had to be—by the field's still-current definitions—because they were *behind.* If those artists happened to be African American, the impression of belatedness chimes harmoniously, if unintentionally, with dominant white-supremacist narratives.[4] If they produced works that weren't commercial, that haven't survived (itself anything but happenstance), then there is, further, no financial and institutional compulsion backing them up. Whether the field has unconsciously accepted racist constructions or has rather shown its discomfort with them by looking the other way, art history has often failed to recognize the challenges black artists in the 1960s and 1970s directed not just at entrenched institutions but also at the presuppositions of the white avant-garde.[5] From this point of view, it was not just a matter of correcting biased aesthetic judgments and producing appropriate demographic representation. Rather, the critique addressed the central preoccupations with aesthetic autonomy and the avant-garde—preoccupations that, consciously or not, supported (and support) a racist worldview. *Art since 1900* is recognizably an extreme, but an extreme that forcefully shapes the landscape of what is possible to think and study about twentieth-century art. What kinds of questions could students whose engagement with the century starts with this book even begin to ask?

In 1950 Clement Greenberg wrote, in an essay on Paul Klee, that the School of Paris "opened our eyes to the virtues of oriental and barbaric art. It became possible to find valid art anywhere in history and geography."[6] Leaving aside the term "barbaric" (coupled quaintly with "virtues"), Greenberg's caveat to this point is notable: "In painting it was demanded of this exotic material only that it be controlled by the primary and still rather inflexible formal requirements of the easel picture, which remains always a most specifically Western and local art form." Greenberg thus opens the 1950s with this admission of the ethnospecificity of the easel picture, an acknowledgement that is, to quote Charles Mills on the racial contract, "simultaneously quite obvious if you think about it . . . and nonobvious, since most whites don't think about it."[7]

Along with the Western easel picture, other basic suppositions within modernist art discourse are a monocultural hierarchy of value and the ideology of an identifiable avant-garde: "advanced art," a single vanguard thread that runs through (or perhaps alongside and stitching into) history. The avant-garde is reputed to be in rebellion against social conditions, yet is by now—indeed was by the 1960s—thoroughly the creature of consumer capitalism.[8] These points may seem obvious, but they bear repeating, in a discipline that loves to critique modernist myths yet at the same time seems oddly addicted to them (or perhaps addicted to a market logic for which they provide cover).

I came to this work from two directions: one was the pedagogical imperative to see that my students, studying on the South Side of Chicago, became aware of the rich histories of the arts that exist in their neighborhood, often just outside the university walls. The other was the sense that contemporary practitioners of socially engaged art were missing out, because the histories of their practices have been occluded, on possibilities for solidarities and learning across race, history, and geography. A segregation of knowledge both mirrors and continually produces the persistent segregation of artist and activist communities. Writing on twentieth-century art remains overly *dependent*, perhaps because and not in spite of the premium it places on "aesthetic autonomy," on art-market-based institutions. Let me pause here: the continued concern with autonomy, I am arguing, is a screen for a form of dependence. The study of twentieth-century art still seems tethered—or as I said earlier, addicted—to assumptions that are based in the dominant value judgments of the historical period it studies. Since the ideology of the avant-garde and aesthetic autonomy also often buttressed racial and gender hierarchies, they obscure the view of history and our perceptions of what research it might even be possible to undertake. From a phase-shifted point of view, the twentieth century might be seen as a century of reflection, consciously conducted by artists and critics, on the social commitments and responsibilities of art—not just as one of an ever-advancing line of superior competitive strategies.[9]

A different example of the ways in which the boundaries of art are policed comes in a statement made by Claire Bishop about Tania Bruguera's experimental art school in Havana, Arte de Conducta. Debating "the status of Arte de Conducta as a work of art," Bishop writes, "My feeling is that everything will depend on how [Bruguera] documents five years of workshops—as a book, an exhibition, or through the students' own work. As a live project it's completely invigorating, but subsequent audiences need to be able to make sense of it."[10] Bishop seems here to be capitulating to external definitions rather than offering up her own—answering the question "Will this be understood as art?" rather than "Is this art?" But these (as Bishop is certainly aware) are two different questions. Indeed, the suggestion that they depend on the same process is somewhat unsettling. It implies that art becomes art—or becomes intelligible as art—only through its representation within specific institutions of art. I take Bishop's remarks as symptomatic not of her own views but of a position in which she finds herself in dealing with Arte de Conducta. Following the logic of this position, either we must resituate art in objects alone (ephemeral performance becomes art through its documentation in material objects) or imagine that the Cuban art students who are the primary actors and recipients of the project do not actually count as actors and recipients. If the latter is the case, the question is why: are they culturally, politically too far outside the institutions of the Euro-American art world? Or does a state that compels collectivity and collectivism frustrate the attempt to define a collective art project as a *critical* one? (In its own context, in other words, is education-as-art not enough of an intervention?) Perhaps it is Bishop's response to the dawning suspicion that she has been othered—as a Euro-American critic, turned by the students into an object of slightly sad curiosity. Perhaps a more embracing way to think about the questions Bishop raises would be to suggest that if art is an intervention into a conversation, we need to have a sense of what that conversation is before evaluating the art. Art is a moment of newness, an event, but one that pushes back against something—whether we call that conversation, as I just did, or medium, institution, or frame. What Bishop reaches for and cannot find is the frame against which Arte de Conducta pushes, and her default is the world of Euro-American art institutions. The remark is an offhanded comment in an otherwise thoughtful body of writing. Yet in its very offhandedness it is symptomatic of more general assumptions and hints at a broader problem in the field: What is the ground against which as-yet-unimagined figures will define themselves? The institutions and discourses of modernist criticism and its postmodern aftermath have provided a convenient and often extremely productive ground for approaching a lot of twentieth-century art. But perhaps it is time to kick the habit.

Art & Soul was not entirely outside the mainstream art world. It was a point of intersection: between the new aspirations of late 1960s museums and forms of creativity born of the desperate conditions of an African American ghetto; between the young Black Arts Movement and older, established African American artists. At base it may have been just a fresh episode in the history of the periphery of mainstream art institutions. But it was a moment of optimism, coalition, and risk-taking that may have lessons for the future. Institutional politics sometimes produced conflicts; the approaches made by the various parties—the museum, the gang, the broader local community—were sometimes tense. Indeed, the risks taken by all sides were considerable. And though it has been largely forgotten, the project as a whole embodied many qualities now accepted not just as adjuncts to the creation of artworks but as components of the work of art itself. Art & Soul and similar projects might indeed be seen as the precursors to more recent projects that go under the rubric of community art or collaboration or "new genre public art." But it can be a struggle to see it in this light. It doesn't fit the standard history of "contemporary" art for a few reasons. It wasn't the project of a single famous artist or even a famous artist group. It doesn't fit with the lingering critical notion of the avant-garde and the historico-aesthetic preoccupations that attend it. Its politics were not revolutionary (though they were certainly risky, and that was part of their importance). It doesn't sit comfortably with narratives of the history of identity politics. To account for stories like this one requires a more expansive notion of the history of the present than art history has yet shown willingness to undertake.[11]

The Experiment

Art & Soul served as a neighborhood art studio with classes for children, a library of books, freely available materials for artists, an artist residency, contests, readings, and exhibitions. Funding from the Illinois Sesquicentennial Commission enabled two storefronts to be joined into a single space, their interiors painstakingly renovated, cleaned, and prepared, and the whole building painted and decorated inside and out. Ann Zelle, a young photographer from Springfield, Illinois, worked on the project with Lawndale artists—the brothers Jackie and Daniel Hetherington and Peter Gilbert—along with a staffer from the Illinois Sesquicentennial Commission, James Houlihan. Zelle kept copious notes and documented the project photographically. Children were involved from the beginning, painting the exterior walls as renovations began.

Lawndale was (and is) one of the poorest neighborhoods of the city, and the project sought to bridge the divide between the ghetto and downtown cultural institutions. It was not merely a white outpost; the Hetheringtons, who served as director and assistant director, were members of the CVL organization, and the advisory council included numerous black artists and community organizers. When Art & Soul opened on November 14, 1968, it was full of visitors. Robert Nolte wrote for the *Chicago Tribune*, "Two months ago, it was a dilapidated building, housing a hat cleaner on 16th Street. Today, it is the brightest spot on the block—Art & Soul, a library, gallery, light and music theater, and workshop for west side artists."[12] Two vacant storefronts (one had been, as Nolte writes, a hat cleaner's; the other a defunct burglar alarm

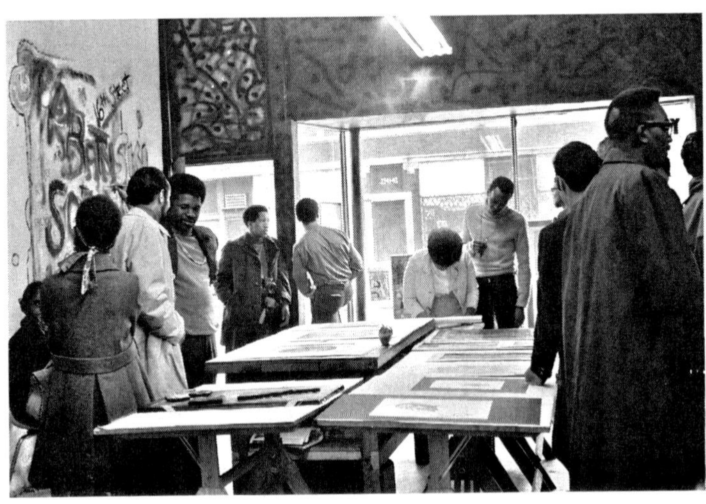

Visitors at the opening of Art & Soul, 1968. Photo © Ann Zelle.

company) had been painstakingly converted into a single space for youth programming, artist residencies, and exhibitions.

The Vice Lords, created as a coalition of several gangs in 1958 by young men incarcerated in the St. Charles Youth Prison, reinvented themselves in the mid-1960s as the Conservative Vice Lords. A turning point came one night when the older gang members were approached by a younger member: "He told us he wanted to take about fifty fellows later that night to make a fall. We asked him why and who he wanted to fall on; had anyone misused him. His reply was we the older lords including the fellows who are in jail had made a name and they wanted to keep it alive."[13] Alarmed at their part in creating an image of violence that had become self-perpetuating—perhaps also anxious to shore up control—the older members decided to form CVL, Inc. They formed a relationship with David Dawley, who had come to Chicago as a Transcentury Corporation staffer to do a study on ghetto residents' attitudes toward the provision of social services.[14] With his Dartmouth training and his personal contacts, Dawley helped the CVL members make contact with businesses and foundations. As spokesman Bobby Gore puts it, the Vice Lords "poured [their] hearts out to them."[15] With Dawley's help, the CVL submitted successful grant proposals to foundations, and these substantial funds enabled them to create several businesses. The West Side was in crisis; foundations and business owners and upstanding community members were taking a risk. But perhaps the alternative seemed a bigger risk. CVL received backing from the Ford and Rockefeller foundations, the retailers Sears and Carson Pirie Scott, and other businesses and individuals.

At its high point, CVL, Inc. ran a diner, ice cream parlors, and a clothing shop—the African Lion, supported by Sammy Davis, Jr.—and promoted neighborhood cleanup programs and helped build playgrounds. The simple idea was that by establishing opportunities for training and jobs for kids, the gang might prevent violence among younger members and promote economic self-reliance for the community, keeping the community's money in the community. It was a bid for economic autonomy for the neighborhood; it was also an attempt to convert illicit forms of power to licit ones, and to maintain a presence within the neighborhood that would be associated with positive, and not negative, effects on the community.

Jan van der Marck had arrived in Chicago in 1967 to direct the new Museum of Contemporary Art. He had originally traveled to the United States as a Rockefeller fellow to study American museums and their relationship to the public. First at the Walker Art Center in Minneapolis and then at the MCA, he started to put his ideas into practice. In early 1968, he met Zelle in New Orleans at the American Association of Museums meeting. He offered her a job, and she quickly packed up and moved to Chicago from New Jersey, where she had just finished an internship at the Newark Museum. The first written record of Art & Soul appears in the MCA timesheet, a set of ongoing records kept by van der Marck and Zelle. This meeting, held in May 1968, was itself the result of previous conversations. The record reads: "Meeting with Robert Stepto, Bernard Rogers, Allen Wardwell, Jan van der Marck to discuss what can be done in the way of art for the black community on the West Side. This meeting was prompted by previous discussions with Bernard Rogers, who for some time has been active with the Conservative Vice Lords, Inc., as well as by the museum conference in New Orleans where a session was devoted to the subject 'How can museums be made more useful.'"[16] It was a high-powered meeting. Wardwell was the head of what was at the time called the Primitive Art Department at the Art Institute of Chicago. Stepto was a trustee of the MCA, an African American physician who was a faculty member at the University of Chicago Medical School. He had taken an interest in the West Side since serving as head of the obstetrics and gynecology department at Cook County Hospital.[17] Rogers was an insurance executive and a member of the Art Institute's board of trustees. Early consultations also included David Dawley and the two Hetherington brothers. Daniel Hetherington was an especially talented artist; Jackie Hetherington had graduated from Crane Tech and Crane Junior College (later to become Malcolm X College) and had worked in a barber shop and in the display department at Compton's Encyclopedia. He also had experience working on another CVL venture, Teen Town.[18]

The notes from an August meeting reveal further development of the project:

> An art workshop-gallery, located in a remodeled store or several adjacent stores in an accessible area would be a center for all the arts from painting to sculpture to films and music, a place to work and a place in which to display, a meeting point for discussion and exposure to art. The center would be run by a neighborhood manager for the people of the neighborhood, and the role of the museum would be to provide ideas, counsel, contacts, and technical advice.[19]

From the beginning, therefore, the museum saw its job as facilitation: it wasn't setting up a branch location or dispensing charity. On July 8, van der Marck approached Ralph Newman of the Illinois Sesquicentennial Commission, the organization set up to commemorate the 150th anniversary of Illinois statehood.[20] Van der Marck hoped Newman would fund the project. Originally, van der Marck had proposed something quite different to the Sesquicentennial: *Hydroscape*, a floating sculpture garden on Lake

Michigan, which would (according to van der Marck's original proposal) have included works by a welter of famous names: Claes Oldenburg, Andy Warhol, Roy Lichtenstein, James Rosenquist, Jean Tinguely, Niki de Saint-Phalle, Christo, Yayoi Kusama, Les Levine, Francois Dallegret, Tony Smith, Robert Morris, Robert Smithson, Hans Haacke, Billy Apple, and others.[21] Newman had been interested in this project, but it hadn't panned out, apparently for lack of funds on the MCA's side. Van der Marck would later say that "it turned out to be a sad case of my eyes being bigger than my stomach and trustees escorted me back from Delaware Riviera to Ontario Street."[22]

When he heard of what was originally called the West Side Project, Newman also expressed immediate interest. He had funds available and was eager to enhance the representation of black Illinoisans in the Sesquicentennial festivities. But Newman was unwilling to use state funds to finance an operation run exclusively by a street gang, and emphasized that the project must involve other community partners and serve the community as a whole. Therefore, many different community groups were invited to initial meetings from which the advisory council developed. Community organizations that sent representatives or offered moral support of one kind or another included the Lawndale Youth Commission, West Side Federation, Lawndale Urban Progress Center, Better Boys Foundation, Boys Brotherhood Republic, the Lawndale People's Planning Conference, the A.B.C. Youth Center, the Chicago Public Library, and the Catholic Church—a very different list from the first Sesquicentennial proposal van der Marck had drawn up.

Early meetings with community members were not overwhelmingly promising. Two women from Concerned Parents criticized the use of storefronts: van der Marck noted, "The point was driven home rather sharply that black people associate storefronts with churches, neighborhood clubs and in general poorly financed, faltering operations." He went on to remark that "neither of the 2 ladies were thinking of the museum in terms other than the traditional concept." While he saw promise in experiment, the women imagined something like the Art Institute; storefronts, they thought, would consign the operation to being a poor substitute for a real museum. They also objected to the use of funds for art at all—as opposed to more basic needs. As van der Marck reported in the timesheet, they asked, "Why do you white people all want to make your mark in the Lawndale area? Is that the way you want to get into the news?"[23]

The mothers' doubts about gang involvement were shared by Lew Kreinberg of the Westside Federation, who proposed a location, a vacant bank building, outside the CVL's territory. Van der Marck was excited by the scale of the building, as well as that of a vacant Oldsmobile dealership proposed by a development company, Greenleigh Associates. But these ideas quietly died—perhaps because they were too expensive or, in the case of the bank building, because it would have been difficult to get the project off the ground without the CVL. Van der Marck's introduction to the concept had come through Rogers, who was the linchpin between Lawndale and the white cultural institutions downtown, and who had formed a specific connection with the CVL. Perhaps more important, the various social services and funding organizations had to reckon with the Vice Lords because they held the power in Lawndale. The CVL had the capacity to make things happen in a way that other organizations couldn't. With this more collaborative approach and the support of the gang organization, Broady was able to proceed in his work.

But if the Vice Lords were needed to make the West Side Project go forward, they could not be the official recipients of Sesquicentennial funds. Newman made this clear. It had been a real priority for him to ensure African American representation in the Sesquicentennial events, and he was enthusiastic about the project in general, but he was wary of Vice Lord involvement. In a meeting at which the project seemed to be at an impasse, Newman proposed that, rather than disbursing funds to the project directly, the Sesquicentennial would hire an administrator who would have control over payments.[24]

This is how James Houlihan came into the picture. Later to become the Cook County Assessor, he was the Sesquicentennial Commission's representative to Art & Soul. His role set him up for conflicts. He was there to ensure broader community participation and to keep control over the Sesquicentennial's funds. As it was described in the August 12 meeting in which Newman proposed the administrator position, in addition to managing the budget, his role was to act "as a go-between among the Commission, the project, and the various elements of the community hopefully broadening community interest and support of the project."[25] Newman saw Houlihan's position as a way to maintain limits on how much the project would belong to the Vice Lords. By contrast, Zelle defended their role. Both believed in community leadership of the project, but different definitions of community were at work. To Newman, the Vice Lords were a potentially nettlesome segment of the community; to Zelle, the Vice Lords—with their particular representatives, the Hetherington brothers—*were* the community with which the MCA was partnering. In notes in the timesheet she describes telling Jackie that she would defend his role as director of Art & Soul.[26] Yet the requirement of a board drawn from different sectors of the community was, she says, a positive thing: "Art & Soul helped integrate the CVL into their community."[27]

But a certain tension was indeed implicit in the institutional relationships. At times Houlihan and Jackie Hetherington found themselves at odds. The routine conflicts are illuminating. In one example, according to Houlihan, Jackie Hetherington asked to bill the Sesquicentennial for expenses that included Ripple, a (mildly) fortified wine produced by the Gallo winery that was popular at the time in the ghetto. As Houlihan put it, "He would say 'Those executives downtown have their three martini lunches and put it on their expense accounts. Why can't I have Ripple [and put it down as an expense]?' I said, 'Your logic is impeccable, but I'm still not going to do it.'" The interaction was jocular, but suggests how philanthropy with strings attached might rankle. A bigger issue in the use of funds was a conflict between spending on building renovation and spending on programs. As the head of the Sesquicentennial, a program of events commemorating Illinois's 150th year of statehood, Newman obviously wanted the project to bear fruit—specifically through programming that could be reported to state government—in the year 1968. The project only got off the ground in the summer; spending too much time on renovations would slow the progress of the opening, and spending too much money would reduce program possibilities. Yet community members wanted to establish some permanence. Jackie Hetherington pushed for more extensive renovations. Once Broady saw the condition of the building, his cost estimates went up. The crumbling interior walls could not be redone without spending more money than Newman would allow. The questions of cost were emotionally and politically charged; recall the two mothers and their concerns about a storefront. If white money was coming into the neighborhood to build something, why couldn't it be something magnificent? In a meeting on September 30, van der Marck, Zelle, and Rogers came to "agree with Jackie that enough money had to be spent to get the job done well and quickly."[28] The next day van der Marck expressed frustration: "Where are we? No payrolls yet. Everything is done piecemeal and nothing is done properly. . . . Forget preliminary budget— do remodeling right with black architect and contractor."[29] As Houlihan remembered it, Zelle had the idea to tack burlap over some of the interior walls and nail down a simple wood border rather than completely replacing the decayed plaster.[30] This had the added benefit of providing a good surface for hanging artwork. The written records don't provide a clear final answer to questions about the renovation costs, but within a month the space was nearly ready to open; a pre-opening Halloween party was held, and Zelle noted with relief that the CVL had come through with support for the event, that it was a "good introduction to Art & Soul as an active, swinging place."[31] Two weeks later, it formally opened.

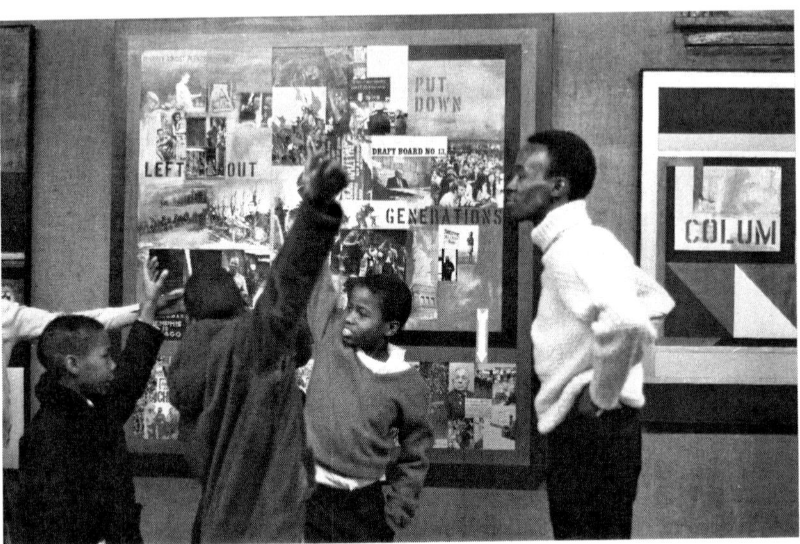

Daniel Hetherington leads children in a discussion of Ralph Arnold's *Columbia*, 1968 and *One Thing Leads to Another*, 1968. Artworks © The Ralph Arnold Estate, Chicago. Photo © Ann Zelle.

The Soul of Art

If anything, these tensions seem to have injected energy into the project. Eventually the collaborators became, as Houlihan put it, "trusted partners." Although he recalls the project as misguided in certain ways, he also describes it as "a wonderful event."[32] Zelle echoes this sentiment: it was "very positive and fun. People were excited and interested. Lots of neighborhood people would come by. It was exhilarating and full of hope. Such a rich, productive, creative time."[33] Early on, Art & Soul hosted Ralph Arnold as artist-in-residence, displaying his collage paintings on its walls. The center held an art contest in which Jeff Donaldson of AFRICOBRA (African Commune of Bad Relevant Artists, a group founded in 1968 by former members of the OBAC Visual Art Workshop) won first prize, and Peter Gilbert, a local sculptor who had been involved from the start and whose medium was animal bones, was second. Reggie Madison, who appears in several of Zelle's photos touching up one of his entries at the last minute, won third place with an abstract kinetic sculpture he titled *Black Madonna and Child*. Art & Soul also hosted a traveling exhibition of African sculpture from the Art Institute's collections. Staff offered classes in papier-mâché, puppets, and screen-printing; the center also held informal studio hours and sponsored visits to the MCA and a poetry reading there by black poets (Eugene Perkins, Sigmonde Wimberli, and Ebon).[34] The photographer Roy Lewis created an experimental installation of his photographs on the outer wall of the building, joining with other black photographers in Chicago—Bobby Sengstacke and Bob Crawford—who were inspired by the *Wall of Respect* on Chicago's South Side to create their own form of mural. These photographic street museums could also serve as political rallying points.[35] Lewis gave his installation the title *West Wall* with the subheading *Proud of Being Black*.[36] It was documented in a booklet of poems entitled *West Wall* by Eugene Perkins. *West Wall* was a doubly meaningful title: it was the west wall of the building and also a wall of images for the West Side, as opposed to the South Side locations of Crawford and Sengstacke's projects.[37] *West Wall: Proud of Being Black* appears in Zelle's photograph against the backdrop of rainbow stripes painted under the direction of the Japanese artist Sachio Yamashita, newly arrived from art school in Tokyo. His rainbow stripes, a signature of his work in the late 1960s and early 1970s, adorn Zelle's color image of the storefronts.[38]

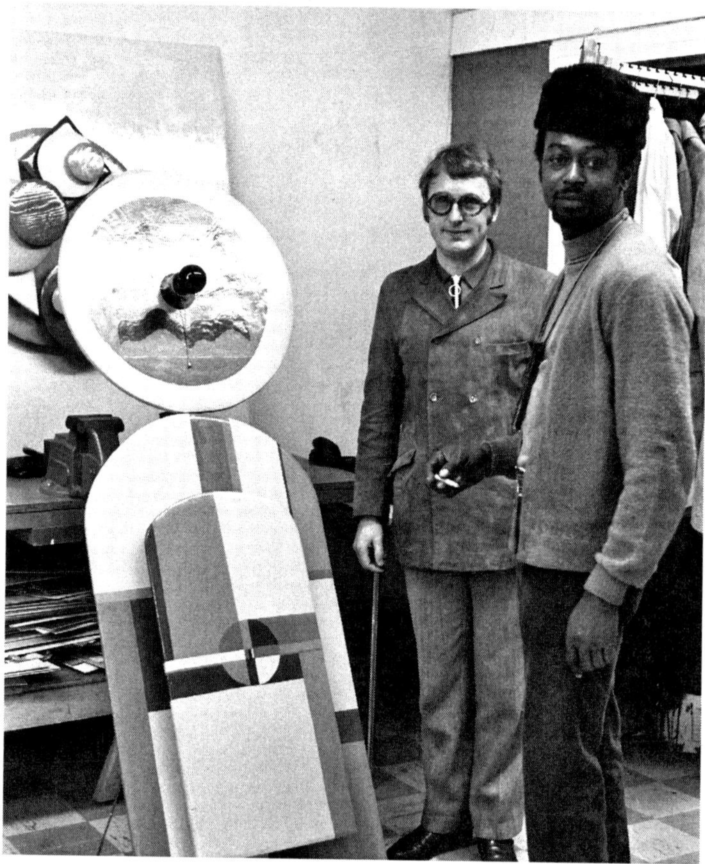

Jan van der Marck and Jackie Hetherington with Reginald Madison's *Black Madonna and Child*, 1968. Artwork © Reginald Madison, by permission of the artist. Photo © Ann Zelle.

Funds from the Sesquicentennial ran out at the end of 1968, and fund-raising efforts occupied much of the next six months. By the summer, most of the original staff had moved on. The details of the transition remain unclear, but from mid-1969 youth programs continued with federal funds administered by the University of Illinois at Chicago. The black mural artist Don McIlvaine, who was not a Vice Lord, took over as director and worked with children to paint powerful, aggressive, insistent murals throughout Lawndale. (His substantial oeuvre has now, tragically, been almost entirely demolished.) The project seems to have continued in a more limited way until 1972, when it was likely the victim of President Nixon's dismantling of the Johnson-era Office of Economic Opportunity.[39]

Interviewed in late 1968 by Steven Pratt of the *Chicago Tribune*, Houlihan said that the work done by "artists here is a different type of art than that you see hanging in the north side galleries. That's why the museum is so interested."[40] In shifting his attention from a project like the proposed *Hydroscape* to the West Side project that was to become Art & Soul, van der Marck had not abandoned the world of contemporary art as it was then understood. The language contained in a February 1969 funding proposal written was carefully modulated to draw on the rhetoric of contemporary art: "'Art & Soul' began as a six-month art happening in Lawndale, an experimental friendship between a street group and a museum." The project was often described as a Happening and was directly inspired by the free stores of the Diggers, a San Francisco radical street theater group.[41] Along with its commitment to children's programming, Art & Soul was a way to be involved in the creation of new forms of art through dialogue between the contemporary white art world and the styles and concerns of black artists. The proposal also suggested that part of the project's innovation was its responsiveness to African American cultural forms: "By providing the opportunity for the application of contemporary art techniques to black moods, the concept of 'Art & Soul' becomes a medium for new forms and styles in art."[42] "Black moods" was an interesting word choice. Other CVL grant proposals refer to overwhelming hopelessness as the "mood" of Lawndale, but here "black moods" seems instead to represent a more expansive and creative feeling. It also suggests the idea of creating, or maintaining, a distinctively African American style of art, something that Jackie Hetherington, too, emphasized in conversations with Zelle. An exhibition of African art was offered by the Art Institute, but Hetherington hesitated to stress African art at the expense of developing contemporary African American artists.[43] He also rejected the MCA's offer of Red Grooms's *Chicago* billboard, which contained a caricatured African American boy.[44]

Van der Marck and Zelle, both relative newcomers to Chicago, had entered into a moment of political ferment that was also a moment of intense artistic ferment among African American artists in Chicago. The notion of a "Black Aesthetic" was being vigorously discussed and debated within the African American arts community of the period, much of it in the pages of *Negro Digest* (which changed its name to *Black World* in 1970), published in Chicago and edited by Hoyt Fuller.[45] Black artists and writers voiced multiple and sometimes conflicting views on the importance of art and the specific aesthetic qualities it should possess, but one of the primary points was the insistence that art be connected to life: that art play a social and political role, that it be in the streets and among "the people."[46] This entailed a revolt against prevailing (white) institutional standards for art in which abstraction was still dominant. As James C. Hall has written, not only did "African-American art in the 1960s [claim] for itself an expansive social capacity" but the challenges it posed to modernist criticism "have been too often ignored as rhetorical or ceremonial."[47] Hall is speaking largely about literature, but his critique holds true for art history and criticism as well. The point was not a turn from art to a purely political form of blackness, but a redefinition of the relationship between art and politics accompanied by a sustained critique of the collusion of notions of aesthetic autonomy and universalism with racist ideologies.

Other Idleness

In May 1969, when Art & Soul had been open for six months, the Cook County State's Attorney, Edward Hanrahan, along with Mayor Richard J. Daley, declared a "War on Gangs." Together, they argued: "Gang claims that they are traditional boys' clubs or community organizations ignore the violence and destruction of social values in the neighborhoods they terrorize."[48] Leaders of the CVL were harassed, arrested, and imprisoned, often with obviously flawed or manipulated judicial processes. And at the indictment of Bobby Gore, one of the Vice Lord leaders, on murder charges that many argued at the time and since were trumped up, Hanrahan pointedly excoriated granting organizations for giving money to gangs: "We think these brutal acts should cause foundations and others to intensify their scrutiny of persons seeking money from them to make certain their funds are not used to arm street gangsters or for other idleness."[49] Why was this war declared? Did Daley and Hanrahan not see the potential the "reformed" gangs offered? Several observers at the time, and historians more recently, have suggested that Daley saw their potential all too well. He knew this from personal experience. As a young leader of the Hamburg Athletic Association, he was a probable participant in the major race riot of 1919 in Chicago; throughout his life he refused to answer questions about his involvement.[50] He knew exactly what could happen when gangs began to legitimize themselves and claim political power, because he had lived through this very experience. By this reading, the Conservative Vice Lords were not the exception to the rule, a force for good unfortunately swept up in an overly indiscriminate but ultimately necessary police operation provoked by the violence of other gangs. They *were* the provocation.

Hanrahan's choice of words is quite striking. What did he mean by idleness—worthlessness, folly, inactivity; the nonfunctional, the nonproductive, the trivial, the fantastical? Did he mean, specifically, crime? Daley and Hanrahan made it clear that the funding offered by foundations was itself part of the provocation to the authorities. "Idleness" seems to roll off the tongue here as a general term for bad things: no matter what, the money is used for purposes not intended by the foundations.

On the other hand, from the point of view of dumbfounded Chicagoans who watched the erection of the Picasso in 1967 and wondered if it was a baboon, it might be art itself that constituted "idleness." In a way, this isn't so far from the art world's own critical discourses. Idleness might be a beneficial condition, when it is understood as freedom from compulsion, or the ability of the imagination to roam. Children making papier-mâché masks in an open-ended art class might, too, be perceived to be idle. For Greenberg in his 1959 essay "The Case for Abstract Art," the virtue of abstract art is that it encourages a meditative form of viewing. He argues that this is necessitated particularly in America as antidote to society's devotion to profit-making, goal-oriented, instrumental activity (otherwise known as capitalism).[51] By this definition, art as idleness—in its Kantian nonpurposive purposiveness—might indeed be salutary.

Yet if an "idle" form of art may be an antidote to profit-making, goal-oriented, instrumental activity, it is less clear how it could be an antidote to the situation of enforced idleness found in Lawndale, where the unemployment rate was three times the city average (and where the youth unemployment rate was 25 to 50 percent).[52] This situation expresses a fundamental divide for modern art in its impulses toward reduction, asceticism, and negation. Where these modernist operations of self-sacrifice require a self to be sacrificed—they require self-possession—black artists were, and needed to be, engaged in a process of self-creation. At the same time, the necessity of construction and creation (that is, affirmative rather than negative operations) transcended race. When artists joined in the *Richard J. Daley* exhibition at the Feigen Gallery to protest the police attacks on protesters at the 1968 Democratic National Convention, Robert Motherwell sent two already completed canvases that were, he stated, without political content. "There is a certain kind of art which I belong to. It can no more make a direct political comment than chamber music can."[53]

But the problematic status of this position, in 1968, is palpable, for he also glossed this *parti pris* a bit by suggesting that context made the works political: "The significance is to participate," he said, and elsewhere, "This show represents the politics of feeling, not the politics of ideology."[54] It might be argued that perhaps the gesture itself—the participation, as performance—was part of the art. The art, as well as "the [political] significance," was to participate—not to stand idly by.

Today, postindustrial shifts in national and global economies to a situation characterized by unemployment and precarity might prompt us to redirect our ideas not only about how art engages with social and political issues but also how it engages with work.[55] Indeed, what kind of "work" can count as the "work" of art? There were art objects made and displayed at Art & Soul. In a way, though, these objects were only the documents of the real work: the building, cleaning, organizing, educating, befriending, negotiating, managing, risk-taking, material gathering, directing, grant-writing, learning, dreaming, schmoozing, protecting, collaborating, remembering, and contributing of cultural knowledge. Many of these tasks would in the coming years be signaled as art and not just adjuncts to it—by Mierle Laderman Ukeles, Andrea Fraser, and others.[56] During this historical period artists and critics began to view the avant-garde as co-opted by capitalism, and a range of practices (performance, feminism, conceptualism) began, in various ways, to challenge modernist assumptions and to herald what would be called postmodernism. As Julia Bryan-Wilson deftly shows in *Art Workers,* the Art Workers Coalition's 1970 Art Strike presents a tension between the desire to recast art as labor, in a gesture of working-class solidarity—and the impulse of refusal, the withdrawal of meaning-making activity, that is both an attempt at political statement and an unintentional rhyme with quietist tropes of mid-century American modernism.

Art & Soul was a bargain struck between two groups—each individually comprising complex interests—that knew, at the outset, very little about one another. For their own separate reasons, each agreed to construct this space both to foster creativity in Lawndale from the ground up and to celebrate African American art and artists in Chicago. If the creation of subjectivity and consciousness were "the work of art"—the productive activity of art—and not just effects of artworks, this means the art itself may be difficult to fasten in our sights, but it also may make this a historical reference point that can reciprocally frame and be framed by later projects such as Havana's Arte de Conducta.

Art & Soul was not a black revolutionary project like the *Wall of Respect*. It was a pragmatic bargain among organizations with rather different interests. It borrowed, and was sometimes a vehicle for, the Black Arts Movement's aspirations, and in making do with limited resources and challenging presuppositions, it also made an art of the labor required to create such a space. One cannot claim any precedence for Art & Soul in relation to the South Side collective black projects (*Wall of Respect*, OBAC and AFRICOBRA, the Museum of African History, the Affro-Arts Theatre). These groups and projects deserve much more attention in their own right, as part of the history of art of the twentieth century. What is most important about Art & Soul is the remarkable fact of the engagement of the MCA and other white institutions, in an aesthetic project, with a street gang, whose members engaged in the project as essential partners and not merely recipients of charity. The multiple kinds of labor that went into allowing this risky, fragile experiment to happen even for a short time express the content of the project as need, crisis, poverty, danger, and power—as well as optimism and creativity. "Other idleness": next to "arming street gangsters" it sounds like an understatement. But then, it is a capacious phrase. It could mean violence, it could mean loitering. It could mean art. If the reported presence of FBI snipers at the unveiling of the *Wall of Respect* in Chicago in 1967 is any indication, some of the "authorities," anyway, believed that black people making art was itself violence.

Both sides ran risks in engaging in the collaboration called Art & Soul, and some of those risks and their effects lie beyond the scope of this essay. From the point of view of the writing of art history, theory, and criticism, to write about elements of work that might seem mundane poses a smaller, but definite risk: the potential loss of the currency we hope to find in aesthetic exquisiteness. But perhaps we might lose it only to find it reinvented in another form. As an experimental friendship, Art & Soul can help us pose questions about the kinds of aesthetic and political risk we are or aren't taking today.

This text was originally published by the College Art Association in *Art Journal* 70, no. 2 (Summer 2011): 66–87, and is reprinted here with minor revisions.

1 Donald Mosby, "Westside Gang Plans Business Ventures" *Chicago Daily Defender*, April 4, 1968, 1.

2 Conservative Vice Lords, Inc., Proposal to Rockefeller Foundation (signed Alfonso Alford, to Joseph Black, Director, Humanities and Social Sciences), December 20, 1967, Rockefeller Foundation Archives, Record group: 01.0002, Series 200, Box 113, folder 997, 2.

3 In "Interventions Reviews," *Art Bulletin* 88, no. 2 (June 2006), many reviewers make this and related points about problematic authorship of these two entries as well as the absence of political art and questions of race and ethnicity; see Nancy Troy (374), Geoffrey Batchen

(376), Amelia Jones (377–79), Romy Golan (382), and Robert Storr (384–85). A note appears on the copyright page of *Art since 1900* to credit the otherwise mysterious "AD" who authored the two entries: "The publishers would like to thank Amy Dempsey for her assistance in the preparation of the book."

4 I use "white-supremacist" in the sense of pervasive and often unstated expectations of racial hierarchy, as in bell hooks's usage in "Overcoming White Supremacy," *Talking Back: Thinking Feminist, Thinking Black* (Boston: South End Press, 1989), 112–19.

5 See Julia Bryan-Wilson, *Art Workers: Radical Practice in the Vietnam War Era* (Berkeley: University of California Press, 2009)

6 Clement Greenberg, "An Essay on Paul Klee," *Collected Essays and Criticism*, ed. John O'Brian, vol. 3, *Affirmations and Refusals, 1950–1956* (Chicago: University of Chicago Press, 1993), 5.

7 Charles Mills, *The Racial Contract* (Ithaca: Cornell University Press, 1997), 30. Later critics writing in Greenberg's wake have insisted even more on the specificity of the medium and on evaluation by comparison with the (European) history of the medium. For Michael Fried, it is a "basic modernist tenet" that new paintings must "'sustain comparison' with older works whose quality is not in doubt." Fried, "An Introduction to My Art Criticism," in *Art and Objecthood* (Chicago: University of Chicago Press, 1998), 1–74; 74, n81—a sentiment repeated several times in essays in the collection (38, 165, 169). The structure of beginning with certainty (or rather absence-of-doubt) recuperates time by mapping the Cartesian cogito onto history just as the "modernist reduction" maps it in space.

8 See for instance Peter Yates, "A Digression around the Subject, Unpopular Criticism is Necessary, or 'Don't Stop the World, I'm Still on It,'" *Arts in Society* 6, no. 1 (1969): 62–69; or Judith Adler, "'Revolutionary' Art and the 'Art' of Revolution: Aesthetic Work in a Millenarian Period," *Theory and Society* 3 (Spring 1976): 417–35.

9 See for instance the now nearly forgotten journal *Arts in Society* published by the University of Wisconsin Extension Division from 1958 to 1976.

10 Claire Bishop, "Havana Diary: Arte de Conducta," *Untitled: A Review of Contemporary Art* 45 (2008): 38–43, 41–42.

11 I am inspired in this research by Greg Sholette's notion of the "dark matter" of the art world. Yet in this context in particular, the phrase makes me uneasy. He does not use it in a racially specific way, and yet it describes the invisibility of the Black Arts Movement all too well. Gregory Sholette, "Dark Matter: Activist Art and the Counter-public Sphere," *Journal of Aesthetics and Protest* 1, no. 3 (2004): 13–24. On exclusions see also Francis Frascina, *Art, Politics, and Dissent: Aspects of the Art Left in Sixties America* (Manchester, UK: Manchester University Press, 1999).

12 Robert Nolte, "Artists Paint a Bright Spot on West Side," *Chicago Tribune*, November 14, 1968, A4.

13 CVL, Inc. "A Unique Friendship between the Street and a Museum: Art & Soul," grant proposal, 1969. Museum of Contemporary Art, Van der Marck papers, 13.

14 Dawley tells the story of the CVL in his book *A Nation of Lords: The Autobiography of the Vice Lords* (Garden City, NY: Anchor Press, 1973).

15 Bobby Gore interview, June 15, 2011.

16 MCA Art & Soul Timesheet, May 29, 1968. All references to the MCA Timesheet refer to a file kept by Ann Zelle and now filed with Jan van der Marck's papers at the MCA in Chicago.

17 Personal communication, Robert Stepto Jr.

18 MCA Timesheet, West Side Progress Report (Trustees' Meeting), October 8, 1968.

19 "Meeting on Proposed West Side Art Project." MCA Timesheet, August 12, 1968.

20 MCA Timesheet, July 8, 1968.

21 Chicago History Museum, Ralph Newman papers, Box 592/394A, Museum of Contemporary Art, June 1, 1967.

22 Meeting of Leadership Group at Sears YMCA. MCA Timesheet, August 8, 1968.

23 Meeting of Leadership Group at Sears YMCA. MCA Timesheet, August 8, 1968.

24 "Meeting on Proposed West Side Art Project." MCA Timesheet, August 12, 1968.

25 Ibid.

26 MCA Timesheet, October 2, 1968.

27 Ann Zelle interview, November 24, 2010.

28 MCA Timesheet, September 30, 1968.

29 MCA Timesheet, October 1, 1968.

30 Houlihan interview, February 10, 2010.

31 MCA Timesheet, October 31, 1968.

32 Houlihan interview, February 10, 2010.

33 Zelle interview, November 24, 2010.

34 "An Evening of Black Poetry," MCA news release, May 2, 1969. MCA, Van der Marck files.

35 Funding was provided to the South Side Community Art Center by the Illinois Arts Council, the Chicago Committee on Urban Opportunity, and the National Endowment for the Arts for three photographic murals. Bob Crawford's was at the Umoja Black Student Center in the Oakland neighborhood, and Robert Sengstacke's was in Englewood at Sixty-second and Halsted Streets. "New Walls for City," *Chicago Defender*, October 22, 1968, 14–15. Roy Lewis's mural also appears in Catalysts Cultural Committee, *Black Cultural Directory Chicago '69* (Chicago: Catalysts, 1969), 29. Crawford's wall is visible in a photograph of the Umoja Center that accompanied an article on a student boycott in *Jet*: "Chicago Pupils Boycott; Board Member Agrees," October 31, 1968, 28.

36 "New Walls for City," *Chicago Defender*, October 22, 1968, 14–15.

37 Eugene Perkins and Roy Lewis, *West Wall* (Chicago: Free Black Press, 1968).

38 Sam Yanari interview, November 17, 2010.

39 See "McIlvaine seeks 24th Ward Seat," *Chicago Defender*, December 5, 1974, 4.

40 Steven Pratt, "Sesquicentennial Group Helps Gang to Open Art Gallery-Studio," *Chicago Tribune*, November 7, 1968, W2.

41 Although the idea of a free bookstore—based on the Diggers' free stores—had been nixed in an early meeting with area pastors, it resurfaced in the description of Art & Soul as "A Community Art/Book Center for All Ages" in its opening program. Program in van der Marck papers; Timesheet, July 10, 1968.

42 CVL, Inc. "A Unique Friendship between the Street and a Museum: Art & Soul," grant proposal, 1969. MCA, Van der Marck papers.

43 MCA Timesheet, October 2, 1968.

44 Ibid.

45 On the Black Arts Movement in Chicago, see an important essay by Margo Natalie Crawford, "Black Light on the *Wall of Respect:* The Chicago Black Arts Movement," in *New Thoughts on the Black Arts Movement*, ed. Lisa Gail Collins and Crawford (New Brunswick: Rutgers University Press, 2006). The collection also contains an essay by Mary Ellen Lennon, "A Question of Relevancy: New York Museums and the Black Arts Movement," that addresses issues in New York similar to those the present essay addresses for Chicago.

46 See for instance the essays collected in *The Black Aesthetic*, ed. Addison Gayle Jr. (Garden City, NJ: Doubleday, 1971).

47 James C. Hall, *Mercy Mercy Me: African-American Culture and the American Sixties* (Oxford: Oxford University Press, 2001), 5.

48 Hanrahan quoted in John Hagedorn, *A World of Gangs: Armed Young Men and Gangsta Culture* (Minneapolis: University of Minnesota Press, 2008), 79.

49 Hanrahan quoted in "Boyle Defends Shamberg in Setting Bond," *Chicago Tribune*, November 15, 1969, 9.

50 Hagedorn, *A World of Gangs*, 66–72.

51 Clement Greenberg, "The Case for Abstract Art," *Collected Essays and Criticism,* ed. John O'Brian, vol. 4, *Modernism with a Vengeance, 1957–1969* (Chicago: University of Chicago Press, 1993), 75–84, 82.

52 Beryl Satter, *Family Properties: How the Struggle over Race and Real Estate Transformed Chicago and Urban America* (New York: Henry Holt, 2010), 403, n101.

53 Motherwell quoted in "Artists vs. Mayor Daley," *Newsweek,* November 4, 1968, 117, cited in Therese Schwartz, "The Politicalization of the Avant-Garde II," *Art in America* 60, no. 2 (March–April 1972): 70–79, 71.

54 "The Politics of Feeling," *Time*, November 1, 1968, online at www.time.com/time/magazine/article/0,9171,839608,00.html, accessed December 18, 2010.

55 Precarity, in both scholarly terminology and movement politics, refers to the normalization and extension of precarious employment prospects and economic conditions for a broad swath of society, from migrant workers to displaced office workers to contingent university faculty. There is an extensive literature on precarity (précarité) in French. See Nicolas Bourriaud, ed., *Open 17: A Precarious Existence: Vulnerability in the Public Domain* (Rotterdam: NAi Publishers, 2009); and Stevphen Shukaitis, Imaginal, *Machines: Autonomy and Self-Organization in the Revolutions of Everyday Life* (London: Minor Compositions, 2009).

56 See, for instance, Mierle Laderman Ukeles, "Maintenance Art Manifesto" (1969), in *Theories and Documents of Contemporary Art: A Sourcebook of Artists' Writings*, ed. Kristine Stiles and Peter Selz (Berkeley: University of California Press, 1996), 622–24; and Andrea Fraser, "What's Intangible, Transitory, Mediating, Participatory, and Rendered in the Public Sphere?" *October* 80 (Spring 1997): 111–16.

Does the Public Work?

Iñigo Manglano-Ovalle

One year after launching *Counter-Proposals: Adaptive Approaches to a Built Environment*, there are aspects of the project that continue in progress, others that have taken on a life of their own, and a few questions still to consider. *Does the public work?* What public are we addressing? How do we define the terms under which the public works? I would like to suggest that both "public" and "work" be considered as independent yet interwoven sites and possibilities, that is: the *public-at-work, a working public,* and the *public-work.*

The notorious "anti-aesthetic" posture of much postmodern art may be seen, in its flouting of the canons of high modernism, as the latest edition of the iconoclastic public icon, the image that affronts its own public—in this case, the art world as well as the "general public." The violence associated with this art is inseparable from its publicness, especially its exploitation of and by the apparatuses of publicity, reproduction, and commercial distribution. The scandalousness and obtrusive theatricality of these images hold up a mirror to the nature of the commodified image, and the public spectator addressed by advertising, television, movies, and "Art" with a capital A. If all images are for sale, it's hardly surprising that artists would invent public images that are difficult (in any sense) to "buy."

—W.J.T. Mitchell, "The Violence of Public Art," *Critical Inquiry* 16, no. 4 (1990).

A whole history remains to be written of space – which would at the same time be the history of powers (both of these terms in plural) – from the great strategies of geopolitics to the little tactics of the habitat.
—Michel Foucault, *Power/Knowledge*, 1980, C. Gordon (ed.)

Debate over critical public art is continually locked in a contest of demarcating and circumscribing the site. Recently this debate has extended itself beyond the tolerable confines of our cultural institutions and public spaces. The contest has shifted from issues of the site to those of the public, from a definition of space to a contestation of space; the city, its political and cultural institutions, the environment, the home, and the site of the body. Private and public spaces collide as do cultural and political sites; both cultural arenas and the public domain shift in and out of each other's overlapping territories. A redefinition of public art no longer fits easily in the civic plaza, rather it necessitates constructing, redirecting, and, more importantly, engaging itself with the everyday experiences and struggles that pass through, live in, and transform our social environment. Increasingly, contention over the public realm is a potential for social change in public life. From the idea of *art in public spaces,* where artists, institutions, and organizations fought for a small percentage of the built environment's capital investment, we find ourselves as part of a larger public seeking other alternatives through the activation of the site. Rather than continuing with a modernist "critique of the site," by merely positing or positioning art in culture, there is an increasing attempt to formulate "sites of possibilities," wherein one can intervene in and engage culture itself.

Counter-Proposals was such an attempt, and it hoped to provide a forum for some of these possibilities. The project as a whole presented itself as a framework for initiating public discourse on key issues including the immediate need for shelter, new affordable housing, and community planning and development. Randolph Street Gallery, the institution, experienced its own shift in regard to how it perceived and presented itself. Issues of space and site were now concerned with use of space, and transformation of site. The gallery had to intermittently change over from display space to workshop and construction site for homeless shelters. Settings changed from the intimate roundtable to the meeting hall. The gallery's physical space was occupied by construction materials as well as an information center for alternative housing. The alternative cultural space modified itself into an active social space. The organization of the project and its programmed events required certain flexibility to accommodate unscheduled meetings of community groups and housing activists. *Counter-Proposals* presented the artists, architect, and activist in the role of direct participant engaged in both cultural and social transformation. To this end, the institution had to engage and invest itself equally as an urban participant. The project necessitated its own programmatic counter-proposals in order to function within its own site and in the extended urban environment it now addressed.

Many of the projects included in *Counter-Proposals* were chosen because of their alternative responses to the built environment. Strategies ranged from the pragmatic to the subversive; underlying all of them was a commitment to devise new models of empowerment and intervention. The work presented and the projects that were developed operated with strategies that linked information access with active dialogue, and education with direct involvement. Audiences for discussions and workshops became participants in design and building projects that provided catalysts for future engagements and actions. The success of the work's individual effort and the public's engagement can be measured to the degree with which each project functioned as a public work. Through contributions offered in open discussions and interchanges of resources and ideas, the public negotiated a flexibility in design and adaptive strategies to suit specific sites and situations. Successful public engagement was also measured by the degree in which theory was able to be adapted as a tool for generating cultural practice concerning the urban experience.

Critical public art posits the problematic role of art and artist as central to shaping society. This notion of public art offers new site(s) for art to interact with, as well as act as a part of, the public. It provides artists with the means of real social production, not just the role of a societal pressure valve. Much of the current discussion focuses on interventionist, activist, and/or collaborative practices that emphasize the artist's direct participation with issues and communities outside the insular confines of the "art world."

There is, though, both in mainstream and progressive circles, a resistance to what seems to be (to them) a breakdown of the once secure territorial boundaries between art and the public. This resistance often points to the term "public" in *public art* as an amorphous void that swallows up everything and everybody but cannot be defined: "What public? Which public? Is art no longer safe from the public? It was much simpler when it stood silent and it minded its own business." They even propose that all the "publics" be considered in order to fully discuss the term *public art*: this in turn is regarded as an impossibility. And so it is resolved that the only public we can speak of is our own, that of the "art public" or "art community." There is a certain tolerance, even an acknowledgement, that artists can be influenced or concerned with "non-art" issues, but they must not breach the boundaries of their "vocation." The work of the artists is considered sincere and true so long as it remains a specialization within his/her concept of "specialized public spheres."

Such posturing serves only to safeguard the sovereignty of art, maintaining art practice in cultural seclusions. An alternative to this isolation and over-specialization may be found through collective approaches to public work. By this I mean initiating a discourse that operates on an interdisciplinary level, not limited to the use of different "art-media," but rather a discourse among and including different fields, disciplines, communities, and sites of social production. This strategy offers the potential for moving beyond a "strategy of public address," to one of dialogue and exchange, beyond art as a cultural barometer or oppositional gesture, to art practice as meaningful social transformation.

Counter-Proposals attempted such a transformation of both site and production. The gallery space unfolded itself, establishing linkages and networks with and amongst a host of organizations concerned with housing, homelessness, and urban planning. These changes allowed the site to function as a resource, providing access to urban issues and interventions within the cultural grid of the city. The difference in stance is as profound and significant as that between the "consumer" and the "citizen." In this regard, our organizational activities paralleled the practices of the artists, architects, and activists in *Counter-Proposals*, To what extent we succeeded in overcoming our own marginalization and isolation in the public domain is still to be determined. To some we continue to be an elitist space catering to only a small "alternative" community; to others we are considered mainstream and part of the real estate problem; still to others we are a cross between a cultural center, community organization, meeting hall, and a conduit for social activism. *Counter-Proposals* made us keenly aware that we are some of all of these, and that it is through this type of public work that the artist organization can further define itself.

The success of public projects may be measured by the degree to which the organization either remains passive as an arts presenter *or* is able to activate itself as a contributing participant in the public domain. The artist organizations can best support artists as agents for change by engendering opportunities for engaged social production. These relationship between *public-work* and the *public-at-work* are key to the understanding of art's role in cultivating a *working public*.

This text was originally published in *Art Papers* 16, no. 5 (1992): 31-33.

Counter-Proposals at Randolph Street Gallery

Iñigo Manglano-Ovalle and Peter Taub in conversation

Iñigo Manglano-Ovalle: At Randolph Street Gallery (RSG), both as artists and curators, we tried to figure out what a space could do or be. And at that time in the late 1980s and early 1990s, we were interested in notions of public space and the public sphere, and some of us were in dialogue with younger architects over these issues. Still the idea did simply spring forth as say; "Let's do something about the built environment, or urban planning or activism." Peter, do you remember how *Counter-Proposals* began?

Peter Taub: You were very interested in the quality and texture of the city and the elements that form the framework of the city by the mid-1980s. But from that time to 1991 when *Counter-Proposals* opened, a lot had happened, not only with your own work but also to clarify the changing notion of what an artist is. As you said, you were an artist and curator; we recognized at RSG that artists aren't only artists when they're in their studios. They're also artists when they're curators, teachers, community organizers, activists, or advocates. The reason that came into focus was partly because in the late 1980s, there was an increasingly virulent attack from the religious Right against artists and they became public punching bags—Robert Mapplethorpe, Andres Serrano, John Fleck, Tim Miller, Holly Hughes. With the rise of Glasnost and the fall of the Berlin Wall in 1989, the volume of those attacks really became high, and the NEA individual artists' fellowships was defunded.

All of this came about at the time when there was a move toward recognizing artists as part of the public rather than part of an avant-garde set of individuals who attack the establishment. We at RSG became very interested in ways the artists could be active and recognized as both working members of the public and catalysts for change. So it was an intriguing notion to make a show of proposals that would in fact be counter-proposals, and that would go outside the familiar reference points to include people in architecture and planning.

IMO: At that time, too, artist spaces or art institutions were becoming contested spaces themselves. There was an alignment of issues outside of and within our own spaces. We became interested in the idea of building different definitions of public space or sites for the public. But then the public had to be redefined as well. So we also became interested in the many definitions of what the public could be.

PT: So when you consider those questions about defining the public —whether the public works, what is a public work, what is a working public—*Counter-Proposals* was a proposition for a construction of publics, not only for the construction of activities or objects. Some of the projects, like Treasure Smith's map of West Town social service agencies, grew up out of a recognition that institutions have different levels of visibility within the city. Within the social service arena, one truism is that people don't know how to get the services they need, so her map was a straightforward way to redress that. However, it was not all straightforward; in fact, even in the neighborhood in which she lived, she had to discover the information for herself and engage a number of different agencies many of whom knew of each other

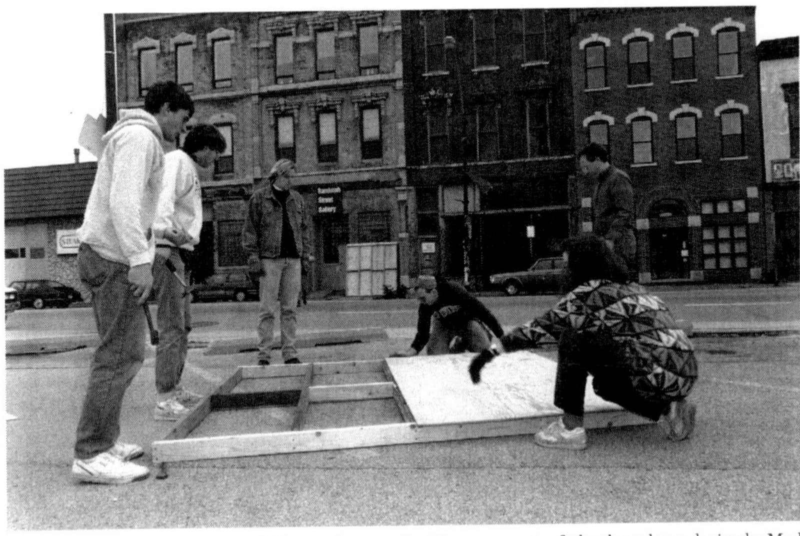

Outside Randolph Street Gallery, volunteers build components of a hut based on a design by Mad Housers of Atlanta, 1991. Courtesy of the Randolph Street Gallery Archives, John M. Flaxman Library, School of the Art Institute of Chicago. Photo: Bill Stamets.

but didn't necessarily work together. So while the map was shown in the exhibition, it ended up having a really useful life beyond the show because it was used in all of those agencies as a local directory.

IMO: The gallery was full of stuff ready to be deployed or activated, but in a way the space was empty. It set itself as a stage, a workshop, a platform, a meeting table, an assembly hall, right?

PT: Mad Housers' display probably changed the most dramatically. At the start of the exhibition, a pile of recycled building materials was on view and a set of questions about what could grow from those materials.

IMO: It set itself up that way. As the show unfolded, we had to respond to the needs of the participants, who eventually far outnumbered the original list of artists and architects. These participants became the owners of the projects, the activators, and made particular demands on us as a space and staff.

PT: Things like building workshops on Saturday afternoon during gallery hours were really different ways of using a gallery as a public meeting space. Another less physical but even more challenging issue was trying to recognize the role and responsibility of RSG in building alliances with other organizations like the Coalition for the Homeless. These relationships hadn't existed; before that we had never recognized that we could be a credible institutional partner. We always thought of ourselves as outside any of those trade routes, existing in a different environment. We didn't recognize the institutional potential to provide a framework or support structure to advance the work of artists in a broader sphere. At that time, we thought, "Oh, my god, can we actually do this? Can we be involved in conversations with the City of Chicago about the way homeless people are treated?" Iñigo, you were particularly involved in brokering such relationships.

IMO: Most of the work during the project was curating partnerships. All the conversations that happened outside of the gallery, in other communities, had to be real dialogues. It wasn't just showing an artwork that talked about something; we were actually in conversation with other institutions and individuals that had something at stake with the activity or the object being proposed.

With Mad Housers, it might have started simply by vacating some square footage in the gallery in order to build the parts that would eventually become a Mad House or a hut. But when we hosted the first planning meetings the participants, who would eventually become Mad Housers Chicago, quickly started to use RSG as their own home, not only during the exhibition but also afterwards. They set their own programming and their own agendas, as well as made their own invitations for others to participate. All of a sudden we were not the hosts. We started to feel intrusive sitting at their table, so we removed ourselves from the table and let them direct the conversation. That was actually a really exciting part.

PT: That's something that I saw you do with Street-Level Video for *Culture in Action*. You were so completely involved in the conception and development of that group, so it was interesting that you ultimately saw the possibility of stepping away and creating a path for yourself to continue doing your own work separate from Street-Level and, at the same time, for them to continue without you. I think that the notion of an artist or artist-activist creating something and being responsible to it, without controlling it, is really interesting.

IMO: This goes back to what you said about the multiple hats artists can wear. In this type of work, sometimes artists want to completely reconfigure themselves as—well, back then the term thrown around was "cultural workers." But there is a responsibility for the artist to protect the role of being an artist. One of the things being contested at that time was the necessity of artists in culture-at-large. So you had to protect yourself as an artist as well. I also remember having many conversations during *Culture in Action* about how important it was to these communities, outside of the museum world, to know there were artists within their street or neighborhood, whether they engaged in politics or activism or were secluded within their own studio. They were still an important aspect of the community. The community on my street in West Town would actually claim them. We all knew where the poet lived.

PT: I love what you're saying about claiming artists. The reason that it was possible to do some of these group projects and have new people come in through groups like Mad Housers was because the entire organization at Randolph Street Gallery was fueled by volunteer artists. The rotating flow of people with new energy and new ideas, wanting to use the platform of the organization, made it easier for us to accommodate working with artists who also saw the opportunity to use whatever momentum was developing around Mad Housers.

IMO: It was of the moment. When I wrote in *Art Papers* about *Counter-Proposals*, I quoted W.J.T. Mitchell's "The Violence of Public Art: Do The Right Thing" in *Critical Inquiry*. He talks about Tiananmen Square and questions the definitions of when something moves from a private into a public sphere. The trajectory of the times is important to know, because after *Counter-Proposals*, not only do you get *Culture in Action*, but we were also in the midst of the breakdown of NEA individual artists funding, which didn't end until 1995, and the LA insurrection after the Rodney King beating in 1992. So the issue of how institutions might engage larger communities and larger publics became a very important topic—one that institutions sometimes approached in a rather naïve fashion.

I think that although we weren't trying to set up a workbook on how to go about doing this, you can look at *Counter-Proposals* as an example of

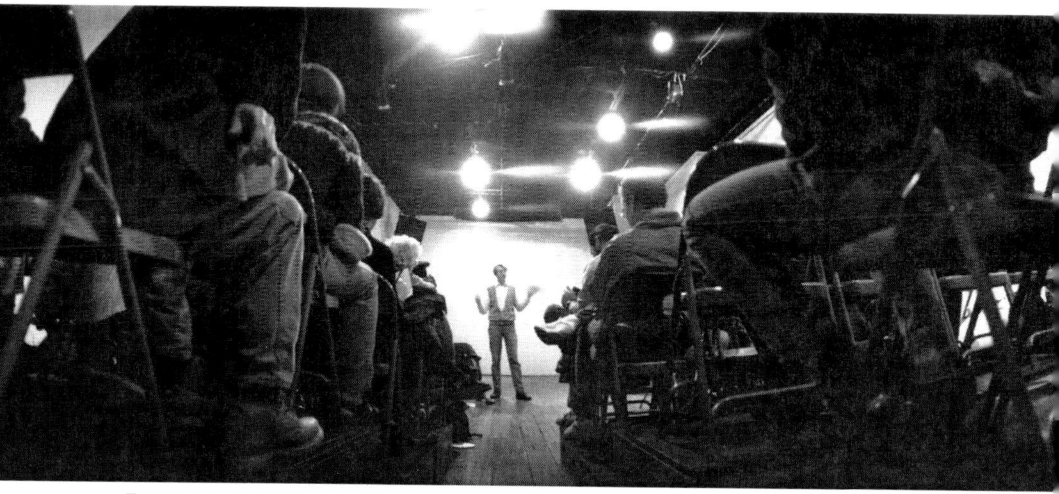

First meeting of Mad Housers of Chicago at Randolph Street Gallery, 1991. Courtesy of the Randolph Street Gallery Archives, John M. Flaxman Library, School of the Art Institute of Chicago. Photo: Bill Stamets.

where we were troubled by what was going on. Everything was a question. Everything was a proposal. This notion of engendering opportunities for engaged social production was a question in and of itself. We knew what opportunities were, but we were trying to figure out what engaged social production was and whether it could be real. So we questioned each other. And there was a sense of always trying to figure out who we were doing it for and whether the intentions were real. One of the ways to gauge it was to remove yourself as director or author to see if it had its own volition—and even that was a kind of experiment.

At the time I don't think other institutions could have done this, since there were a lot of problems with regard to zoning and liability and so forth. RSG was really invested in *Counter-Proposals* as proposals for transgressive action and was open to radicality as content. When those things come together, why not deploy seventeen or eighteen huts without any permission or permits? Artists can be ad hoc guerilla producers, right?

PT: With Mad Housers, we were also working in an arena where there were a lot of polarized positions. It was high stakes for the people involved in it. There was one point when people were using the huts, many for really practical reasons. They felt safer there. They had jobs but their work schedule didn't allow them to get to the shelters in time for the cutoff. But there was a point at which hut dwellers were removed and then the city came along and tore down the huts. That was confrontational. Housing commissioner David Alvarez said something along the lines of, "Well, the people who were using the huts are no longer there and therefore the huts aren't needed anymore, so we just wanted to take them away because we don't need extra stuff on the landscape."

There was a lot of conceptual and political posturing going on around this stuff. And there were public demonstrations where we tried to get Mad Housers to be part of larger debates around the homeless. This challenged RSG to consider, "Do we have the capacity, credibility, and knowledge to participate in this way?" I think what the organization did best was to be a catalyst. We can't claim ownership over this. There were other efforts that sprang up in other cities.

IMO: But don't you think that Chicago was uniquely suited for this? We might not have thought about it that way then, but we were in a city of plans. Chicago was and still is a place of prominent architectural schools. It has its own architectural history, its own history in urban planning, the legacy that is the Burnham Plan, as well as the rift of the Robert Taylor Homes. And like any big city, let's say, Atlanta where the Mad Housers sprang up, it was also undergoing gentrification. Those issues affected Chicago, not only the citizens of Chicago but also artists who were constantly having to relocate. Even RSG needed to consider relocation.

PT: It's true. Around that same time we were trying to purchase the building to create a stable platform for the organization, while trying to put a stake in the ground to say that alternative practice can be stable, essential, and recognized. But I don't know that that was distinct to Chicago.

IMO: I was thinking about how the issues are still around. It's a little disheartening to go back and think that after twenty years the juggernaut of development is still out there.

PT: One thing that's changed is that there are engaged publics. There's a recognition of creativity on all fronts in Chicago and it's known to be a strong center for DIY practice. So that's really different. I also feel that within the creative economy, there are more opportunities for like-minded people to cluster. Through social media and online communications, people can find communities of support more rapidly, more readily, more democratically. So I think now, there's potential for self-determination within perhaps narrower spheres. There are opportunities, at least, for self-definition.

IMO: I'm not sure people refer to *Counter-Proposals* in terms of how it might have affected current discussions around social practice. These terms pop up and seem to be the new flavors. I'm not opposed to artists, curators, and writers proposing new terms of engagement, but whenever you think you've invented a new form, be careful, because relational aesthetics was very much a part of something we did at RSG and social practice was, in a sense, the underpinning of *Counter-Proposals*.

As artists, we wanted to remain connected to historical practice. We wanted to be clear that whether it had occurred in Europe, New York, or LA, whether we were talking about Fluxus, Joseph Beuys, or Alan Kaprow's happenings, there is a historical lineage. The idea that a "new genre" could set up a way to look at contemporary practice separate from those previous histories is, I think, disempowering to an artist. If we claim these histories, then we have to consider the shifting role of the artist as well as the role of the art community.

Randolph Street was always questioning its space in that community, its history, its connections to alternative spaces of the late 1970s. Often we were bringing in artists who were untested in much more renowned spaces and giving them a chance to use us as a laboratory, because we recognized RSG was not just an exhibition space but a think tank. I think some artists who started in Chicago in the 1990s, such as Temporary Services, were affected by what we did. So I think there is a little bit of legacy. There certainly was with *Culture in Action,* although the critiques that came out afterward really didn't approach the artists' projects or even the project overall in a very complex way. We were always looking to see how we positioned ourselves, not only in Chicago, but nationally and internationally. *Counter-Proposals* was part of that, even if—or maybe even because—we were very invested at that moment with it being as local as possible.

This conversation occurred on April 10, 2014, in Chicago.

Remembering the *Culture in Action* Bus Tour

Lisa Corrin

I first heard about *Culture in Action* when I met Mary Jane Jacob at an event in Europe in early summer 1993. I remember not understanding what the title meant and, when she described the exhibition, it was something I could not conceive of because nothing like it had ever been done. It was clear that the vocabulary of large-scale extravaganzas like *Skulptur Projekte Münster* and the discourse of public art generally could not accommodate the concept as it was unfolding. I would definitely use the word "unfolding" because no matter how cogently she described it, these projects were in motion, and it was impossible at that point to be certain what the outcome would be. Only later, after I had experienced it, did I understand that what I saw was not really what *Culture in Action* was; it was a manifestation of many processes.

Each artist had worked with a community or a constituency and those constituencies were in most cases equal collaborators. It was in the dynamic between the artist and those collaborators that the word "art" began to take on some meaning, or the "art" in the piece began to be made concrete. While an outcome, like the paint chart of Kate Ericson and Mel Ziegler, was a public artwork, what led up to it was just as essential and just as much a part of it, though not necessarily visible. One of the exciting things to me was that I would never ever fully know the art. It locked me out because it was so much about a specific constituency and audience and those artists. Suddenly being in the art world didn't give you privileged access to the work at all. You could never fully know its meaning because you weren't part of the ongoing conversations that had occurred. You could never know from the inside the decisions that would have been held jointly by the public housing residents with Kate and Mel, or the confectionary union workers and Simon Grennan and Christopher Sperandio.

I did get to experience some of those public parts of the work, however, and have conversations with some of the participants on a bus tour that took groups of art world guests to visit the sites around the city where *Culture in Action* projects were occurring. Uncharacteristically for me, I was not very talkative, and I think that's because I was working very hard to internalize the whole range of experiences I was having, and to come to terms with what this new emerging form was. The only person, in fact, whom I have a clear memory of speaking to was Buddy Mayer [Beatrice Cummings Mayer], who sat next to me. There was a lot of sitting on the bus and going around the city, which took a very long time. But Buddy and I didn't talk directly about the works of art. Our conversation focused on the city of Chicago. It was at that moment that I think I understood that, while Chicago had a center or perceived center called the Loop, it was actually a city of many centers depending on who you were and where you had grown up. It's a cliché to call an urban place a "city of neighborhoods," but it's especially true of Chicago.

My experience of Chicago up until this point had been the typical art-world tourist. I went to the major institutions; I went to some of the outliers in Hyde Park; and then I knew a couple of the galleries. That was Chicago for me. What *Culture in Action* did was to make me a traveler. First, to experience this exhibition, you had to go very great distances and to places where tourists would never go, then have encounters with people you would never otherwise meet and look at art outside the kinds of sites where you're used to seeing it. Your vision of art was enlarged, but your vision of Chicago was enlarged, too. I don't recall conversations with art-world colleagues on the bus, but I do remember the outdoor installation of Iñigo Manglano-Ovalle's video piece, talking to the people in the neighborhood sitting on their folding chairs and meeting the kids who participated in the project. When I went to Lincoln Park to see the Mark Dion project, I was much more engaged with the teenagers than I was with the artist, who was actually a friend of mine. To access what was at stake in these works, you needed to engage with those who had engaged with the artist. In fact, the whole role of the artist was really displaced in a very significant way by the high pitch of the voices of the participants in the different neighborhoods. At a certain point it no longer mattered to me whether I had a language for talking about what I saw: it really became about conversations with people, about their lives, and what it meant to live in the places that they lived, and to have the lives they had, and to find common ground.

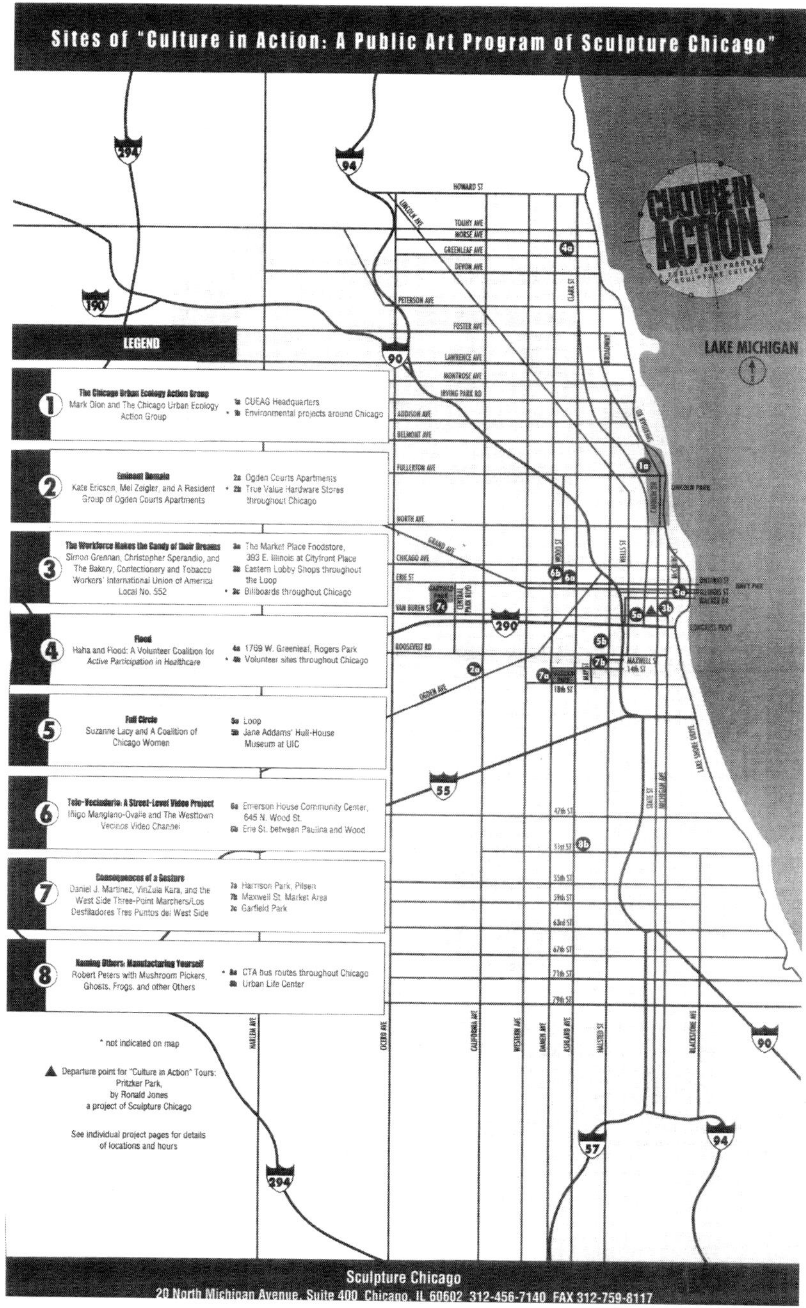

Map of *Culture in Action* sites around Chicago. Courtesy of Sculpture Chicago.

My experience with Haha was really profound. We had just gone through the worst of the AIDS crisis. The art world was hit hard and we had watched many friends die. I remember the smell of the room in the storefront location where Haha's hydroponic garden was installed because it was so alive. That's something about *Culture in Action* that often is passed over in the writing about the project —the multisensory experience of art merging with the smells and sounds of the city and how that became part of the work. Haha was producing vegetables for people who had AIDS—making their project literally a life-giving work of art. We tend to be a little uncomfortable in the art world with anything sentimental or maudlin. Haha's project was, without question, very direct. Yet because of the way in which it functioned on a day-to-day basis, it elided that boundary between art and everyday life making this aesthetic strategy tangible. You could see the transformative capacity of what they were doing in that particular community, a community that had been shunned by many. Here was a work of art that was not just touching but feeding and becoming one with the body politic and the physical bodies of that community. It was extremely poignant.

I remember hearing some of the residents of the public housing community who worked with Ericson and Ziegler talking about their experience, and how they came to name the colors on the color chart and the histories that they had dug up. I was astounded at the level of sophistication of the conversations about the history of public housing in Chicago that had taken place. Later on, knowing that I was going to move here, my experience catalyzed an interest in reading about that history which is now, of course, completely erased in parts of the city that have been gentrified. Their artwork has become more meaningful as time goes on because it's a vestige of the voices of the people who lived there and were forcibly displaced.

While *Culture in Action* was primarily for the people of Chicago and for the collaborators in specific neighborhoods, one of the other things that happened, art historically speaking, was that this was a museum-scale exhibition undertaking but held in the realm of public art, where languages around the public sphere and sculpture came together. In that way, I think, *Culture in Action* was building on a conversation that had been developing since *Chambres des Amis* in Ghent, Belgium. But it added a very important missing dimension. It made me realize that some of the strategies being used within *Culture in Action* by the artists could have a place within more traditional institutions, if they were willing. It has as much to do with the ways museums think about their relationships to audience and community as it does with the way they think about public art and sculpture. *Culture in Action* was part of an evolving and important discourse taking place at that moment but it remains part of a much bigger, ongoing conversation that continues to be relevant and urgent.

Reconsidering *3 Acres on the Lake: DuSable Proposal Project*

A. Laurie Palmer

But the fact of the matter is that the world needs improving (re-improving) every day. Just as one can't prepare an all purpose meal and dine once and be done with (it), so... victories are particular, local, and almost always temporary.
— Lyn Hejinian, *The Language of Inquiry*

In 2000, the Chicago Park District announced plans to turn a three-acre piece of prime lakefront land that had been dedicated to become a memorial park into a parking lot. At that time, wildflowers, tall grasses, and a ring of trees grew opportunistically on this little spit, extending out under Lake Shore Drive. Fourteen years later, neither the park nor the income-generating parking lot have been built, though the land has been disturbed, the trees and wildflowers are gone, and what's left is mostly bare dirt. Rumors that a park may finally be built are tied to the prospects of whether Santiago Calatrava's dramatic Chicago Spire, a 2000-foot-tall, 150-story luxury condo tower meant to be the tallest building in the western hemisphere, will go up on the other side of Lake Shore Drive. The Spire was abandoned in 2008 when the project went into foreclosure, leaving only the magnificent abyss that is its foundation hole. With the upturn in the stock market in 2013 (due to an economic recovery benefiting investors but neglecting everyone else), the Spire developer has rekindled his plans for the second tallest building in the world and for the park, which the city gave to him in exchange for developing it as part of Calatrava's overall design.

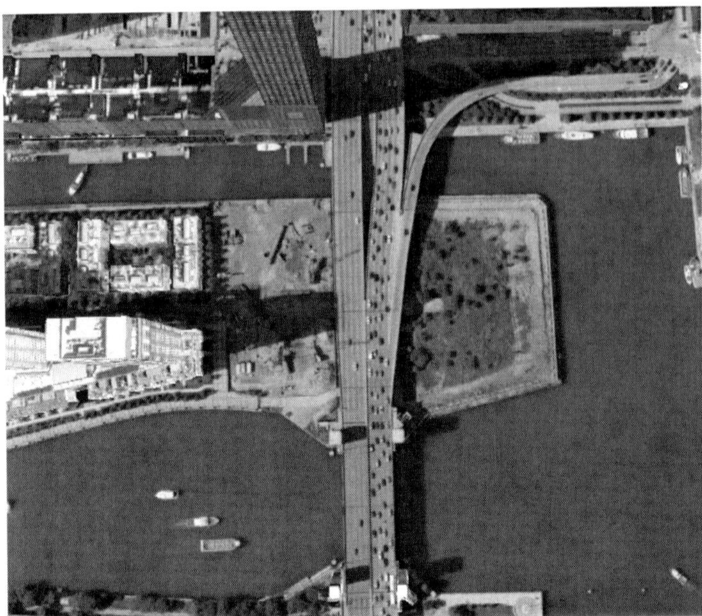

Aerial view of DuSable Park. Map courtesy of Google Earth.

In the intervening years, at least sixty-five other parks have virtually occupied this tiny piece of land, projected onto it by participants in an art project that called for public participation in city planning processes, and for accountability by the city to its promises to the black community in particular. In the 1980s, this land had been dedicated as a memorial park by Mayor Harold Washington to commemorate Chicago's first permanent non-native American settler and first African American settler, Jean Baptiste Pointe DuSable. The fact that the park had not yet been developed, and the insulting possibility that it might have been forgotten by the city when plans to pave it over for paid parking were announced, so incensed some city residents that a coalition was formed in 2000 to advocate for, and insist on, the development of the park. I joined this coalition at the time because, coincidentally, my attention as an artist had been drawn to the park precisely because of its romantic, overgrown, and seemingly abandoned state.

The *3 Acres on the Lake: DuSable Park Proposal Project* was developed in response to the claustrophobic climate of increasingly privatized urban space and the dwindling of habitats and haunts for opportunistic plants and curious persons. It was also a response to the suspiciously delayed materialization of the promised memorial, which seemed tied to the discriminatory and devastating effects of city policies favoring high-income development. The project invited, without sanction or authority, speculative proposals for how this small plot of public land in Chicago might be used (with the dedication to DuSable maintained front and center). There was no jury, no winner, and no prize. It was an invitation to irony, fantasy, and utopian imaginings, but also an attempt to pry open city planning processes for public scrutiny and participation.

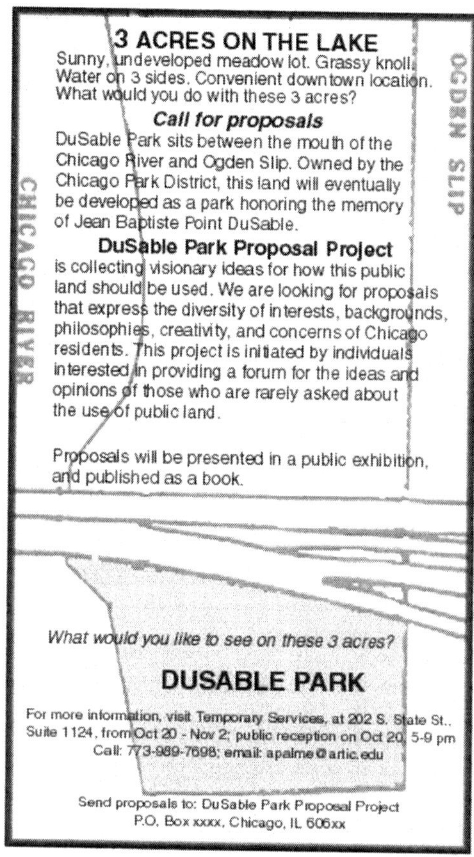

The DuSable Park Proposal Project's call for proposals.
Courtesy of A. Laurie Palmer. Design: A. Laurie Palmer.

The speculative/imaginary art project and the actual/political coalition work exerted considerable influence on each other. The initial coalition included the Chicago DuSable League, an organization of African American women on the South Side who had been working towards official recognition of DuSable for more than seventy years; Friends of the Parks, a park district watchdog/advocacy group; the Haitian Physicians of America

(DuSable was part Haitian); Friends of the Chicago River, a non-profit environmental organization; a few individuals like myself; and a neighborhood organization representing property owners who lived near the park (an area which hosts the most expensive real estate in the city). Eventually we became The Friends of DuSable Coalition. None of us wanted exactly the same thing, but we shared suspicion that the promised park and its memorial status would evaporate if we didn't act. The awkwardness of this coalition was a version of "public" that I was also interested in exploring with the art project: one that included multiple and conflicting claims.

The Chicago Park District had been sued by the federal government in 1983 for "benign neglect" of communities of color. The dedication of this park in 1988 was clearly an attempt to reach out to the African American community, but also fraught with contradictions since the park is located in an extremely wealthy, and increasingly white, neighborhood. In spite of what I assume was an intention at the time of dedication—that this memorial park might symbolically address, and even somehow, if minutely, assuage, the histories of racial division that continue to split Chicago—there was neither public input nor an open call regarding its commission. Instead, a monument was initially commissioned directly from the well-respected African American sculptor, Martin Puryear, through the Art Institute of Chicago's Ferguson Fund. If a monument is going to effectively gather and symbolize some aspect of a plural public's emotional reservoir, it has to come from a plural public process. While the DuSable League, for instance, did not like Puryear's proposed monument, my argument was not with who they

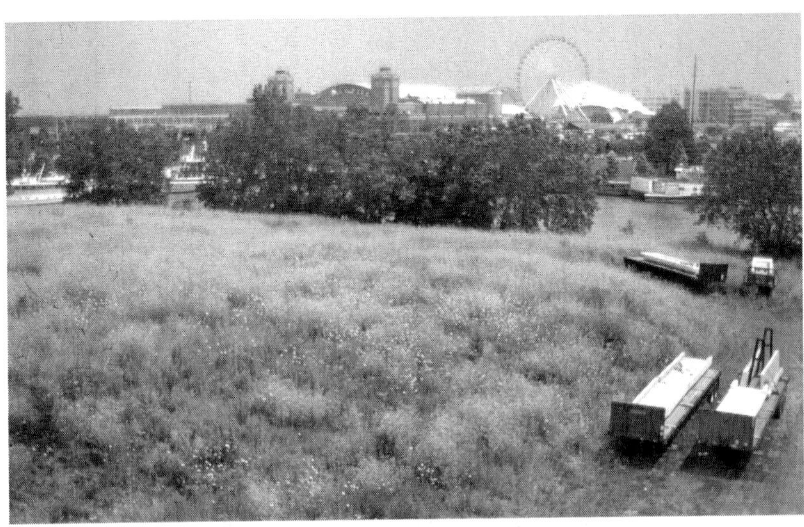

DuSable Park, 2001. Courtesy of A. Laurie Palmer.

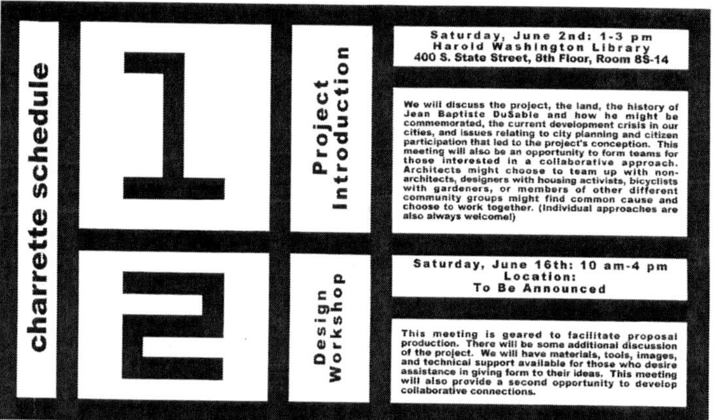

Brochures publicizing the DuSable Park Proposal Project's charrettes. Courtesy of A. Laurie Palmer. Design: Andres and Yamani Hernandez.

chose, but how. A more open process might acknowledge, if not remedy, long-term experiences of racial division and exclusion and also address problems with some of the city's existing public monuments (which includes a bronze plaque marking the spot where Chicago's "first white child" was born).

An exhibition at Temporary Services's space in October 2000 introduced the *3 Acres* project. By August 2001, sixty-five proposals had been submitted, approximately 60 percent from the Chicago area, the rest from cities across the U.S. and abroad, including Lima, Guadalajara, London, Paris, Berlin, and Victoria, Australia. The first exhibition opened on September 14, 2001. Despite the date, there was a lot of press, many public presentations followed, the Chicago Architecture Foundation mounted a second exhibition a year later, and the alderman of the ward where the park was located sent a personal letter committing, again, to following through with the memorial park's development.

To my delight, the members of the coalition, including members of the DuSable League, had no problem with the outrageousness of some of the submissions (including a lesbian retirement home in the form of a large bathtub). They understood that you don't need to police the imagination in order to leverage its energy toward a shared political project. The proposals took many forms, including hi-tech digital images, an oil painting, a hand-built sculptural ship, an interactive website, text spelled in trash, notes written in longhand on a legal pad, a paper cut-out model, watercolor drawings, audiotaped bird sounds, and an audio/visual interview. Contributions ranged in attitude from earnest to ironic to critical; some were historical or playful and a few supremely egomaniacal. Several proposals attempted to reconcile or even dampen conflict—to create spaces for everyone—although unseating the assumption of everyone was a fundamental reason to do the project, as someone is always excluded by that term. The point was to accept and to show them all.

One proposal, by Esther Parada, celebrated all the women, past and present, of the DuSable League itself. The league was founded in 1928 and at its height had about forty active members, though by 2000, it was down to six, most of whom were in their eighties. Parada had made another project in 1992 (*Who Dis/covers, Who Dis/Colors*) highlighting the league's campaign to erect a replica of DuSable's cabin during the 1933–1934 Chicago World's Fair. It showed letters documenting the league's polite but insistent demands met with faintly veiled racist rebuffs by the fair committee. The cabin replica was finally erected for the fair, due to the persistence of the league women. Though this was an important victory, a permanent public monument to DuSable — their primary goal — has yet to be constructed.

While *3 Acres* began in curiosity about an anomalous place and ended with two exhibitions, a website, and a book[1], the story of the park continues to unfold in an intricate tale relevant to many urban spaces, punctuated by contradictions and conflicts involving public and private interests, toxic residues, repressed histories, racism, and real estate development. The land's extended state of limbo is not a function of lack of interest, but precisely the opposite—the civic promise of a memorial park conflicts with economic interests. *3 Acres on the Lake* experimented with how art might play a role in generating and leveraging public participation to counter the hegemony of high finance over historical memory and public process, and for an extended moment we won: we occupied the park.

---

1 Laurie Palmer, *3 Acres on the Lake: DuSable Park Proposal Project,* (Chicago: White Walls, 2005).

Revisiting *Enemy Kitchen*

Greg Broseus, Aaron Hughes, Michael Rakowitz, Maikl Shaer, and Milad Shaer in conversation

Michael Rakowitz: I began *Enemy Kitchen* back in 2003 as a series of workshops exploring the effects of the Iraq war. For the project I worked with my mother to compile Baghdadi recipes and share our culinary heritage with different public audiences. My mother had pointed out that there were no Iraqi restaurants in New York City, and I began to consider ways to counter the CNN broadcasts of green-tinted, night-vision images of the violence in Iraq and to create an act of resistance that would humanize Iraqis. I thought that preparing food and eating together might open up new contexts in which participants could discuss the topic of war and draw parallels with their own lives. *Enemy Kitchen (Food Truck)* evolved from this initial iteration for the *Feast* exhibition at the University of Chicago's Smart Museum. For the run of the show, the food truck would travel around Chicago serving a rotating menu of regional Iraqi dishes prepared by chefs from the city's Iraqi community, with American veterans of the Iraq War acting as servers and sous-chefs. The truck later developed into a nightclub opened up by Milad and Mikey. It was a wonderful extension of the food truck and can maybe help us think about the sustainability of projects such as this. I am thrilled to be here today with you all to reflect on our various experiences collaborating on *Enemy Kitchen*.

Aaron Hughes: I became involved with *Enemy Kitchen (Food Truck)* when Michael held an *Enemy Kitchen* session at the Experimental Station. Personally, I was drawn to re-engaging with Iraqi culture, because my deployment experience was always about distancing myself from the Iraqi community. For me, it was so moving, and I felt other veterans could find it

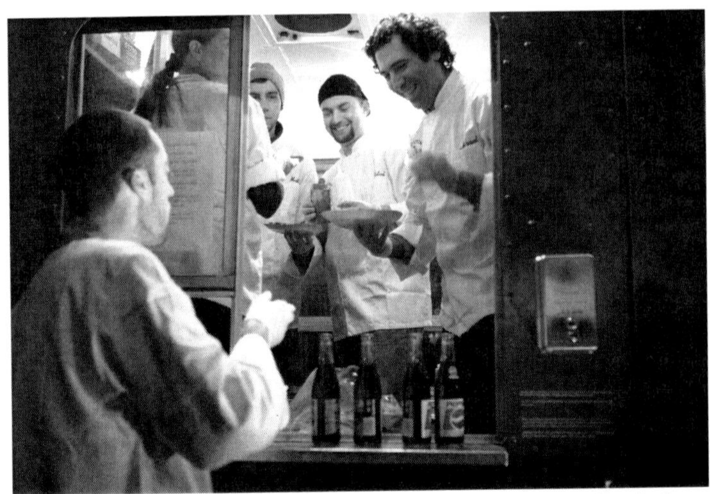

Michael Rakowitz serving food as part of *Enemy Kitchen (Food Truck)* at the Smart Museum of Art, February 15, 2012. Courtesy of the artist and Smart Museum of Art. Photo: Jeremy Lawson.

transformative. Then in 2009, at the National VeteransArt Museum here in Chicago, Michael taught a group of Iraq and Vietnam veterans how to make an Iraqi barbecue. I was so thrilled about the whole thing; there were a lot of beautiful, quirky moments.

MR: I think it's important to mention that Aaron invited me to bring *Enemy Kitchen* to the veterans' museum. The event also took place on Memorial Day.

AH: For me, just watching these old Vietnam vets running the grill—but with these little kebabs—was such a mind shift from their traditional Memorial Day barbecue, at the same time it *was* their traditional Memorial Day barbecue. It was a great moment of interaction. Michael, when you told me you were expanding the project by making a food truck with veterans serving Iraqi cuisine [as a commission for the exhibition *Feast: Radical Hospitality in Contemporary Art* at the University of Chicago's Smart Museum], it sounded like such a powerful gesture, and I just went into organizing mode. I wanted to get other people involved who could be inspired by this project. So we had a dinner at my house and that really cemented things. Michael is one of the most amazing hosts and makes people feel really good about their involvement in a project. I felt like that my contribution to this work was to make connections, so I introduced Michael to Ash Khyrie, Alejandro Villatorro, Greg Broseus, and Crystal Colon. But there was a veteran who had a hard time joining the project because of the amount of psychological distrust of Iraqis that built up during his deployment. Yet, I feel like that's what this project is starting to expose and unravel. I think it's a healing and transformative way to confront those exact feelings. It's a space for people to find their relationship to these internal and external conflicts and human connections.

Greg Broseus: The first time that I heard about the project was through you, Aaron. I said, "Hell, yeah, I want to be involved," but it wasn't until after doing *Enemy Kitchen (Food Truck)* that I realized why I had that immediate response. In Iraq, before we started doing our route clearance missions, we got assigned to escort local Iraqis onto the base who were there to provide some service. I did that for four or five days before I started doing actual missions. I escorted this same guy onto the base for three days in a row. Every day he'd say, "Hey, you should come to my house and have fruit and we'll drink tea," and every single time I had to tell him, "I would love to go sit and have fruit and tea with you, but I can't. They won't let me. It's not safe." I think he understood that just fine, but it still didn't stop him from inviting me each day. I think subconsciously that was playing in my mind when I was invited to come and work on this project: the idea of sitting down with Iraqis, making and serving and eating food together. It brought me full circle back to one of my first days in Iraq.

I enjoyed the experience. I loved working with Mikey and Milad on the truck. It was interesting watching the range of reactions. I didn't take any hostility personally; I didn't really give much thought about it. But it was interesting to watch people who really understood what was going on, especially those who would make the connection that the Chicago flag had Iraqi colors, seeing the ways the two cultures were being brought together. Of course some other people were just blinded by the word "Iraq," and that's where the hostility came from because they couldn't see beyond their own preconceived ideas of who an Iraqi is. Then there were those who were skeptical; they stood back wondering what was going on. They'd ask what's happening and I would explain that it was an art project. Then they would start to put two and two together and you could just see them warm up to it.

MR: Aaron and I did a scouting mission together when I was looking for other partners for the project. Milo's Pita Place was the last Iraqi restaurant we tried, and it was perfect. Milad and Mikey proved to be great partners, not just because of the amazing food but because they were ready to collaborate. You were totally into it—you got it, and saw it as something that could grow.

Maikl (Mikey) Shaer: I think the meaning of the food truck was very powerful—that's why I was interested when you and Aaron came in. I told my brother and we got very excited about the project. Later, we started talking about it on Facebook and posted some pictures. Once they found out about the project some of our good friends were concerned. They said, "But you are not Iraqi, you're Assyrian and Christian. You're representing yourself as Iraqi Muslim."

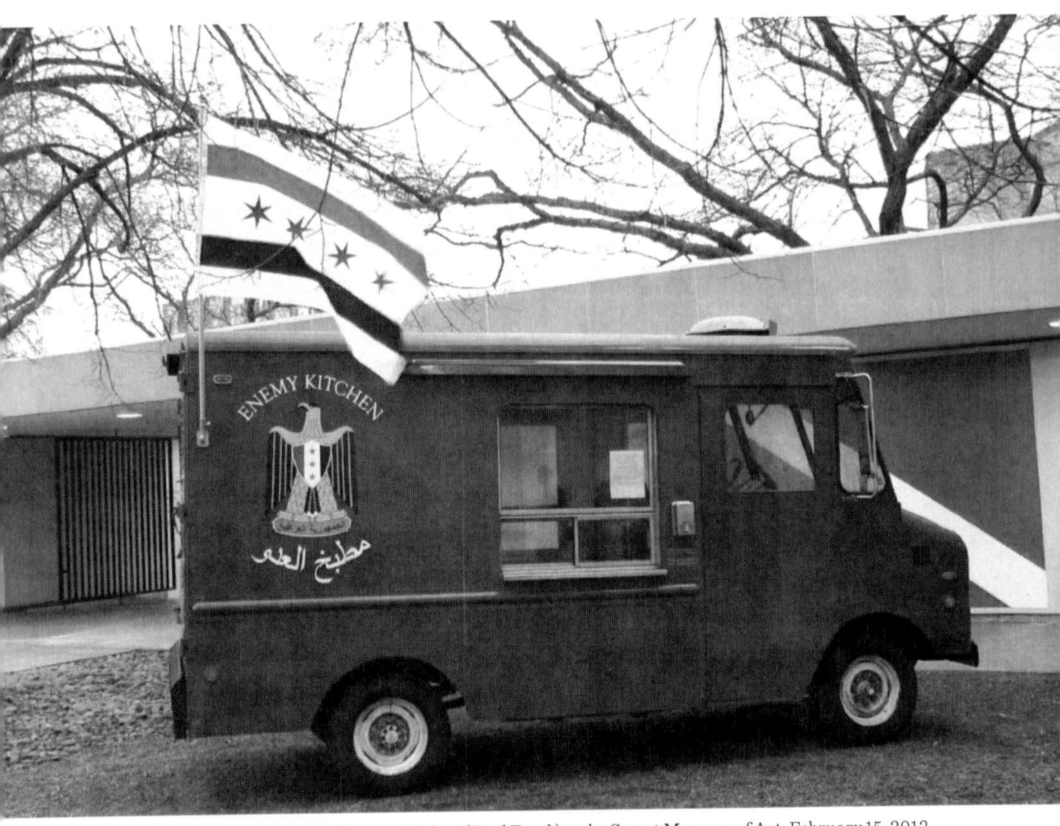

Enemy Kitchen (Food Truck) at the Smart Museum of Art, February 15, 2012.
Courtesy of the artist and Smart Museum of Art.

Milad Shaer: If you don't specify that you're Assyrian from Iraq or that you're Jewish from Iraq, "Iraqi" to most of the world means you're Muslim, so some people misread that side of the project. But it didn't bother us. It didn't back us off. And, honestly, I was more interested every day. Every day we would experience new things.

MR: At Milo's you call your food "Mediterranean cuisine." We know that Iraq doesn't have a border on the Mediterranean. But there seems to be a need to conceal origins that has always been a part of the immigrant story in the US, because of the xenophobic relationship to strangers. So even members of the Assyrian community sometimes distance themselves from Arabs. In a way the project galvanized your own identity, but you also faced antagonism. The truck was vandalized. That was a bit of a surprise because the majority of reactions were generative, transformative, and healing. Still there were these marks of hate. But if you build a chimney you're going to have a fire. If you have a truck called *Enemy Kitchen,* you're asking a question.

Milad: I think it got everybody's attention, as we were driving or parked. Necks were turning: whoa, what is that? Some people thought it was an army truck.

MR: I have to say that the green of the truck wasn't about being military green. It was the color of my grandfather's company, Davison's & Co., in Baghdad, and it's been following me my whole life; I've used it in several projects.

Milad: It was hard for people to understand, but after understanding it, they wouldn't be so mad. We saw people get upset seeing the truck parked; we'd get called names, flipped off, honked at … you name it. In the beginning we would get upset as well—like, what's wrong with you guys?

MR: There was that moment with the Iraqi cab driver who jumped out of his cab saying, "Why? Why 'Enemy Kitchen' with my flag? Iraq was never the enemy." That was great—and then we sent him along with a box of food.

Mikey: The sign on the truck, the writing, and the flag—people didn't understand what this was. Even when we parked the truck on our own property at home, neighbors or other business people would tell us it was wrong. We didn't see it that way because we were trying to make a point. But they didn't want to listen; they just judged us, thinking it was a threat, even though food was involved. Food should always make peace. That's what I believe.

Milad: Some of those people had families who had fought in the Iraq War. I don't know exactly what happened to them, but a lot of them were saying, "Shame on you guys. This shouldn't be happening," then they'd just walk away. They wouldn't give us a chance to explain the project. The Arabic writing kept some people away, but the Chicago flag in Iraqi colors brought people in. They'd see an Iraqi logo, Saddam's main logo. People who wanted to understand usually gave us a chance to talk and explain.

One night when the truck was parked, someone broke the windshield and popped the tires. It was definitely prompted by the Saddam emblem, because a lot of people in this community came from Iraq as refugees. Many worked for the American government and had been threatened. So I guess seeing a symbol like that just brought out the anger in them. Once again, it comes back to the point that some people never took the time to realize what the project was. But I think if we take the truck out again in the future, it could definitely change a lot of minds, because of what you can bring out with the food.

MR: To be clear, the darker aspect of the project was intentional. Also it's not actually Saddam's emblem. That emblem existed well before; then he only personalized it when he wrote *Allahu Akbar* between the three green stars, which symbolize Pan-Arabism. So again, symbols end up being fueled by misunderstandings and xenophobia. These responses are shaped by the fact that Iraq continues to be perceived by many non-Iraqis as this dangerous entity. By calling the project *Enemy Kitchen*, there was an intentional antagonism that was mixed with the hospitality of serving food and being a host. The name was crucial. If we called it "Iraqi Kitchen," it wouldn't have done the same thing.

GB: That reminds me of a great moment of connection that I experienced years after a misunderstanding. Saba was one of the refugees from the Iraqi Mutual Aid Society who worked with us on the food truck. One of the things that I do whenever I meet people who have recently come from Iraq, and who were probably there the same time that was, is ask them where they were. She told me that she lived in Baghdad, and I asked what area; she said an area that I'd never heard of. The only way that I know Baghdad is through US routes, like Route Michigan or Route Tampa. So I looked up Baghdad on Google on my phone and zoomed in, and it so happened that her neighborhood was right along the route that we would constantly patrol with four Humvees and a really big vehicle with a robotic arm. She was there in 2005 when I was there, and she says, "Yeah! I remember you guys. I got stuck behind you one day when I was trying to get to work while this soldier was playing music and dancing on top of a truck with his machine gun just dancing. I was like, 'What the hell are you dancing about? What is so great that you're up there dancing?'" It turned out that that was me. But we had a good laugh about it at Milo's Pita Place.

AH: Michael, you suggested that the *Tea* project should be a part of the truck and that was a really generous of you. And so I did a tea performance on the anniversary of the invasion of Iraq at the *Enemy Kitchen* truck.

Tea is about creating a space to dive into cultural barriers, because tea is one of those things that brings us together; it transcends national, cultural, political, religious boundaries. It's also an opportunity for me to host, share stories, and listen to others stories. The project stems from a moment when I went back to Iraq in 2009 as a civilian to attend a labor conference. I was asked to give a short talk about the US peace movement. During the talk I took responsibility for contributing to the destruction of Iraq and spoke about the organization Iraq Veterans Against the War. Afterword, this gentleman stands up in the back of the auditorium, yelling something in Arabic (and I don't know any Arabic), and starts walking up toward the stage, shaking his hand. I thought he was coming up to punch me in the face. But then the translation comes through: "I just want to come on stage and give this gentleman a hug." He grabs me and I cry. He was in the Iraqi military during the invasion; I got to Kuwait in April, a month after the invasion, and my first mission into Iraq was in May. So literally, we were indirectly trying to kill each other, and he's hugging me. For me, that's generosity and humanity, when people see through the systems of violence we live in, and that's what I've been trying to share through these *Tea* performances. When oppression and violence are still happening, this kind of liberal notion that we can have reconciliation

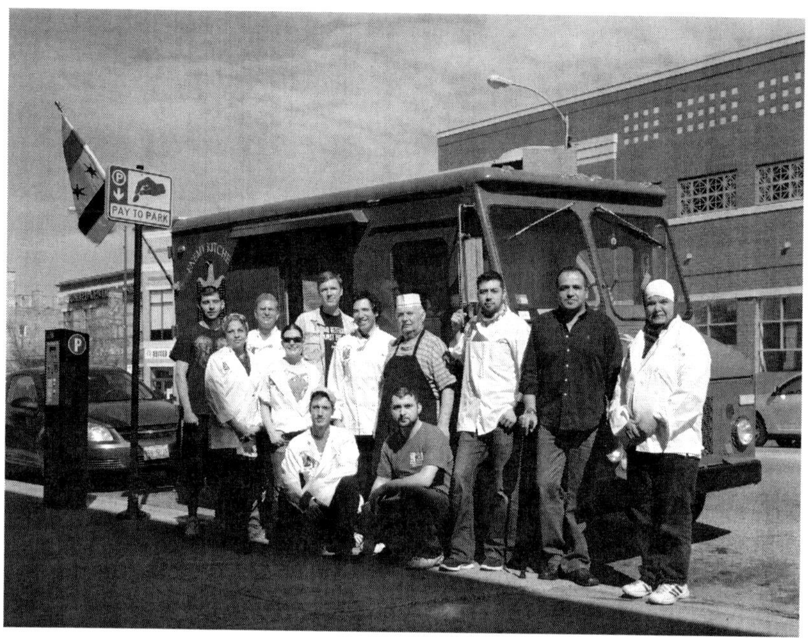

Enemy Kitchen (Food Truck) project team, Chicago, 2012. Courtesy of the artist and Smart Museum of Art. Photo: Greg Broseus

and everyone is going to be okay, is actually not okay. I still hold that guilt as a service member; the Iraqis still live in a destroyed, and now war torn country, and that's what *Tea* is about—all the generosity provided me by the Iraqi community, by citizens of countries that we see as our enemies.

The chance to share *Tea* with a people who had just participated in an anti-war march on the anniversary of the invasion was perfect. We did it at sunset, which was just like every night in Iraq when we would pull these massive convoys into motor pools, and the third-country nationals would pull out a rugs, make tea, and always offer it to everybody in my unit or platoon that was on the mission; we'd all refuse. That refusal of generosity is not okay. Despite that refusal, the generosity continues, and I'm just slowly learning how to accept it. I hope that through the process of hosting tea other people are learning how to accept that as well. For me it was an honor and a blessing to hold *Tea* as part of *Enemy Kitchen*. I don't know if I would have done it if it weren't for Michael's invitation and all the support from Milo's and everyone from the Iraqi Mutual Aid Society.

You know Paulo Freire has this great quote that is something like: Oppressors can never liberate the oppressed. Only the oppressed have the power to liberate themselves and their oppressor. I fundamentally believe that. I've experienced that liberation, and I feel like that's what *Enemy Kitchen* is—all of a sudden, folks who were literally the oppressors are now in the role of serving. I think the connections go beyond any specific story. They are about that fundamental relationship to our humanity.

Mikey: I want to say thank you. We were focused and hungry for the project and for life in general. This project changed us to be better in life.

Milad: I feel the same way and I want to say thank you to Michael and to the Smart Museum. I walk with my head high. The project opened our eyes and gave us a lot of amazing experiences. We met many great people and became a part of art. Now they call me an artist.

MR: A perfect way to end.

This coversation occurred on February 16, 2014 in Chicago.

Political People: Notes on Arte de Conducta

Carrie Lambert-Beatty

Dissent Dissent

"I'm a political artist, so I decided that I was going to give my space to people I admire as political people." So said Tania Bruguera from the back of a crowded Chicago lecture hall, as part of the brief speech with which she turned the attention of some two hundred audience members over to Bill Ayers and Bernardine Dohrn on May 1, 2009 and shifted our expectations: from radical art performance to radical political discourse.

It was just months after Barack Obama's acquaintance with 1960s radicals Ayers and Dohrn (now an eminent education professor and the director of a center for juvenile justice, respectively) had been churned into pseudo-scandal by his opponents in the US presidential election. So the couple had more than a little celebrity status among the left-leaning art crowd gathered for Bruguera's presentation, which was held at a commercial art fair but organized as part of the experimental art history conference *Our Literal Speed*.[1] This star power compensated for the disappointment some of us felt at Bruguera's own abdication of the stage. We craned our necks to see the faces of the former leaders of the Weather Underground. We chuckled at their self-deprecating jokes about their age and welcomed their message that artists had a political role to play breaking "out of that controlling frame that limits the horizon of our imaginations." Everyone seemed to nod appreciatively when Ayers contrasted two different memories of

Chicago's Grant Park: the first when he was beaten by police during the Days of Rage around the 1968 Democratic Political Convention; the second on election night forty years later, when he stood together with nearly a million other onlookers to hear the country's first black president acknowledge his victory.

Everyone, that is, except a young man, perhaps in his early twenties, sitting a few rows from the back. Not long into the presentation, as Dohrn was taking a look back at the Haymarket uprisings in Chicago in 1886, he interrupted, loudly. "Isn't that all still going on, though?"

"That's what's interesting," replied Dohrn, who had been noting the recurrence in the contemporary immigrants' rights movement of issues that had rallied Americans a century earlier. "But then I don't know where the change is," the young man insisted, referring back to Ayers's two Grant Park scenarios. The couple continued with an inspiring, if somewhat practiced, series of comments about the challenges facing the left early in the Obama administration—"Obama's not going to save us, but with any luck, we can save Obama"—but the heckling continued. Ayers and Dohrn responded like the generous and experienced teachers that they are. But their equanimity and his aggression competed for control of the room. Artist and activist Gregg Bordowitz urged the heckler to "cool out a bit" and remember an adage of the left: "When the enemy's not in the room, we practice on each other." Others, however, jumped in to press Dohrn and Ayers about the kind of change they wanted to see. ("Are you in la-la land?" one questioner asked, exasperated by their argument for prison abolition.) For nearly an hour, the discussion shifted in this way. Congressional budgeting of the war in Iraq. Earnest entreaties about artists' role in society. The prison-industrial complex. And plainly generational squabbling. In one exchange, the young man reminded the couple that they, too, had once been rash and extreme, to which Dohrn responded with a mixture of bemusement and indignation. "We never sounded like you, baby . . . we were way off the deep end, but we never sounded like you."

Everyone in the audience responded differently to what happened in the wake of Bruguera's decision to give over her spot to Ayers and Dohrn, of course. But I suspect many felt, as I did, simultaneously annoyed by and grateful to the unnecessarily argumentative members of the audience. For as distracting and sometimes illogical as they were, they had thoroughly invigorated the conversation. It felt like something real was happening. Ayers and Dohrn seemed to acknowledge as much in the smiles they flashed one another, and an occasional whispered aside—"this is great"—audible over the microphone when the cross-talk in the audience grew particularly impassioned. Dissent had erupted in a conversation about dissent.

Or had it?

Some may have suspected it right away. I didn't, but somehow by the second day of the conference I knew (strangely, I can't remember exactly how I found out) that four of the most strident interlocutors of Dohrn and Ayers the day before had been planted by Bruguera (she didn't tell them what to say, only to interrupt when they disagreed with the speakers). This simple revelation raised a number of questions. What does it mean that the most interesting leftist political conversation I've been in on in a while was partially staged—its most convention-rupturing moments actually ordained from behind the scenes? Was it necessarily less "real" because it was prodded into being? Was the conversation less democratic, because controlled? Or more so, because dissent is closer to democratic process than is peaceful preaching to the choir? Had we in the audience been lab rats, used in a political experiment? As some audience members complained later, there is a basic affront to dignity in being deceived. As a gesture, moreover, planting combative interlocutors in a political discussion has unpleasant connotations. It recalls the history of infiltration of leftist groups, including Dohrn and Ayers's own, by FBI counterintelligence agents charged with producing discord. And it almost eerily anticipates the wave of falsely spontaneous disruptions of public meetings that American conservatives would use as a tactic later in 2009 to try to block reform of the US healthcare system.

Bruguera calls experiments like this Arte de Conducta. This art of behavior is aimed at "not representing the political but provoking the political," and the Chicago example (titled *Generic Capitalism*) is among the most benign. Other works from the last ten years include bomb-making in an art gallery, a school for critical political performance in a communist state, the supervision of art viewers by security officers and guard dogs, even a very literal game of Russian roulette. In a period in which free meals and bean-bag lounges, cafés, and rural retreats have been mobilized as art and interpreted in terms of a kind of politics of conviviality, Bruguera is driven to explore forms of oppression, force, and regulation—and often mimetically to inflict versions of them, herself. What is this artist up to?

It would be argumentative, unnecessarily argumentative, to propose that what she is up to is a self-reflexive commentary on art itself.

Arte de Conducta

Bruguera came to international attention in the mid-1990s with a decidedly theatrical form of performance. Hers was a politically inflected body art featuring resonant materials like hair, a butchered lamb carcass, soil, and her own naked body. Joseph Beuys's photogenic actions seem a relevant precedent for these works, or the dramatic tableaux of Marina

Abramović. She was also influenced by the Cuban American artist Ana Mendieta (whose oeuvre Bruguera systematically reenacted in and for Mendieta's native Cuba, early in her own career), and there are faint echoes of Mendieta's evocative imprints of a female form in natural settings, connected to Afro-Cuban religious rites. But in 1973, before the *siluetas*, Mendieta had explored the corporeal trace in a very different way. Leaving a pool of blood on a city sidewalk, she sat back to photograph the reactions —or more disturbingly, non-reactions—of passers-by to the gory puddle. And it is this piece that Bruguera cites as the precedent for Arte de Conducta, the kind of work she has been doing since around 2000.

Bruguera's category of Arte de Conducta overlaps with various versions of performance-in-the-world that artists have explored since at least the 1960s, in attempts to subtract the theatrically from "performance" and overcome its dichotomy of active performer/passive audience, while retaining the duration, unpredictability, and immateriality of art as action. The later "social sculpture" works of Beuys are an example, and Beuys was frequently referenced in Bruguera's Cuban art education. But I find it helpful to look to the American artist Allan Kaprow to understand the evolution of non-theatrical performance. He is best known for coining the word "happening," and for the complex and largely theatrical art events the term designated in the early 1960s. But, frustrated by the ease with which the happenings were recuperated as artworld spectacles (Bruguera, too, found her more theatrical early performances "immediately accepted" and "too easy"[2]), Kaprow spent much of his career thereafter articulating alternatives, using terms like "events," "non-theatrical performance," "unart," "lifelike art," and "research" for a practice that sometimes looked like strange sociology experiments—a man and a woman repeatedly passing through a doorway, trying every combination of holding and not holding the door for one another—and sometimes like meditation—wetting a stone and carrying it until it dried. Indeed, behavioral experimentation and meditative practice might be the two structural poles of the category of non-theatrical performance. On one end, an interest in mindfulness, a commitment to experience and attentiveness for their own sakes (sometimes, as for Kaprow, connected with Zen or other meditative disciplines). And, on the other, practices that take their cue from the scientific study of human behavior.

More directed to public than private experience, based in outward rather than inward attentiveness, and more critical than ameliorative, Bruguera's recent work leans towards the latter pole, as the term Arte de Conducta—"Behavior Art"—suggest. The techniques of Arte de Conducta often evoke social psychology investigations like Stanley Milgram's experiments of 1961. Like Mendieta's *People Looking at Blood* (or in a more benign register, like the audience in Chicago), these experiments involved participants who did not have all the facts about their participation. Believing they were in a study of learning, Milgram's subjects in fact demonstrated how many of us would hurt, perhaps even kill, another person if instructed to by someone in authority. Likewise the infamous 1971 Zimbardo experiments at Stanford, in which students pretending to be guards and prisoners took only days to sink into intergroup hatred and abuse. Debate around these experiments eventually resulted in the strict guidelines and review procedures for behavioral human subject research that are now the norm; protocols designed to cleanse from scientific practice the very insensibility to others' pain that the initial experiments had so dramatically revealed.

No such guidelines regulate art. It's disturbing, but perhaps not surprising that mid-century behavioral science, shaped by a post-World War II imperative to understand human cruelty and aggression, has had currency for artists in the age of Abu Ghraib and Guantanamo. Some of these recurrences have been quite literal (Rod Dickinson's restaging of the Milgram experiment with actors; Artur Zmijewski's Zimbardo redux), but consider Zmijewski's *THEM (SIE)* (2007), a video documenting a series of sessions in Poland in which the artist brought together activists representing four different political positions (nationalist youth, Catholic conservatives, Jewish activists, and socialists). Given paper and paint, they were invited first to make a large-scale tableau representing their beliefs, then to edit the self-representation of another group. Initially polite, the gestures soon progressed to outright desecration and destruction. By the end, offensive images were being thrown from the window or set aflame.

Like much of Bruguera's art, Zmijewski's workshop can be understood as a precise reversal of the positive visions of sociability in art since the mid-1990s. The paradigmatic example is the Austrian group WochenKlausur, whose art works often brought together representatives of opposing social groups. These individuals were sequestered in small spaces like a boat or a specially constructed cabin and provided with a professional mediator and some light refreshment. Privacy and the label of "art"—and perhaps the power of table manners—seemed to suspend established patterns of enmity, producing opportunities for interchange person-to-person that were foreclosed in public discourse.[3] The goal of such socially ameliorative projects—as in the larger category of what Nicolas Bourriaud named "relational" art practices—is to generate sociality itself. But, as critic Claire Bishop has incisively argued, the implied model of interchange in many of these convivial experiments, and in most of writing about them, is a strangely depleted one: their goal is to produce peaceful accord, but the basis of democracy is dissensus.[4]

Dangerous Play

Bruguera can be accused of many things, but not of discouraging dissensus.

In *Tatlin's Whisper # 5* (2008), a pair of mounted police officers used crowd-control techniques to herd art viewers around the huge Turbine Hall at London's Tate Modern. Blocking the exits, grouping and then dispersing the crowd, the officers and their horses treated the audience as if it were convened for a demonstration or rally. Instead of encouraging an ideal of the art audience as a proto-public, Bruguera treated it like a mob. In a place we'd like to consider a zone of freedom, she introduced coercive force. Likewise, in *The Dream of Reason* (2008), an art gallery was patrolled by an increasing number of uniformed security officers with guard dogs. In a second version museum-goers arriving at an exhibition were patted down and their bags searched before they could enter. ("There is some political art in the show," Bruguera explained to visitors, "we've got to be careful.")

The deployment of security forces in an art space reverberates in many ways, most of them unpleasant. Coming from a society in which censorship is always a possibility, does Bruguera want to remind us of what it means for art not to be free? Or does she want us to give up the illusion that we are free of repression in the Western democracies? Is the uniformed surveillance a vision of where we are heading in the paranoid, post-9/11 West? Is it simply an old-fashioned attempt to shock us out of our placidity? Does it critique oppressive, even fascistic tendencies? Or does it exhibit them?

Zmijewsky was able to produce an extraordinary portrait of antagonisms in the particular crucible of post-communist Poland, and a generalizable document of escalation of commitment in political debate—but most likely only at the cost of actually radicalizing, then sending out into the world, the individuals who performed for his camera. Such effects on participants are precisely what regulations and review boards for human-subject research are designed to avoid in the sciences. By contrast, they are what Tania Bruguera seeks out; what she considers the work itself. In this she differs somewhat from Zmijewski, whose Polish workshop existed in order to be made into an art video. (In fact, its subject matter amounts to an argument for the social relevance of, of all things, painting.) Bruguera doesn't make videos—those that exist are produced as documentation by the host institution—or exhibit photographs of her behavior art. (She has actually tried to sell her performances, but only in a way that mocks the whole idea of non-theatrical performance as a product: offering for sale the ownership of whatever performance she does next, for example.) In Zmijewski's case, the art audience contemplates conflict. In Bruguera's, they experience it.

Yet precisely for this reason, it seems to me that it is art and art viewing that this set of projects tries, forcibly, to redefine. The appearance of the crowd-controlling policemen at the Tate implies a crowd that requires control. As Dionorah Pérez-Rementería has pointed out, it presumes the possibility, however unconscious or remote, of violence among normally docile art viewers.[5] Bruguera represents the art audience—represents it to itself—as a potentially dangerous assembly. This is a remarkable twist on the paradigm in recent art that seems dedicated to reviving interchange and conversation among art viewers, so as to make the art audience less a collection of contemplators than a proto-public sphere. Bruguera, too, wants to change our view of being an art audience, but in the opposite direction. In 2006 she showed how far she would take this tendency when she hosted a Molotov cocktail party: viewers arriving at the opening of her show at a commercial art gallery in Madrid found themselves in a workshop, led by the artist, on producing homemade bombs. (Bruguera describes the dealer, getting into the spirit of the evening, pouring out bottles of wine she had put out for the opening so the lessons could continue.) Here again, art and art viewing are treated as, or rather, made to be dangerous activities. Bruguera happily sent her audience out into the night armed with Molotov cocktails and the knowledge of how to make them: she *actually* made them *potentially* dangerous. Her Arte de Conducta assumes that art viewers are all "political people." And if we are not, she makes it so.

Artistic Freedom, Incorporated

Bruguera is deeply committed to the avant-garde project of breaking down the boundary between art and life. She speaks about it often. She has expressed her discomfort "with the visual arts and their inevitable distance from life,"[6] and she gave up her more theatrical performances because she wanted "an art in which the artistic nature was not that easy to define and which worked in the realm of life."[7] Unafraid of instrumentalizing art, she is committed to the possibility of rejecting once and for all the modern separation of art and utility, stating that "artwork should not only be useful but should exist in the realm of reality; otherwise, it automatically becomes a representation again, one that exists only in the realm of possibility."[8] She strives for a mode in which art is not "a sample, art is . . . something of real consequence," and wants art "to go from being a proposal to be a working temporary reality."[9]

In fact, Bruguera speaks more and more readily about what art is and should be than most other artists I know. Is it possible that she—whose practice involves activities as unartistic as publishing a newspaper and running a school, who happily accepts that her works are not even always recognized as art—is art's fierce defender? This, at least, is how I understand the many gestures in her recent practice that seem to imagine art and art audiences as forces of disruption.

Bruguera grew up in an art culture that assumed art had a functional social role. In capitalism, art's social function is of course often denied, but more importantly, it is always double: art functions ideologically, reflecting or building culture, and art functions as a market, tied into and supporting the economy. But in revolutionary Cuba, the connection of art to the social is not—or was not supposed to be—double. Cuba's history on artistic control differs significantly from other instances of state communism—for there has never been an imposed state style. But, understood as an integral part of the revolution, for nearly fifty years Cuban art has been held to standards of "ideological rigor." Bruguera is of a generation that came of age just as this system began to falter. Contemporary Cuban visual art has been successful in international markets, and since the collapse of the Soviet Union and the "special economic period" that followed, art has become a valued industry, both for the revenue it brings in directly and for of the cultural tourism it attracts. Moreover, according to sociologist Sujatha Fernandes, as the government has cracked down on political dissidence, it has increasingly tolerated criticality within artistic expression. Fernandes calls this a new mode of "incorporation" in Cuban cultural politics.[10] It sounds familiar: once valued for its meaning, art is now prized for its exchange value. Once controlled as a potentially dangerous signifying force, now it appears tolerated as a source of revenue and a social safety valve. And, as Luis Camnitzer and others have pointed out, the two functions are interrelated: political content in Cuban art is one of its selling points.[11]

These are simplifications, of course, of a complex and quickly changing situation (and one I don't know intimately). But I wonder if in Bruguera's recent work we see an underlying sense of loss. One of the most ambitious of her Behavior Art projects was the Cátedra Arte de Conducta, a long running workshop based at but largely independent from the art institute in Havana. There, over seven years, Bruguera brought in artists, critics, and curators to meet with Cuban students and artists in a series of discussions about political, performative art. Perhaps creating a community of critical artists in Cuba is at least metaphorically comparable to arming a European art audience with homemade bombs. Each appears to be tolerated, but each dares its respective regime to recognize its power. Bruguera is anything but nostalgic, but perhaps it could be put this way: she grew up in a social experiment, in which art had a function. Now she enacts social experiments to try to give it one, again.

Crafting Confrontation

During the conversation in Chicago, Bill Ayers and Bernardine Dohrn, themselves former revolutionaries, repeatedly looked to artists as contributors to social change. The role they seemed to propose was for artists as agents of imagination—Dohrn suggested that they might be the ones to come up with alternatives to the American prison system; Ayers, that they could counter the limited and limiting narratives created in the news media. Bruguera, a self-proclaimed political artist, would seem just the person to volunteer such imaginative reframing. But the overall structure of her event—her relinquishment of her space and audience to Dohrn and Ayers—suggested instead that the most an artist could do politically was to sacrifice art to the political.

Of course, once you know that Bruguera had not actually removed herself from that conversation but intervened in it by proxy, the situation gets more complex. She only seemed to make art a window into politics; only seemed to remove form in favor of content, or the aesthetic in favor of the political. In a sense, this pattern is repeated on a larger scale in her work as a whole, where art seems to disappear into life, but is in fact bolstered and renewed. In Chicago, disagreement *was* form—or better, medium. (*Conducta* translates not only to *behavior*, but also *conduit*.) However open-endedly, Bruguera shaped—imagined—that experience. Does that mean that she fulfills the role of artist as imagination agent? Not if we insist on the benevolence of that role, on the artist as the generator of civility and accord, or even of inventive social solutions and narratives. Bruguera has a different technique: her craft is confrontation.

What does it mean that we seem to need her? That the art Left needs this daughter of the revolution to conjure confrontation itself?

This text was originally published in Helaine Posner, Geraldo Mosquera, Carrie Lambert-Beatty, *Tania Bruguera: On the Political Imaginary* (Milan: Charta, 2009): 37-45.

1 More precisely, the venue was a hall at the Merchandise Mart in Chicago. The performance was presented as part of both a lecture series attached to Art Chicago International Fair of Contemporary and Modern Art, which was being held at the time in the same building, and the experimental art and theory conference *Our Literal Speed*. In addition to my own memories, my descriptions here draw on conversations with other audience members, an interview with Bruguera at her Chicago studio, August 10, 2009, and an audio recording of the performance. Bruguera did not document the event, but the artist Rainer Gahnal photographed this along with most of the other conference proceedings and was kind enough to share his archive with me.

2 Francesa di Nardo, "Arte de Conducta: an interview with Tania Bruguera," *Janus 22* (January 2007): 79, 81.

3 See, for example, their project in Nuremberg, documented at http://www.wochenklausur.at/projekte/13p_kurz_en.htm.

4 Claire Bishop, "Antagonism and Relational Aesthetics," *October* 110 (Fall 2004). Not surprisingly, Bishop has written approvingly of Bruguera's practice. See "Speech Disorder," *Artforum* (Summer 2009).

5 The piece might suggest the argument that disciplinary measures presume and even *create* the very threats they are meant to deter.

6 Francesa di Nardo, "Arte de Conducta: an interview with Tania Bruguera," *Op.cit.*

7 Bruguera interviewed by Gerald Matt in Matt, *Interviews* (Cologne: Walther König, 2006).

8 Ibid.

9 Ibid.

10 Sujatha Fernandes, *Cuba Represent! Cuban Arts, State Power, and the Making of New Revolutionary Cultures* (Durham and London: Duke University Press, 2006).

11 Luis Camnitzer, "Epilogue: Luis Camnitzer with Rachel Weiss," in *New Art of Cuba*, rev. ed. (Durham: Duke University Press, 2003), 336.

Contributors

Bill Ayers has written extensively about social justice, democracy and education, the cultural contexts of schooling, and teaching as an essentially intellectual, ethical, and political enterprise. He is a distinguished professor of Education and senior university scholar at the University of Illinois at Chicago (retired), member of the executive committee of the Faculty Senate and founder of both the Small Schools Workshop and the Center for Youth and Society. Ayers taught courses in interpretive and qualitative research, oral history, creative non-fiction, urban school change, and teaching and the modern predicament. He is a graduate of the University of Michigan, the Bank Street College of Education, Bennington College, and Teachers College at Columbia University, as well as past vice-president of the curriculum studies division of the American Educational Research Association. Ayers's articles have appeared in many journals including the *Harvard Educational Review*, the *Journal of Teacher Education, Teachers College Record, Rethinking Schools, The Nation, Educational Leadership*, the *New York Times* and the *Cambridge Journal of Education*.

Mike Bancroft is the co-founder and executive director of Co-op Image, owner of Co-op Sauce as well as the sauce in Sauce and Bread Kitchen. He has been teaching interdisciplinary art practice and entrepreneurship with young people in Chicago since 1998 with institutions like CAPE, the Museum of Contemporary Art, and Street Level Youth Media. He is an active community artist with projects ranging from street installations (Piñata Factory, Garage Spaces) to pop-up cuisine (Bun Pow, The Stew Supper Club).

Carol Becker is dean of faculty and professor at Columbia University School of the Arts, New York. Previously she was dean of faculty and senior vice president for Academic Affairs at the School of the Art Institute of Chicago. With research interests ranging from feminist theory, American cultural history, the education of artists, and art and social responsibility, to South African art and politics, she has published books on cultural criticism, including *The Invisible Drama: Women and the Anxiety of Change*; *The Subversive Imagination: Artists, Society, and Social Responsibility*; *Zones of Contention: Essays on Art, Institutions, Gender, and Anxiety*; *Surpassing the Spectacle: Global Transformations and the Changing Politics of Art*; and *Thinking in Place: Art, Action, and Cultural Production*.

Sara Black works both individually and collaboratively as an artist, artist-teacher, and arts organizer. She received her MFA from the University of Chicago in 2006 and is currently assistant professor of Sculpture at the School of the Art Institute of Chicago. Her work uses conscious processes of carpentry, wood-working, and repair as a time-based method, inherited building materials or other exhausted objects as material, and creates works that aim to expose the complex ways in which things and people are suspended in worlds together.

Greg Broseus is an artist, Iraq veteran, and member of Iraq Veterans Against the War. Broseus participated in Michael Rakowitz's *Enemy Kitchen (Food Truck)*. He earned his BFA from the School of the Art Institute of Chicago in 2013.

Terry Nichols Clark is professor of Sociology at the University of Chicago. He has written and published extensively on the ways that cities use culture to transform themselves, particularly, *The City as an Entertainment Machine* and *Trees and Real Violins*, an oral history of Chicago from Mayor Daley I to the present. With Daniel A. Silver and Stephen W. Sawyer, and through The Scenes Working Group, he has built a practice that joins aesthetics with urban analysis. Together they have consulted in this manner, working alongside mayors and artists for cities from Seoul to Toronto to Paris. In their contribution to this volume, they probe the aesthetic foundations of the city of big shoulders. See the sites: scenes.uchicago.edu and www.faui.org.

Lisa Corrin is the Ellen Philips Katz Director of the Mary and Leigh Block Museum of Art and a senior lecturer in Art History at Northwestern University. She was previously the Director of the Williams College Museum of Art, and the Deputy Director of Art/Jon and Mary Shirley Curator of Modern and Contemporary Art at the Seattle Art Museum, where she served as the artistic lead for the new Olympic Sculpture Park. From 1997-2011 she was the chief curator at The Serpentine Gallery in London. Corrin's museum career began as the first curator of Baltimore's Contemporary Museum, a nomadic museum without walls. Corrin has published widely on contemporary art and museology. Her book on Fred Wilson's landmark installation, *Mining the Museum*, and exhibition organized by The Contemporary Museum in collaboration with the Maryland Historical Society, was awarded the Wittenborn Prize.

Phil Cotton is a practicing multimedia visual artist and an Arts and Design teacher at Daniel Hale Williams Preparatory School of Medicine in Chicago. His Bauhaus influenced arts/design classes explore the contemporary art world, highlighting the global influences of the arts on past and present modern civilizations. Students are given fine art and societal-directed projects that aid them in taking positive ownership of their lives. Class projects are designed to educate and inspire students to use the arts to make a lasting, productive contribution to our world. Past projects have included developing community-based "Identity Museums," neighborhood needs assessments, community center design, family history mapping art works, and the development of affordable prosthetic design products to aid handicapped individuals. He collaborates regularly with Margy Stover, a teaching artist for the Frank Lloyd Wright Trust and CAPE.

Jim Duignan is an artist and professor of Visual Art in the College of Education at DePaul University. He started the Stockyard Institute as an artist project and space in the Back of the Yards area of Chicago. The Stockyard Institute was influenced by a small group of community artists, radical teachers, local activists, and individuals no one has ever heard of, all considering how the social and civic forms of engagement are integral to their life. The efforts of the Stockyard Institute and the studio work of Jim Duignan has been exhibited, written about, and collaborated with everywhere.

Marc Fischer is a Chicago-based artist. Since 1998, Fischer has been a member of the long-running artist group Temporary Services. The group's current members are Fischer and Brett Bloom. Temporary Services has produced over 110 publications and a similar number of exhibitions and projects. In 2008 Temporary Services founded a publishing imprint and web-based store named Half Letter Press. Fischer was also a co-founder of Mess Hall, an experimental cultural center in Chicago's Rogers Park neighborhood, which closed in 2013 after ten years of programming. In 2007, Fischer founded the initiative Public Collectors.

Theaster Gates creates platforms. In Chicago, Gates's leadership of artist-led spaces has catalyzed an evolution in perceptions of poorer parts of the city and their human and cultural resources. As evident in the synergistic design process of his building practices and persistent challenging of organizational structures, Gates's development projects function as an extension of his studio work. Gates takes on the problem of Black space as a formal exercise, reminiscent of Beuys's concept of social sculpture. The latest example of this work is the Stony Island Arts Bank, set to open for the Chicago Architecture Biennial in October 2015.

Amanda Gutierrez was born in Mexico City in 1978. She earned her MFA at the School of the Art Institute of Chicago, specializing in Performance and New Media. In Mexico, she completed her undergraduate studies in Stage Design at the INBA/ENAT. For twelve years, she has worked in the field of performance and sound art, fusing the two disciplines in installation projects. Among the video series she has made, *A brief history of fictions*, *Tracking Memory*, and the trilogy *Time Topographies* have won several awards: The Fellowship Competition 2007 and CAAP 2008. Gutierrez was awarded the EMAN-EMARE prize in 2012 and The National System of the Arts Fellowship in 2015.

Ronne Hartfield is an essayist, poet, and author of the acclaimed memoir, *Another Way Home* (2004). She served as Women's Board Endowed executive director for Museum Education at the Art Institute of Chicago throughout the 1990s, and before that was executive director of Urban Gateways: the Center for Arts Education, at that time the largest program of its kind in the United States. Hartfield was dean of students at the School of the Art Institute where she also taught world literatures. With undergraduate and graduate degrees from the University of Chicago, she has been awarded fellowships from the Rockefeller Foundation, the Goethe Institut, and the Institute for International Education, among others.

Tempestt Hazel is an independent curator, writer, artist advocate, and executive director of Sixty Inches From Center, a Chicago-based online magazine and archiving organization. Additionally, she is the arts program manager and curator at the Arts Incubator in Washington Park with the University of Chicago. Her curatorial practice often uses archives and collections as a starting point to draw connections between a variety of histories and the work of contemporary, emerging artists. With Sixty Inches From Center, she advocates for artist legacy-building through arts journalism and ephemera while working to increase visibility of the Chicago Artists' Archive, a collection of over 10,000 records documenting artists in Chicago since the 1940s housed in the Harold Washington Library.

Aaron Hughes is an artist, activists, organizer, teacher, and Iraq War veteran whose work seeks out poetics, connections, and moments of beauty in order to construct new narratives, connections, and meanings out of personal and collective traumas. He uses these narratives to create projects that attempt to deconstruct systems of dehumanization and oppression. He works with a variety of art, veteran, and activist organizations and projects including: Iraq Veterans Against the War, Warrior Writers Project, Dirty Canteen, National Veterans Art Museum, Iraq Veterans Against the War, Justseeds Artists' Cooperative, and the Center for Artistic Activism.

Mary Jane Jacob is a curator, professor, and executive director of Exhibitions and Exhibition Studies at the School of the Art Institute of Chicago. Shifting her workplace from museums to the street, she critically engaged the discourse of public space with landmark exhibitions *Places with a Past* in Charleston, South Carolina, *Culture in Action* in Chicago, and *Conversations at the Castle* in Atlanta. Among her publications are the co-edited books *Buddha Mind in Contemporary Art*; *Learning Mind: Experience into Art*; *The Studio Reader: On the Space of Artists*; and *Chicago Makes Modern: How Creative Minds Changed Society*.

Lisa Junkin Lopez is a public historian, educator, and organizer. She is the associate director at the Jane Addams Hull-House Museum, where she has worked for six years. Junkin is a faculty member of Museum and Exhibition Studies at the University of Illinois at Chicago and serves on the National Board of Editors for *The Public Historian*. Lisa earned an MA in Arts Education from the School of the Art Institute of Chicago and a BA from the College of William and Mary. She has worked in museums and art organizations since 2004.

Carrie Lambert-Beatty is an art historian at Harvard University, with a focus on art from the 1960s to the present and a special interest in performance in an expanded sense. Her 2008 book *Being Watched: Yvonne Rainer and the 1960s* brought together aspects of her research on minimalism, dance, performance documentation, theories of spectatorship, and the American avant-garde's response, often at the level of the political unconscious, to the period's burgeoning media culture. Published by MIT Press, *Being Watched* was awarded the de la Torre prize for dance studies. Lambert-Beatty's writing on recent art appears in journals such as *Artforum* and *October*, of which she is an editor. She is writing a book about practices of artistic deception and the politics of knowledge since 1990.

Jorge Lucero is an artist and assistant professor of Art Education at the University of Illinois, Urbana-Champaign. Most of his work exists at the intersection of art and education. Lucero's work is manifested through symbolic works such as art objects, performances, videos, images, lectures, and publications. He also participates in actual socially engaged art works—such as teaching—that test the pliability of duration, documentation, and relationality. Not too long ago, Lucero was a Chicago Public School teacher.

Duncan MacKenzie is an artist, pundit, educator, and a founder of Bad at Sports (B@S) podcast and badatsports.com. With B@S he has produced over 450 interviews with artists and cultural luminaries such as Suzanne Lacy, Kerry James Marshall, Luc Tuymans, Jeff Wall, and Helen Molesworth. Alongside his work with B@S he regularly shows his own artwork internationally with his collaborator Christian Kuras. Between B@S and Kuras he has realized exhibitions and projects with art fairs like NADA Miami, EXPO Chicago, PULSE Miami, and Volta NYC, and institutions like the Contemporary Art Museum of St. Louis, The Walker Art Center, and apexart. His work has been written about in *Afterall*, artforum.com, *Flash Art*, and the *New York Times*. He is currently enjoying a post as an assistant professor in the Art + Design/Art and Art History Department at Columbia College, Chicago.

Edward Maldonado is an artist, independent writer, and curator. He previously worked as a curator with the City of Chicago Department of Cultural Affairs, the director of the Clarke House Museum in Chicago, and as an adjunct professor at the School of the Art Institute of Chicago. Maldonado is a graduate of SAIC with a BFA in painting and an MA in Art History, Theory, and Criticism. He has been a board member with various arts non-profit organizations in Chicago, including: The Chicago Public Art Group, Randolph Street Gallery, and The Puerto Rican Arts Alliance, as well as served as a panelist for the Illinois Arts Council. Maldonado was recently the guest curator for the Festival de Mayo in Guadalajara, Mexico.

Iñigo Manglano-Ovalle is a conceptual artist working across media to create works that challenge our notions of the political and the cultural. He is internationally recognized for his activist-inspired public art and studio-based works. He has received numerous awards including a United States Artists Guthman Fellowship (2011), a Guggenheim Memorial Foundation Fellowship (2009), and a John D. and Catherine T. MacArthur Foundation Award (2001), as well as a fellowship from the National Endowment for the Arts (1995). Manglano-Ovalle has presented major projects at SITE Santa Fe, New Mexico; Ernst Schering Foundation, Berlin; The Power

Plant Contemporary, Toronto; The Art Institute of Chicago; Musée D'Art Contemporain de Montréal; Massachusetts Museum of Contemporary Art; Documenta 12, Kassel; Krefelder Kunstmuseen, Krefeld; Barcelona Pavilion, Mies van der Rohe Foundation, Barcelona; the Guggenheim Museum, New York and Bilbao; and Museum of Contemporary Art, Chicago. Currently he holds a professorship for Art Theory and Practice at Northwestern University.

Mark Messing is a composer and musical agitator. He is musical director of circus punk marching band Mucca Pazza and has led the band from coast to coast through concert halls, public parks, neighborhood pubs, and a dozen canoes on the Chicago River. He has composed music for numerous independent films including *The First Breath of Tengan Rei* (2009) by Junko Kajino and Ed M. Koziarski, and has been musical director for hundreds of theater performances. As musical director for Redmoon Theater he composed a piece for 100 tiny radios at the Museum of Contemporary Art, a 35-foot drum tree at Millennium Park, and for musicians on stilts at Puppetropolis. His new company, Opera-Matic, performs Lullaby Parades on bicycle powered floats in Chicago neighborhoods at twilight.

Anne Elizabeth Moore is an award-winning journalist and Fulbright scholar born in Winner, South Dakota. Her writing has appeared in *The Baffler, Al Jazeera, Salon, Wilson Quarterly, The Los Angeles Review of Books, The Onion, Tin House,* and *Truthout.* Her art has been featured in solo exhibitions at the Museum of Contemporary Art, Chicago, and in the Whitney Biennial, and she has been on CNN, NPR, Australian Broadcasting Corporation, Georgian National Television, Voice of America Khmer, and in the *New York Times.* She has been banned from American Girl Place for ten years.

A. Laurie Palmer is an artist, writer, and teacher living in Chicago and California. She teaches in the Department of Sculpture and the Low-Residency Master of Fine Arts program at the School of the Art Institute of Chicago. She collaborated with the artist group Haha for twenty years on site- and community-based projects and currently collaborates with Chicago Torture Justice Memorials Project and the Prison Neighborhood Arts Program, both prison justice groups based in Chicago. Palmer's individual practice takes form as sculpture, installation, public projects, writing, and interdisciplinary research. Among her writings, she has published the book *In the Aura of a Hole: Exploring Sites of Material Extraction.*

Robert Peters is an artist and professor emeritus at the Department of Visual Arts at the University of Chicago. His art works often explore how language and other institutional structures shape perception and experience. These interests have been expressed through a variety of forms: installations, performances, artist's books, drawings, and audio works. Peters often collaborates and his collaborators are often non-artists: historians, decorators, anthropologists, economists, magicians, critics, architects, etc. He has exhibited widely and is currently preparing for an exhibition at Chiang Mai University Art Museum. He has received numerous awards, including grants from the National Endowment for the Arts, the Illinois Arts Council, and the Lila-Wallace Reader's Digest Foundation (an International Arts Award to Indonesia). His pursuit of his art interests came after an initial education in science and a brief career as a biometrician with the U.S. Forest Service.

Jon Pounds is an artist and organizer whose early work involved temporary non-permission street installations. After joining Chicago Public Art Group (CPAG) in 1984 he began creating collaborative public artworks including playground structures, sculptures, murals. As Director of CPAG (since 1989) he has expanded the ability of the organization and its artists to respond more fully to a wide range of community needs. A fifteen-month-long Chicago Community Trust fellowship allowed him to study the intersection of urban planning, community activation, and public art. In 2012, Pounds was elected to the Americans for the Arts, Public Art Network Council.

Aay Preston-Myint is an artist, printmaker, and educator based in Chicago. His practice currently employs visual and collaborative strategies to investigate memory, memorial, self-reflection, and self-projection within the context of queer community and history. In addition to his own work in interdisciplinary media, he is a founder of No Coast, an artist partnership that prints and distributes affordable contemporary artwork, serves as a DJ and organizer for Chances Dances, a regularly occurring party that supports and showcases the work of queer artists in Chicago, and is editor-in-chief of an online and print journal called Monsters and Dust.

Michael Rakowitz produces conceptual works charged with geopolitical narratives and the history of his own Iraqi Jewish heritage. Intended to incite conversation and exchange, his projects take shape outside conventional art spaces. *Enemy Kitchen*, an ongoing project, compiles and teaches Baghdadi recipes to public audiences ranging from middle school students to museumgoers. In 2012, *Enemy Kitchen* became a food truck, staffed by Iraqi refugees who cooked the food and US veterans of the Iraq War who operated as sous chefs and servers. Recent projects also include, *Return,*

2006, where Rakowitz reopened his grandfather's import and export business first operated in Baghdad, then relocated to New York when his family was exiled in 1946, offering free shipping to Iraq three months after the US declared trade restrictions on the country. Rakowitz is also professor of Art Theory and Practice at Northwestern University.

Dieter Roelstraete is currently Manilow Senior Curator at the Museum of Contemporary Art, Chicago, and a member of the curatorial team convened by artistic director Adam Szymczyk to organize Documenta 14 in Kassel, Germany, in 2017. Roelstraete has published extensively on contemporary art and related philosophical issues in numerous catalogues and journals including *Afterall, Artforum, Frieze,* and *Mousse Magazine.*

Abigail Satinsky is a writer, curator, and organizer. She is currently the interim executive director at Threewalls in Chicago where her work includes organizing exhibitions and programming, editing *Phonebook* (a national directory of artist-run spaces and projects), and co-founding Hand-in-Glove, a national conference for grass-roots and small non-profit organizers, and Common Field, an emerging national organization aimed at building resources and advocacy for small-scale arts organizing. She is also a founding member of InCUBATE and co-initiator of Sunday Soup, an international micro-granting project. InCUBATE's work has been shown nationally, most notably with Creative Time and the Smart Museum of Art at the University of Chicago. She is a regular contributor to the Bad at Sports podcast and her writing has appeared in *the Journal of Aesthetics and Protest, AREA Chicago, Art Practical,* and *Proximity Magazine.* She has taught at University of Illinois at Chicago and teaches courses on socially engaged art and curatorial practice at School of the Art Institute of Chicago.

Stephen W. Sawyer is chair of the History Department at The American University of Paris, associate editor for the English edition of the *Annales Histoire et Sciences Sociales,* and director of publication of the *Tocqueville Review.* He has published widely on transnational influences in urban and political history and theory.

Allison Schein is the archive manager for the Studs Terkel Radio Archive, collaborating with such partners as the Library of Congress, WFMT The Radio Network, the Chicago History Museum, and Dominican University's Graduate School of Library and Information Science. After receiving her archivist certification in 2013 she became the archivist for the Creative Audio Archive at Experimental Sound Studio, where she had been the archive manager since 2011. She earned a Bachelors degree in Audio, Arts and Acoustics from Columbia College Chicago and a MLIS from Dominican University in 2012 in order to become an audio archivist.

David Senior is the bibliographer at the Museum of Modern Art Library, where he manages collection development, including the library's artists' books collection. Senior lectures often on the history of artists' publications and contemporary art and design publishing. He also curates exhibitions of MoMA Library materials including, most recently: *Ray Johnson Designs, Please Come to the Show, Millennium Magazines, Access to Tools: Publications from the Whole Earth Catalog, 1968–74*, and *Scenes from Zagreb: Artists' Publications of the New Art Practice. Please Come to the Show*, a book documenting his exhibition of artists' invitations and show flyers from the MoMA Library collection, was published by Occasional Papers in 2014.

Maikl and Milad Shaer are co-owners of Milo's Pita Palace, a Chicago North Side restaurant that serves Iraqi cuisine under the neutral label "middle eastern," and participated in Michael Rakowitz's *Enemy Kitchen (Food Truck)*.

Gregory Sholette is a New York-based artist and writer whose recent art projects include *Our Barricades* at Station Independent Gallery, and *Imaginary Archive* at Las Kurbas Center, Kyiv, Ukraine, and whose recent publications include *It's The Political Economy, Stupid*, co-edited with Oliver Ressler, and *Dark Matter: Art and Politics in an Age of Enterprise Culture*. A graduate of the Whitney Independent Studies Program in Critical Theory in 1996, he received his MFA from the University of San Diego in 1995, and BFA from The Cooper Union, 1979, and served on the board of the College Art Association (1999-2004). Sholette was a founding member of the artists collectives Political Art Documentation/Distribution (1980-1988), and REPOhistory (1989-2000), remaining active today with Gulf Labor Coalition, as well as serving on the Curriculum Committee of Home WorkSpace Beirut, Lebanon. Sholette is an associate faculty for the Art, Design and the Public Domain program of Harvard University's Graduate School of Design, and an associate professor in the Queens College CUNY Art Department where he co-developed and teaches in its new MFA concentration: Social Practice Queens.

Scott Sikkema is education director at Chicago Arts Partnerships in Education (CAPE). CAPE nurtures authentic collaborations in schools between teaching artists, classroom teachers, and students from kindergarten through twelfth grade. With CAPE Program and Research staff, he oversees partnerships, professional development, research, and public sharing. At CAPE, he engages questions such as: what can be generated from the tensions of clarity and ambiguity; what is the nature of nonlinear teaching and learning in relation to expectations of immediacy; how is space created, entered, or existed in pedagogically; how does shifting or introducing components in an educational encounter become art making itself and produce learning?

Daniel A. Silver is associate professor of Sociology at the University of Toronto.

Stephanie Smith is chief curator at the Art Gallery of Ontario. Previously she was deputy director and chief curator at the University of Chicago's Smart Museum of Art where she has helped establish the museum as a home for challenging thematic exhibitions addressing complex relationships between contemporary art and larger social issues—*Feast: Radical Hospitality in Contemporary Art*; *Heartland*; *Beyond Green: Toward a Sustainable Art*; and *Critical Mass*. She participated in the Getty Foundation's Museum Leadership Institute (2007) and held prior curatorial positions at Contemporary Arts Museum, Houston and the Rice University Art Gallery. Her writings have appeared in journals and books, including *Afterall*, *Parkett*, *Service Media*, and *Land, Art: A Cultural Ecology Handbook*.

Deborah Stratman is an artist and filmmaker based in Chicago. She makes work that investigates issues of power, control and belief, exploring how places, ideas, and society are intertwined.

Peter Taub is a curator and arts manager with over twenty-five years of experience in developing and producing artist-centered projects. He currently directs the performing arts program at the Museum of Contemporary Art Chicago, presenting artists working in crossdisciplinary dance, theater, and music; and engaging audiences with artists around the creative process. From 1986-1996 Taub led Randolph Street Gallery (RSG), an artist-run center focused on the work and ideas of artists, presenting a multi-faceted program of thematic exhibitions, performances, installations, and public art. During this period, RSG grew more than five-fold, and became the leading organization of its kind in the region. The key RSG initiatives that Taub worked on include: a Midwest regional program of grants to artists, major public art projects with Group Material and Krzystof Wodiczko, an extensive community youth arts program, and commissioned projects with Guillermo Gomez-Pena/Coco Fusco, Natsu Nakajima, Antonio Muntadas, and others.

Studs Terkel (1912 – 2008), prize-winning author and radio broadcast personality, was born Louis Terkel in New York on May 16, 1912. His family moved to Chicago in 1922 and opened a rooming house at on the Near West

Side. Terkel credited his knowledge of the world to the tenants who gathered in the lobby and the people who congregated in nearby Bughouse Square, a meeting place for workers, labor organizers, dissidents, the unemployed, and religious fanatics of many persuasions. Terkel attended the University of Chicago and received a law degree in 1934. After a brief stint with the civil service in Washington D.C., he returned to Chicago and worked with the WPA Writers Project in the radio division. In 1944, he landed his own show on WENR, and a year later had his own television show called Stud's Place. In 1952 Terkel began working for the radio station WFMT, developing shows that later became the award-winning, "The Studs Terkel Program." His published works include *Giants of Jazz* (1956), *Division Street: America* (1966), and his last oral history book *Will the Circle Be Unbroken: Reflections on Death, Rebirth, and Hunger for a Faith* (2001).

travis. 23SEP46. Itawamba County, Mississippi. Chickasaw/African. Male. BS & MA/Northwestern University. U.S.Navy 1963-69 www.travistravis.com

Philip von Zweck is an artist and painter currently based in Chicago. He is the founder of the Chicago Artificial Birding Society (C.A.B.S.) and serves as the director of D Gallery.

Hamza Walker is director of education and associate curator for the Renaissance Society at the University of Chicago and co-curator of *Made in L.A.* 2016, at the Hammer Museum. Recent exhibitions include *Teen Paranormal Romance* (2014), *Suicide Narcissus* (2013), and *John Neff* (2013). He is the recipient of the 1999 Norton Curatorial Grant and the 2004 Walter Hopps Award for Curatorial Achievement. In 2010 he was awarded the Ordway Prize for his significant impact on the field of contemporary art.

Kate Zeller is director of exhibitions and associate curator in the Department of Exhibitions and Exhibition Studies at the School of the Art Institute of Chicago. She has worked in recent years with artists Moon Kyungwon and Jeon Joonho, Kimsooja, and Wolfgang Laib to create site-specific installations for the School's Sullivan Galleries. Collaborating with the Italian Cultural Institute of Chicago, Zeller curated *A Sense of Place*, presented as part of the 54th Venice Biennale's Italian Pavilion. Zeller is assistant editor of *Chicago Makes Modern: How Creative Minds Changed Society* and *The Studio Reader: On the Space of Artists*.

Rebecca Zorach is professor of Art History at the University of Chicago. She teaches and writes on medieval and Renaissance art, contemporary activist art, and art of the 1960s and 1970s, particularly African American artists in Chicago. Recent articles have addressed AfriCOBRA's gender and family politics; Claes Oldenburg's lawsuit challenging the copyright of the Chicago Picasso; and the experimental art center Art & Soul, founded on the West Side of Chicago in 1968 by the Museum of Contemporary Art and the Conservative Vice Lords, a former street gang. She is currently at work on a book on Art & Soul and the larger landscape of the Black Arts Movement in Chicago.

Index